Grammar Sense 1

SERIES DIRECTOR
Susan Kesner Bland

Cheryl Pavlik

OXFORD
UNIVERSITY PRESS

OXFORD
UNIVERSITY PRESS

198 Madison Avenue
New York, NY 10016 USA

Great Clarendon Street
Oxford OX2 6DP England

Oxford   New York
Auckland   Bangkok   Buenos Aires   Cape Town   Chennai
Dar es Salaam   Delhi   Hong Kong   Istanbul   Karachi   Kolkata
Kuala Lumpur   Madrid   Melbourne   Mexico City   Mumbai
Nairobi   Sâo Paulo   Shanghai   Taipei   Tokyo   Toronto

OXFORD is a trademark of Oxford University Press.

Copyright © 2004 Oxford University Press

ISBN 0-19-436565-4

Library of Congress Cataloging-in-Publication Data

Pavlik, Cheryl, 1949-
    Grammar Sense 1 / series director, Susan Kesner Bland;
    Cheryl Pavlik.
        p. cm.
    Includes index.
    ISBN 0-19-436565-4
    1. English language—Textbooks for foreign speakers. 2. English
language—Grammar—Problems, exercises, etc. I. Title: Grammar
Sense one. II. Bland, Susan Kesner. III. Title.

PE1128.P374 2004
428.2'4—dc21   2003054875

Editorial Manager: Janet Aitchison
Senior Editor: Stephanie Karras
Editor: Pietro Alongi
Associate Editors: Katya MacDonald, Ashli Totty
Art Director: Lynn Luchetti
Design Manager: Mary Chandler
Designer (cover): Lee Anne Dollison
Senior Art Editor: Jodi Waxman
Art Editor: Judi DeSouter
Production Manager: Shanta Persaud
Production Controller: Eve Wong

Book Design: Bill Smith Studio
Composition: Compset, Inc.
Indexer: Leonard Neufeld

Printing (last digit): 10 9 8 7 6 5 4 3 2 1

Printed in Hong Kong.

Acknowledgments

Cover image: © Kevin Schafer / Peter Arnold, Inc.

Illustrations by:
Barbara Bastian, Lyndall Culbertson, Paul Hampson,
Mike Hortens, Randy Jones, Jon Keegan, Raymond Lee,
Scott MacNeill, Laura Hartman Maestro, Karen Minot,
Tom Newsom, Roger Penwill, Alan Reingold, Don Stewart,
Bill Thomson

*The publisher would like to thank the following for
their permission to reproduce photographs:*
Action-Plus; Alamy images; Bananastock; Bettman/Corbis;
Stefano Bianchetti/Corbis; Bruce Burhardt / Corbis; Jacques M.
Chenet / Corbis; Chicago Historical Society; Comstock; Philip
James Corwin / Corbis; Corbis; Courtesy of the Bostonian Society
/ Old State House; CUMULUS; Araldo de Luca / Corbis; Lee
Anne Dollison / OUP; Getty; Hulton-Deutsch Collection / Corbis;
ImageState; Index Stock Imagery; Karen Minot; PhotoDisc;
PhotoDisc Green; Pictures Coulour Library; Anthony
Redpath/Corbis; Robert Harding World Imagery; Rochester
Democrat & Chronicle / Corbis Sygma; Royalty-Free / Corbis;
Ariel Skelley / Corbis; StockPhotoAsia; SuperStock; Syracuse
Newspapers / The Image Works; Brian Sytnyk / Masterfile; Liba
Taylor / Corbis; Tim Thompson / Corbis; Jodi Waxman/OUP;
Michael S. Yamashita / Corbis

Acknowledgements

It takes a village to write a grammar series. I am humbled by the expertise of all those who have contributed in so many ways.

I am grateful to Cheryl Pavlik for her intellectual curiosity, creativity, wit, and for her friendship. A special thanks goes to Stephanie Karras for putting all of the pieces together with such commitment and superb organizational and problem-solving skills, mixed with just the right amount of levity. I owe a special debt of gratitude to Janet Aitchison for her continued support and encouragement from the very beginning, and for her help with the big issues as well as the small details.

It has been a pleasure working closely with Diane Flanel Piniaris, Pietro Alongi, Andrew Gitzy, James Morgan, Nan Clarke, Randee Falk, and Marietta Urban. Their comments, questions, grammar insights, and creative solutions have been invaluable. Many thanks also go to the talented editorial, production, and design staff at Oxford University Press; to Susan Lanzano for her role in getting this project started; and to Susan Mraz for her help in the early stages.

Finally, I owe everything to my family, Bob, Jenny, and Scott, for always being there for me, as well as for their amusing views about everything, especially grammar.

Susan Kesner Bland,
Series Director

The Series Director and Publisher would like to acknowledge the following individuals for their invaluable input during the development of this series:

Harriet Allison, Atlanta College of Art, GA; **Alex Baez,** Southwest Texas State University, TX; **Nathalie Bailey,** Lehman College, CUNY, NY; **Jamie Beaton,** Boston University, MA; **Michael Berman,** Montgomery College, MD; **Angela Blackwell,** San Francisco State University, CA; **Vera Bradford,** IBEU, Rio de Janerio, Brazil; **Glenda Bro,** Mount San Antonio Community College, CA; **Jennifer Burton,** University of California, San Francisco, CA; **Magali Duignan,** Augusta State University, GA; **Anne Ediger,** Hunter College, CUNY, NY; **Joyce Grabowski,** Flushing High School, NY; **Virginia Heringer,** Pasadena City College, CA; **Rocia Hernandez,** Mexico City, Mexico; **Nancy Hertfield-Pipkin,** University of California, San Diego, CA; **Michelle Johnstone,** Mexico City, Mexico; **Kate de Jong,** University of California, San Diego, CA; **Pamela Kennedy,** Holyoke Community College, MA; **Jean McConochie,** Pace University, NY; **Karen McRobie,** Golden Gate University, CA; **Elizabeth Neblett,** Union County College, NJ; **Dian Perkins,** Wheeling High School, IL; **Fausto Rocha de Marcos Rebelo,** Recife, Brazil; **Mildred Rugger,** Southwest Texas State University, TX; **Dawn Schmidt,** California State University, San Marcos, CA; **Katharine Sherak,** San Francisco State University, CA; **Lois Spitzer,** University of Nebraska-Lincoln, NE; **Laura Stering,** University of California, San Francisco, CA; **Annie Stumpfhauser,** Morelios, Mexico; **Anthea Tillyer,** Hunter College, CUNY, NY; **Julie Un,** Massasoit Community College, MA; **Susan Walker,** SUNY New Paltz, NY; **Cheryl Wecksler,** California State University, San Marcos, CA; **Teresa Wise,** Georgia State University, GA.

Contents

PART 7: The Future

PART 8: Modals

PART 9: Objects, Infinitives, and Gerunds

PART 10: Comparatives and Superlatives

Introduction

Grammar Sense: A Discourse-Based Approach

Grammar Sense is a comprehensive three-level grammar series based on the authentic use of English grammar in discourse. The grammar is systematically organized, explained, and practiced in a communicative, learner-centered environment, making it easily teachable and learnable.

Many people ask, why learn grammar? The answer is simple: meaningful communication depends on our ability to connect form and meaning appropriately. In order to do so, we must consider such factors as intention, attitude, and social relationships, in addition to the contexts of time and place. All of these factors make up a discourse setting. For example, we use the present continuous not only to describe an activity in progress (*He's working.*), but also to complain (*He's always working.*), to describe a planned event in the future (*He's working tomorrow.*), and to describe temporary or unusual behavior (*He's being lazy at work.*). It is only through examination of the discourse setting that the different meanings and uses of the present continuous can be distinguished from one another. A discourse-based approach provides students with the tools for making sense of the grammar of natural language by systematically explaining *who, what, where, when, why,* and *how* for each grammatical form.

Systematically Organized Syllabus

Learning grammar is a developmental process that occurs gradually. In *Grammar Sense* the careful sequencing, systematic repetition, recycling, review, and expansion promote grammatical awareness and fluency.

Level 1 (basic level) focuses on building an elementary understanding of form, meaning, and use as students develop basic oral language skills in short conversations and discussions. Level 1 also targets the grammar skills involved in writing short paragraphs, using basic cohesive devices such as conjunctions and pronouns.

At **Level 2 (intermediate level)** the focus turns to expanding the basic understanding of form, meaning, and use in longer and more varied discourse settings, and with more complex grammatical structures and academic themes. Level 2 emphasizes grammar skills beyond the sentence level, as students begin to initiate and sustain conversations and discussions, and progress toward longer types of writing.

Finally, at **Level 3 (high intermediate to advanced level)** the focus moves to spoken and written grammar in academic discourse settings, often in contexts that are conceptually more challenging and abstract. Level 3 emphasizes consistent and appropriate language use, especially of those aspects of grammar needed in extended conversations and discussions, and in longer academic and personal writing.

Introduction of Form Before Meaning and Use

Form is introduced and practiced in a separate section before meaning and use. This ensures that students understand what the form looks like and sounds like at the sentence level, before engaging in more challenging and open-ended activities that concentrate on meaning and use.

Focus on Natural Language Use

Grammar Sense uses authentic reading texts and examples that are based on or quoted verbatim from actual English-language sources to provide a true picture of natural language use. To avoid unnatural language, the themes of the introductory reading texts are only subtly touched upon throughout a chapter. The focus thus remains on typical examples of the most common meanings and uses.

Exposure to authentic language helps students bridge the gap between the classroom and the outside world by encouraging awareness of the "grammar" all around them in daily life: in magazines, newspapers, package instructions, television shows, signs, and so on. Becoming language-aware is an important step in the language-learning process: Students generalize from the examples they find and apply their understanding to their independent language use in daily living, at work, or as they further their education.

Special Sections to Extend Grammatical Knowledge

Understanding grammar as a system entails understanding how different parts of the language support and interact with the target structure. *Grammar Sense* features special sections at strategic points throughout the text to highlight relevant lexical and discourse issues.

- **Beyond the Sentence** sections focus on the structure as it is used in extended discourse to help improve students' writing skills. These sections highlight such issues as how grammatical forms are used to avoid redundancy, and how to change or maintain focus.

- **Informally Speaking** sections highlight the differences between written and spoken language. This understanding is crucial for achieving second language fluency. Reduced forms, omissions, and pronunciation changes are explained in order to improve aural comprehension.

- **Pronunciation Notes** show students how to pronounce selected forms of the target language, such as the regular simple past ending -*ed*.

- **Vocabulary Notes** provide succinct presentations of words and phrases that are commonly used with the target structure, such as time expressions associated with the simple present and simple past.

Student-Centered Presentation and Practice

Student-centered presentation and practice allow learners at all levels to discover the grammar in pairs, groups, and individually, in both the Form and in the Meaning and Use sections of each chapter. Numerous inductive activities encourage students to use their problem-solving abilities to gain the skills, experience, and confidence to use English outside of class and to continue learning on their own.

Flexibility to Suit Any Classroom Situation

Grammar Sense offers teachers great flexibility with hundreds of intellectually engaging exercises to choose from. Teachers may choose to skip chapters or sections within chapters, or teach them in a different order, depending on student needs and time constraints. Each Student Book is self-contained so teachers may choose to use only one book, or the full series, if they wish.

Components at Each Level

- The **Student Book** is intended for classroom use and offers concise charts, level-appropriate explanations, and thorough four-skills practice exercises. Each Student Book is also a useful reference resource with extensive Appendices, a helpful Glossary of Grammar Terms, and a detailed Index.

- The **Audio Cassettes and CDs** feature listening exercises that provide practice discriminating form, understanding meaning and use, and interpreting non-standard forms.

- The **Workbook** has a wealth of additional exercises to supplement those in the Student Book. It is ideal for homework, independent practice, or review. The Answer Key, on easily removable perforated pages, is provided at the back of the book.

- The **Teacher's Book** has many practical ideas and techniques for presenting the Form and the Meaning and Use sections. It also includes troubleshooting advice, cultural notes, and suggestions for additional activities. The Answer Key for the Student Book and the complete Tapescript are also provided.

- **TOEFL®-Style Tests** and Answer Keys, along with advice on conducting the tests and interpreting the results, are available for teachers to download from the Internet. (See *Grammar Sense Teacher's Book 1* for the website address.)

Tour of a Chapter

Each chapter in *Grammar Sense* follows this format:

The **Grammar in Discourse** section introduces the target structure in its natural context via a high-interest authentic reading text.

• *Authentic reading texts show how language is really used.*

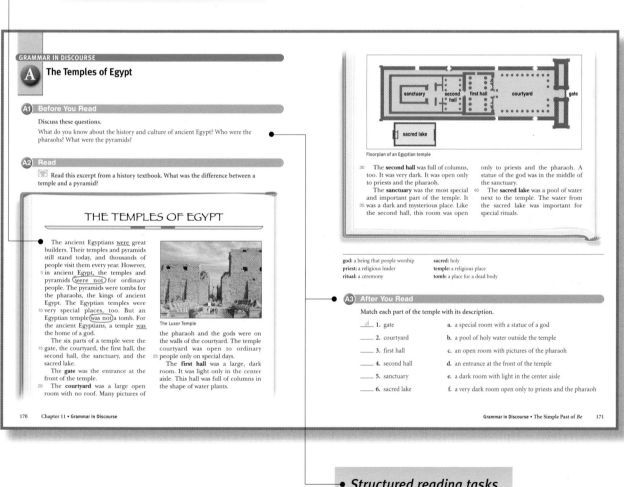

• *Structured reading tasks help students read and understand the text.*

The **Form** section(s) provides clear presentation of the target structure, detailed notes, and thorough practice exercises.

• *Inductive **Examining Form** exercises encourage students to think about how to form the target structure.*

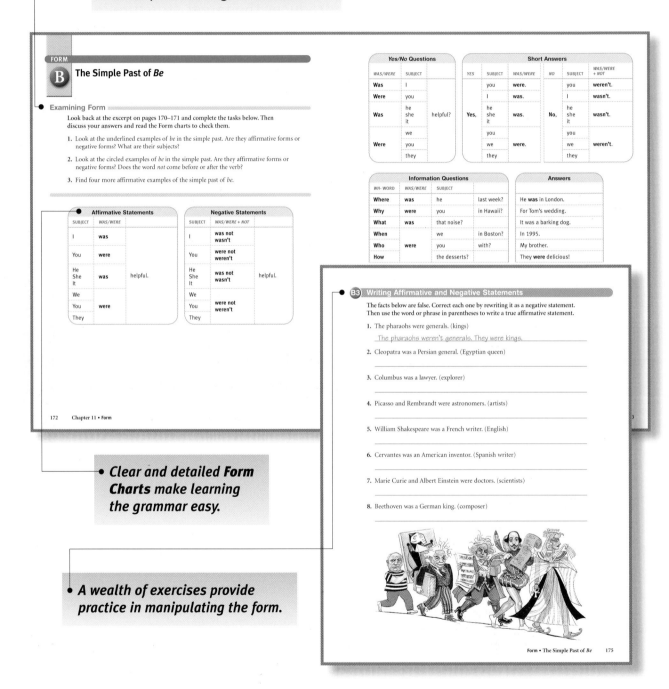

FORM

B The Simple Past of *Be*

Examining Form

Look back at the excerpt on pages 170–171 and complete the tasks below. Then discuss your answers and read the Form charts to check them.

1. Look at the underlined examples of *be* in the simple past. Are they affirmative forms or negative forms? What are their subjects?

2. Look at the circled examples of *be* in the simple past. Are they affirmative forms or negative forms? Does the word *not* come before or after the verb?

3. Find four more affirmative examples of the simple past of *be*.

Affirmative Statements

SUBJECT	WAS/WERE	
I	was	
You	were	
He She It	was	helpful.
We		
You	were	
They		

Negative Statements

SUBJECT	WAS/WERE + NOT	
I	was not wasn't	
You	were not weren't	
He She It	was not wasn't	helpful.
We		
You	were not weren't	
They		

Yes/No Questions

WAS/WERE	SUBJECT	
Was	I	
Were	you	
Was	he she it	helpful?
	we	
Were	you	
	they	

Short Answers

YES	SUBJECT	WAS/WERE	NO	SUBJECT	WAS/WERE + NOT
	you	were.		you	weren't.
	I	was.		I	wasn't.
Yes,	he she it	was.	No,	he she it	wasn't.
	you			you	
	we	were.		we	weren't.
	they			they	

Information Questions

WH- WORD	WAS/WERE	SUBJECT	
Where	was	he	last week?
Why	were	you	in Hawaii?
What	was	that noise?	
When		we	in Boston?
Who	were	you	with?
How		the desserts?	

Answers

He **was** in London.
For Tom's wedding.
It was a barking dog.
In 1995.
My brother.
They **were** delicious!

B3 Writing Affirmative and Negative Statements

The facts below are false. Correct each one by rewriting it as a negative statement. Then use the word or phrase in parentheses to write a true affirmative statement.

1. The pharaohs were generals. (kings)

   The pharaohs weren't generals. They were kings.

2. Cleopatra was a Persian general. (Egyptian queen)

3. Columbus was a lawyer. (explorer)

4. Picasso and Rembrandt were astronomers. (artists)

5. William Shakespeare was a French writer. (English)

6. Cervantes was an American inventor. (Spanish writer)

7. Marie Curie and Albert Einstein were doctors. (scientists)

8. Beethoven was a German king. (composer)

172   Chapter 11 • Form

Form • The Simple Past of *Be*   175

• *Clear and detailed **Form Charts** make learning the grammar easy.*

• *A wealth of exercises provide practice in manipulating the form.*

The **Meaning and Use** section(s) offers clear and comprehensive explanations of how the target structure is used, and exercises to practice using it appropriately.

> • Inductive **Examining Meaning and Use** exercises encourage students to analyze how we use the target structure.

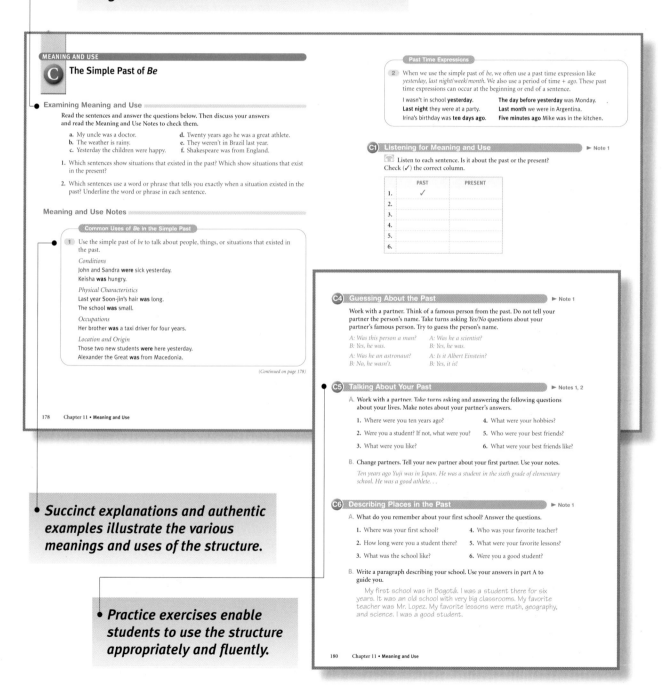

MEANING AND USE

C The Simple Past of *Be*

Examining Meaning and Use

Read the sentences and answer the questions below. Then discuss your answers and read the Meaning and Use Notes to check them.

a. My uncle was a doctor.
b. The weather is rainy.
c. Yesterday the children were happy.
d. Twenty years ago he was a great athlete.
e. They weren't in Brazil last year.
f. Shakespeare was from England.

1. Which sentences show situations that existed in the past? Which show situations that exist in the present?

2. Which sentences use a word or phrase that tells you exactly when a situation existed in the past? Underline the word or phrase in each sentence.

Meaning and Use Notes

Common Uses of *Be* in the Simple Past

1 Use the simple past of *be* to talk about people, things, or situations that existed in the past.

Conditions
John and Sandra **were** sick yesterday.
Keisha **was** hungry.

Physical Characteristics
Last year Soon-jin's hair **was** long.
The school **was** small.

Occupations
Her brother **was** a taxi driver for four years.

Location and Origin
Those two new students **were** here yesterday.
Alexander the Great **was** from Macedonia.

(Continued on page 178)

Past Time Expressions

2 When we use the simple past of *be*, we often use a past time expression like *yesterday, last night/week/month*. We also use a period of time + *ago*. These past time expressions can occur at the beginning or end of a sentence.

I wasn't in school **yesterday**.
Last night they were at a party.
Irina's birthday was **ten days ago**.

The day before yesterday was Monday.
Last month we were in Argentina.
Five minutes ago Mike was in the kitchen.

C1 Listening for Meaning and Use   ► Note 1

Listen to each sentence. Is it about the past or the present? Check (✓) the correct column.

	PAST	PRESENT
1.	✓	
2.		
3.		
4.		
5.		
6.		

C4 Guessing About the Past   ► Note 1

Work with a partner. Think of a famous person from the past. Do not tell your partner the person's name. Take turns asking *Yes/No* questions about your partner's famous person. Try to guess the person's name.

A: Was this person a man?
B: Yes, he was.
A: Was he an astronaut?
B: No, he wasn't.

A: Was he a scientist?
B: Yes, he was.
A: Is it Albert Einstein?
B: Yes, it is!

C5 Talking About Your Past   ► Notes 1, 2

A. Work with a partner. Take turns asking and answering the following questions about your lives. Make notes about your partner's answers.

1. Where were you ten years ago?
2. Were you a student? If not, what were you?
3. What were you like?
4. What were your hobbies?
5. Who were your best friends?
6. What were your best friends like?

B. Change partners. Tell your new partner about your first partner. Use your notes.

Ten years ago Yuji was in Japan. He was a student in the sixth grade of elementary school. He was a good athlete. . .

C6 Describing Places in the Past   ► Note 1

A. What do you remember about your first school? Answer the questions.

1. Where was your first school?
2. How long were you a student there?
3. What was the school like?
4. Who was your favorite teacher?
5. What were your favorite lessons?
6. Were you a good student?

B. Write a paragraph describing your school. Use your answers in part A to guide you.

My first school was in Bogotá. I was a student there for six years. It was an old school with very big classrooms. My favorite teacher was Mr. Lopez. My favorite lessons were math, geography, and science. I was a good student.

> • Succinct explanations and authentic examples illustrate the various meanings and uses of the structure.

> • Practice exercises enable students to use the structure appropriately and fluently.

The **Review** section allows students to demonstrate their mastery of all aspects of the structure. It can be used for further practice or as a test.

• **Thinking About Meaning and Use** exercises consolidate students' understanding of all aspects of the structure.

• **Editing** exercises teach students to correct their own writing.

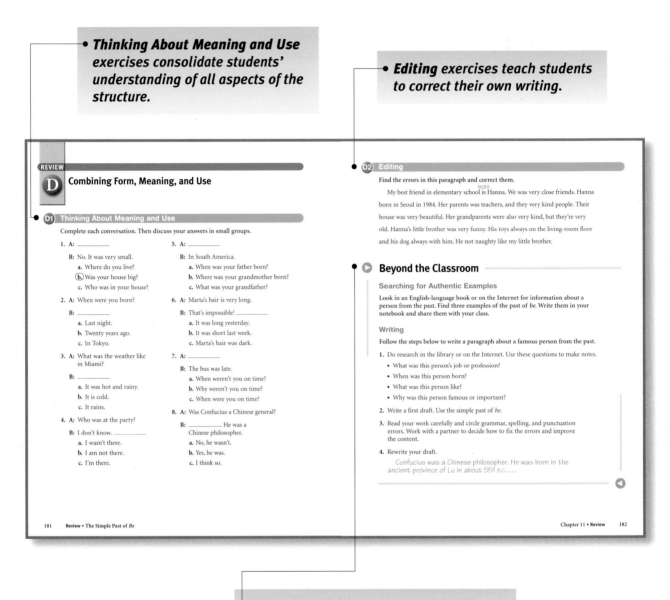

REVIEW

D Combining Form, Meaning, and Use

D1 Thinking About Meaning and Use

Complete each conversation. Then discuss your answers in small groups.

1. A: _____

    B: No. It was very small.
    a. Where do you live?
    b. Was your house big?
    c. Who was in your house?

2. A: When were you born?

    B: _____
    a. Last night.
    b. Twenty years ago.
    c. In Tokyo.

3. A: What was the weather like in Miami?

    B: _____
    a. It was hot and rainy.
    b. It is cold.
    c. It rains.

4. A: Who was at the party?

    B: I don't know. _____
    a. I wasn't there.
    b. I am not there.
    c. I'm there.

5. A: _____

    B: In South America.
    a. When was your father born?
    b. Where was your grandmother born?
    c. What was your grandfather?

6. A: Marta's hair is very long.

    B: That's impossible! _____
    a. It was long yesterday.
    b. It was short last week.
    c. Marta's hair was dark.

7. A: _____

    B: The bus was late.
    a. When weren't you on time?
    b. Why weren't you on time?
    c. When were you on time?

8. A: Was Confucius a Chinese general?

    B: _____ He was a Chinese philosopher.
    a. No, he wasn't.
    b. Yes, he was.
    c. I think so.

D2 Editing

Find the errors in this paragraph and correct them.

My best friend in elementary school is Hanna. We was very close friends. Hanna born in Seoul in 1984. Her parents was teachers, and they very kind people. Their house was very beautiful. Her grandparents were also very kind, but they're very old. Hanna's little brother was very funny. His toys always on the living-room floor and his dog always with him. He not naughty like my little brother.

Beyond the Classroom

Searching for Authentic Examples

Look in an English-language book or on the Internet for information about a person from the past. Find three examples of the past of *be*. Write them in your notebook and share them with your class.

Writing

Follow the steps below to write a paragraph about a famous person from the past.

1. Do research in the library or on the Internet. Use these questions to make notes.
    • What was this person's job or profession?
    • When was this person born?
    • What was this person like?
    • Why was this person famous or important?

2. Write a first draft. Use the simple past of *be*.

3. Read your work carefully and circle grammar, spelling, and punctuation errors. Work with a partner to decide how to fix the errors and improve the content.

4. Rewrite your draft.

    Confucius was a Chinese philosopher. He was born in the ancient province of Lu in about 551 B.C. . . .

• **Beyond the Classroom** activities offer creative suggestions for further practice in new contexts.

Special Sections appear throughout the chapters, with clear explanations, authentic examples, and follow-up exercises.

• **Pronunciation Notes** *show students how to pronounce selected forms of the target language.*

• **Beyond the Sentence** *sections show how structures function differently in extended discourse.*

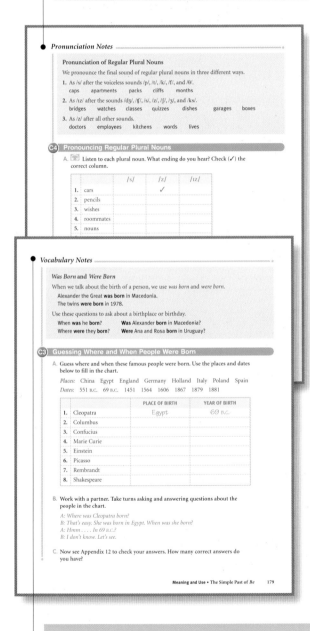

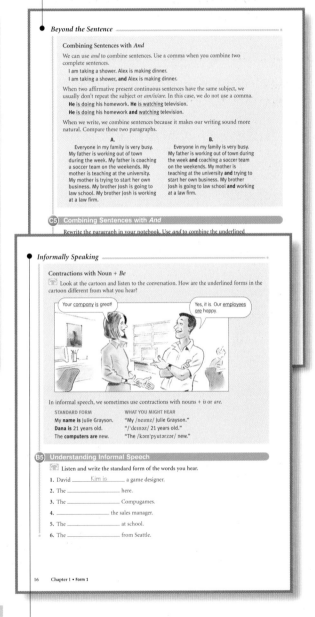

• **Vocabulary Notes** *highlight the important connection between key vocabulary and grammatical structures.*

• **Informally Speaking** *sections show the differences between written and spoken language.*

Before You Begin

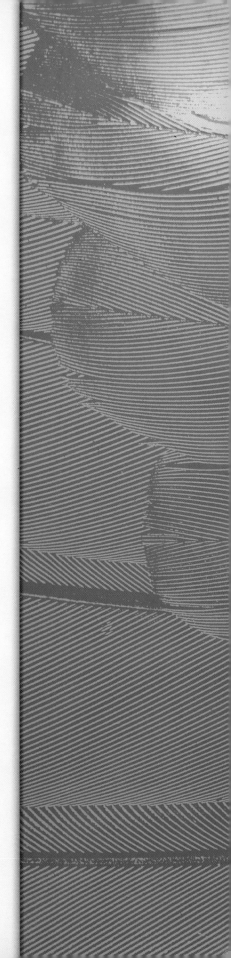

Grammar Language

▶ Nouns refer to people, animals, places, things, or ideas. To form the plural of many nouns, add *-s*.

A. Write the correct noun.

SINGULAR (one)	PLURAL (two or more)	SINGULAR (one)	PLURAL (two or more)

1. pencil   _pencils_

4. desk   _____

2. computer   _____

5. _____   calendars

3. _____   books

6. student   _____

B. Circle the correct noun.

1. two   chair / (chairs)   **3.** four   book / books   **5.** six   teacher / teachers

2. one   house / houses   **4.** three   pencil / pencils   **6.** a   girl / girls

2 Verbs

▶ Most verbs express actions. These verbs are called *action verbs*.

A. Read and follow the instructions.
1. **Work** with another student.
2. **Say** your full name to your partner.
3. **Write** your partner's full name on the line. _____
4. **Underline** your partner's first name.
5. **Circle** your partner's family name.

▶ Some verbs do not express actions. They express states or conditions such as feelings, mental states, or physical states. These verbs are called *stative verbs*.

B. Write *A* for action verb or *S* for stative verb for each statement.

___A___ 1. We **eat** in the cafeteria.   _____ 4. **Write** your name.

_____ 2. The chairs **are** small.   _____ 5. **Close** the door.

_____ 3. I **feel** sick.   _____ 6. We **are** students.

C. Look at the words. Underline the verbs.

<u>say</u>   desk   pencil   word   sit   am   girl   read

3 Adjectives

▶ Adjectives describe nouns.

Look at the pictures. Match the phrases to the pictures.

A.   **B.**

___A___ 1. a **white** car   _____ 3. a **big** car   _____ 5. an **expensive** car

_____ 2. a **black** car   _____ 4. a **small** car   _____ 6. a **cheap** car

▶ Prepositions tell direction, origin, location, or time.

A. Study the picture. Then read the sentences below.

Class is **at** 8:00.	The bag is **under** the desk.
The flowers are **in** the vase.	The teacher is **next to** the desk.
The book is **on** the desk.	Betty Lin is **from** China.

B. Work with a partner. Describe things in your classroom. Use *in, on, next to,* and *under.*

The pencil is on the desk.

C. Read the sentences. Look at the underlined words. Write *A* for adjective or *P* for preposition above each word.

1. The <u>new</u> movie is <u>at</u> 1:30.
   A   P

2. John is <u>in</u> the <u>red</u> car.

3. The student <u>from</u> Japan is <u>young</u>.

4. Put the <u>dirty</u> dishes <u>next to</u> the sink.

5. The paper is <u>under</u> the <u>green</u> book.

6. The <u>expensive</u> shop is <u>on</u> the corner.

5 Subject Pronouns

▶ Pronouns replace nouns. A subject pronoun comes before the verb in a sentence.

A. Study the pictures.

SINGULAR SUBJECT PRONOUNS

PLURAL SUBJECT PRONOUNS

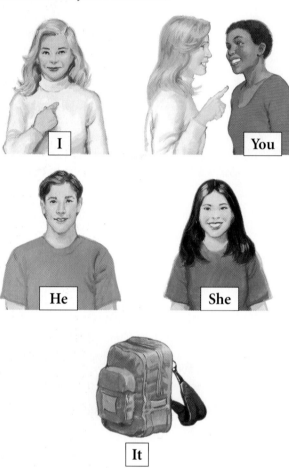

B. Complete the sentences with subject pronouns.

1. Mrs. Harris is a teacher. _She_ is a good teacher.

2. Juan is in the car. _____ is in the blue car.

3. Mr. and Mrs. Welch are Americans. _____ are from New York.

4. The chair is new. _____ is not old.

5. You and your friend are new students. _____ are in my class.

6. Derek and I are students. _____ are in college.

The Verb *Be* and Imperatives

Simple Present Statements with *Be*

A Meet the Staff

A1 Before You Read

Discuss these questions.

Do you work or study? What is your job? What do you study? Do you like it?

A2 Read

Read these conversations. Who is Carol?

Carol: Mr. Goodrich?

John: Sorry. Mike Goodrich isn't at work today. I'm his assistant. My name is John Louis.

Carol: My name is Carol Cheng. I'm a new employee.

John: Of course! You're the new sales manager.

John: Dana, Diego, this is Carol Cheng. Carol is from Taiwan. Carol, meet Dana Sullivan and Diego Chavez.

Carol: It's nice to meet you.

Dana and Diego: Nice to meet you, too.

Dana: We're new employees, too. I'm a computer technician and Diego is a game designer.

John: And Dana and Diego are students, too. Diego is 19 and Dana is 21. They're in college in the morning. In the afternoon, they're at work.

---

assistant: a helper
computer technician: a person who fixes computers
employee: a person who works for a company

game designer: a person who makes new games
sales manager: a head of a sales department

A3 **After You Read**

Match each person to his or her job.

_b_ **1.** John Louis   **a.** game designer

___ **2.** Carol Cheng   **b.** assistant

___ **3.** Dana Sullivan   **c.** sales manager

___ **4.** Diego Chavez   **d.** computer technician

B Affirmative Statements with *Be*, Subject Pronouns, and Contractions with *Be*

Examining Form

Read the sentences and complete the tasks below. Then discuss your answers and read the Form charts to check them.

    a. I am a new employee.
    b. Dana and Diego are new employees, too.
    c. Carol is from Taiwan.
    d. You are the new sales manager.

1. Circle the subjects and underline the verbs.

2. Which subjects are singular? Which is plural? Which subjects are pronouns?

3. Which verb form can have both singular and plural subjects?

4. Look back at the conversations on pages 10–11. Find one more sentence with a singular subject and verb, and one more sentence with a plural subject and verb.

AFFIRMATIVE STATEMENTS WITH *BE*

Singular			Plural		
SUBJECT NOUN or PRONOUN	*BE*		**SUBJECT NOUN or PRONOUN**	*BE*	
I	am	an employee.	**Dana** and **I** / We	are	employees.
You	are	young.	**You** and **Diego** / You	are	young.
Diego He / **Dana** She	is	in college.	**Diego** and **Dana** / They	are	in college.
Compugames It	is	a company.	**Compugames** and **DSL** / They	are	companies.

Singular	
SUBJECT PRONOUN + *BE*	CONTRACTION
I am	I**'m**
You are	You**'re**
He is	He**'s**
She is	She**'s**
It is	It**'s**

Plural	
SUBJECT PRONOUN + *BE*	CONTRACTION
We are	We**'re**
You are	You**'re**
They are	They**'re**

Affirmative Statements with *Be*

- Every sentence has a subject and a verb. The subject is a noun or pronoun.
- The verb *be* has three present tense forms: *am, is, are.*

Subject Pronouns and Contractions with *Be*

- The singular subject pronouns are *I, you, he, she, it.* The plural subject pronouns are *we, you, they.*
- Use *it* for things and animals. Sometimes we use *he* or *she* for animals.
- A contraction with *be* combines a subject pronoun and the verb *be.* An apostrophe (') replaces the missing letters of the verb (**I'm** = I am).
- You can use contractions with *be* in speaking and writing.

B1 **Listening for Form**

Carol and John are employees at Compugames. Listen to their statements. What form of *be* do you hear in each sentence? Check (✓) the correct column.

	AM OR 'M	IS OR 'S	ARE OR 'RE
1.		✓	
2.			
3.			
4.			
5.			
6.			
7.			
8.			

B2 Working on Affirmative Statements

Complete the paragraph with *am, is,* or *are.*

My name ___is___ Mike Goodrich. I _____ the president of
                1   2

Compugames. Compugames _____ an Internet videogame company. Our
                                     3

employees _____ from all over the world. I _____ from Seattle. Celia
              4   5

Rivera _____ the vice president of Compugames. She _____ from
            6   7

Puerto Rico. Ruth McMaster and Carol Cheng _____ two new employees.
                                                      8

Ruth _____ from New York, and Carol _____ from Taiwan. Diego and
         9   10

Dana _____ new employees. They _____ also college students.
         11   12

B3 Working on Pronouns and Contractions

A. Complete the sentences. Use subject pronoun + *be* contractions.

1. Mr. Walsh is our computer technician. __He's__ from Canada.

2. Compugames is a company. _____ in Seattle.

3. Mark and Pete are new employees. _____ game designers.

4. Ana and I are students. _____ from Mexico.

5. Some employees are in college. _____ busy.

6. My name is Hiro. _____ from Japan.

7. Carol is at work. _____ a sales manager.

8. You and Donna are new employees. _____ in my department.

9. *Rocket Race* is our new video game. _____ fun!

10. Our offices are on Jackson Street. _____ big.

**B. Work with a partner. Take turns saying the sentences with contractions
in part A.**

He's from Canada.

Complete the conversations. Add *am, is,* or *are* in the correct place. Use contractions with pronouns when possible.

Conversation 1: At the office

John: My name ^*is* John Lucas.

Sara: Hi, John. I Sara Walker.

John: Oh, you the new game designer. Welcome!

Sara: Thank you. It nice to meet you.

John: It nice to meet you, too.

Conversation 2: On campus

Beth: Steve, this my roommate, Lisa.

Steve: Hi, Lisa.

Beth: Steve, you from California. Lisa from California, too.

Steve: Really? I from San Francisco.

Lisa: I from San Diego.

　　　　(Lisa and Beth leave.)

Lisa: Steve handsome!

Beth: Yes. And he nice, too.

Conversation 3: At a party

Rosa: Jenny and I computer technicians at ElectroDesign.

Juan: Oh! You lucky!

Rosa: Yes, ElectroDesign a great company.

Jenny: The employees very happy.

Juan: My sons computer technicians, too. They employees at Reed.

Informally Speaking

Contractions with Noun + *Be*

🎧 Look at the cartoon and listen to the conversation. How are the underlined forms in the cartoon different from what you hear?

> Your <u>company is</u> great!

> Yes, it is. Our <u>employees are</u> happy.

In informal speech, we sometimes use contractions with nouns + *is* or *are*.

STANDARD FORM	WHAT YOU MIGHT HEAR
My **name is** Julie Grayson.	"My /neɪmz/ Julie Grayson."
Dana is 21 years old.	"/ˈdeɪnəz/ 21 years old."
The **computers are** new.	"The /kəmˈpyutərzər/ new."

B5 Understanding Informal Speech

🎧 Listen and write the standard form of the words you hear.

1. David _____*Kim is*_____ a game designer.

2. The _____ here.

3. The _____ Compugames.

4. _____ the sales manager.

5. The _____ at school.

6. The _____ from Seattle.

C Negative Statements and Contractions with *Be*

Examining Form

Read the sentences and complete the tasks below. Then discuss your answers and read the Form charts to check them.

> **1a.** He is not here.
> **1b.** They are not small.
>
> **2a.** He isn't here.
> **2b.** They aren't small.
>
> **3a.** He's not here.
> **3b.** They're not small.

1. Look at sentences 1a and 1b. Underline the verb in each sentence. Is *not* before or after the verb?

2. Underline the contractions of *be* + *not* in 2a and 2b. How are they different?

3. Circle the contractions of subject + *be* before *not* in 3a and 3b. How are they different?

NEGATIVE STATEMENTS WITH *BE*

Singular			
SUBJECT	BE	NOT	
I	am		
You	are		
He She	is	not	a game designer.
It	is		a new company.

Plural			
SUBJECT	BE	NOT	
We			
You			
They	are	not	game designers.
They			new companies.

> • Add *not* after *be* to make a sentence negative.

(Continued on page 18)

NEGATIVE CONTRACTIONS WITH *BE*

Singular	
SUBJECT PRONOUN + *BE* + *NOT*	CONTRACTION
I am not	I'm not
You are not	You aren't You're not
He is not	He isn't He's not
She is not	She isn't She's not
It is not	It isn't It's not

Plural	
SUBJECT PRONOUN + *BE* + *NOT*	CONTRACTION
We are not	We aren't We're not
You are not	You aren't You're not
They are not	They aren't They're not

- *Am not* has only one contracted form.
- *Are not* and *is not* have two different contracted forms.
- You can use negative contractions with *be* in speaking and writing.

C1 Listening for Form

Listen to each sentence. Is the sentence affirmative or negative? Check (✓) the correct column.

	AFFIRMATIVE	NEGATIVE
1.	✓	
2.		
3.		
4.		
5.		
6.		
7.		
8.		

Forming Negative Statements

Form negative statements with the words and phrases. Use contractions when possible. Punctuate your sentences correctly. Compare them with a partner.

1. in California/not/Seattle/is

   Seattle isn't in California.

2. is/Larry/not/from France

   _____

3. Lisa and I/not/students/are

   _____

4. big/our school/is/not

   _____

5. am/I/not/Canadian

   _____

6. in my class/are/not/you

   _____

C3 **Working on Pronouns and Negative Contractions**

Rewrite the sentences using subject pronouns and contractions. Use two different contracted forms.

1. Sara is not happy.

   She's not happy.

   She isn't happy.

2. Bob is not a manager.

   _____

   _____

3. You and Steve are not teachers.

   _____

   _____

4. The school is not big.

   _____

   _____

5. Rick and Yuki are not in class.

   _____

   _____

6. Eva and I are not Italian.

   _____

   _____

A. Complete the conversations with negative forms of _be_. Use contractions when possible.

Conversation 1

A: Hello. I'm a new student here.

B: <u>I'm not</u> the teacher. He _____ here.
      1   2

Conversation 2

A: Your pens are on the table.

B: No, they _____. My pens _____ blue. They're black.
                1   2

Conversation 3

A: Marta _____ in class.
            1

B: That's right. She and her sister _____ in school today. They're sick.
                                   2

Conversation 4

A: Hurry! Your class is at 12:00. It's 12:10. You're late.

B: I _____ late. My class _____ at 12:00. It's at 1:00.
      1   2

Conversation 5

A: Your computer is very fast.

B: It _____ my computer. My computer _____ very fast at all.
        1   2

Conversation 6

A: Carla and Roberta _____ in the office today.
                      1

B: No, they _____. They're at a meeting.
                2

B. Practice the conversations in part A with a partner.

A: Hello. I'm a new student here.
B: I'm not the teacher. . . .

D Descriptions with *Be*

Examining Meaning and Use

Read the sentences and answer the questions below. Then discuss your answers and read the Meaning and Use Notes to check them.

a. David is 25 years old.   **c.** She is sick.
b. I am from Mexico.   **d.** Mr. Grant is a teacher.

Which sentence talks about someone's:

_____ health?   _____ age?   _____ job?   _____ country?

Meaning and Use Notes

Conditions and Characteristics

1 Use *be* with adjectives to describe conditions, physical characteristics, age, and personality.

Condition	*Physical Characteristic*	*Age*	*Personality*
Jada **is sick.**	The school **is big.**	Josh **is ten (years old).**	Lee **is friendly.**

Identifying and Describing Nouns

2 Use *be* with nouns to identify or define something, describe occupations, and describe relationships.

Identifying	*Describing Occupations*	*Describing Relationships*
It**'s a map.**	He**'s a game designer.**	Lisa **is my friend.**

Location and Origin

3A Use *be* with prepositions to describe location (where people or things are). We also use words such as *here, there, upstairs,* and *downstairs.*
She**'s not in class.** She**'s at home.**   They**'re not here.** They**'re upstairs.**

3B Use *be* with prepositions or adjectives to describe origin (the country where people or things are from).

With Prepositions: They**'re from Chile.**   *With Adjectives:* They**'re Chilean.**

(Continued on page 22)

Talking About Time, Dates, and Weather

4 We use *it* with *be* for the time, the day/date, and the weather.

Time	*Day*	*Weather*
It's eight o'clock.	**It's** Thursday.	**It's** cold and windy.

D1 **Listening for Meaning and Use** ▶ Notes 1–3B

🎧 Listen to each sentence. Does it describe an age or characteristic, an occupation, or a location or origin? Check (✓) the correct column.

	AGE OR CHARACTERISTIC	OCCUPATION	LOCATION OR ORIGIN
1.			✓
2.			
3.			
4.			
5.			
6.			

D2 **Defining and Describing Nouns** ▶ Note 2

A. Complete the definitions using the words below.

colors   Europe   fruits   pizza
dictionary   flower   June   Rome and Venice

1. __Europe__ is a continent.

2. A daisy is a _____.

3. _____ are cities.

4. Green and yellow are _____.

5. A _____ is a book

6. Apples and oranges are _____.

7. _____ is a month.

8. _____ is Italian.

B. Write four more sentences using some of these words.

animal   colors   countries   flower   language   months

Brazil and Peru are countries in South America.

Describing Nouns ► Note 1

Work with a partner. Look at the pictures. Write one affirmative and one negative statement in your notebook with the words below.

beautiful   big   old   small   ugly   young

1.

He's old. He isn't young.

3.

5.

2.

4.

6.

D4 **Talking About Time, Dates, and Weather** ► Note 4

Complete the conversations with a time, a date, or the weather.

1. A: The weather is beautiful

    B: Yes, <u>it's warm and sunny</u>.

2. A: We are late! It's 3:00.

    B: We are not late. _____.

3. A: It's late in New York. It's 11:00 P.M.

    B: _____ in Los Angeles.

4. A: Oh no! The bank is closed.

    B: Of course, it's closed. _____.

5. A: When is your birthday?

    B: _____

Introduce yourself to three classmates. Include your name, age, country of origin, and occupation.

A: *My name is Kathy Lim. I'm 22 years old. I'm from Korea. I'm a student.*
B: *Nice to meet you, Kathy. My name is . . .*

Beyond the Sentence

Using Pronouns in Paragraphs

In paragraphs the first time we talk about the subject of a sentence we use a subject noun. After that, we often use the subject pronoun form to refer to the same noun.

Read the paragraphs below. Notice how the pronouns make the second paragraph more interesting.

Paragraph with No Pronouns

Carol Cheng is from Taiwan. Carol is a new employee at Compugames. Carol is the sales manager. Compugames is a videogame company. Compugames is a new company. Compugames is in Seattle.

Paragraph with Pronouns

Carol Cheng is from Taiwan. **She**'s a new employee at Compugames. **She**'s the sales manager. Compugames is a videogame company. **It**'s a new company. **It**'s in Seattle.

D6 Using Pronouns in Paragraphs

Rewrite the paragraph. Use pronouns to replace some of the nouns.

Sally is 17 years old. Sally is not a normal teenager. In the afternoon Sally is an employee at Macro Ads. Sally is not the only teenager there. Mark is an employee, too. Mark is only 16 years old. Both teenagers are students at West Valley High School. West Valley High School is near the offices of Macro Ads.

<u>Sally is 17 years old. She . . .</u>

_____

_____

_____

Combining Form, Meaning, and Use

E1 Thinking About Meaning and Use

Complete each sentence. Then discuss your answers in small groups.

1. John is an employee at Compugames.

   _____ is an assistant.

   a. She

   (b.) He

   c. It

2. Pedro is from the Dominican Republic.

   He _____ from Puerto Rico.

   a. is

   b. are

   c. isn't

3. Lynn and I are game designers. We

   _____ sales managers.

   a. isn't

   b. am not

   c. are not

4. Bangkok is a large city. _____

   is the capital of Thailand.

   a. It

   b. He

   c. She

5. The company is new. _____ old.

   a. They're

   b. They aren't

   c. It isn't

6. Brazil _____ in North America.

   a. not

   b. is not

   c. is no

E2 Editing

Some of these sentences have errors. Find the errors and correct them.

1. Lucy a̶m̶ a teacher. *(is)*

2. India in Asia.

3. We are at home.

4. She in the classroom.

5. They happy.

6. I amn't a student.

7. Paulo no is Brazilian.

8. You're not in my English class.

Beyond the Classroom

Searching for Authentic Examples

Look at English-language books and newspapers, or on the Internet. Find examples of subject pronouns + *be*. Write them in your notebook. What is the noun that the subject pronoun replaces? Share the sentences with your class.

Writing

Reread the paragraph in exercise D6 on page 24. Then follow these steps to write a paragraph about someone you know.

1. Use the form below to make notes.

Someone I Know

Name: _____

Age: _____

Country: _____

School or Company: _____

Job: _____

Other: _____

---

2. Write a first draft. Use affirmative and negative statements with the correct form of *be*.

3. Read your work carefully and circle grammar, spelling, and punctuation errors. Work with a partner to decide how to fix the errors and improve the content.

4. Rewrite your draft.

> Mark Hunter is my best friend. He is 20 years old. He is from England. Mark is in college. In the afternoons, he is a salesperson.

Questions with *Be*

A ## Are You Best Friends?

A1 **Before You Read**

Discuss these questions.

Do you have many good friends? Are your good friends similar to you? Describe your best friend.

A2 **Read**

🎧 **Read this conversation and the magazine quiz about friends on the following page. Then take the quiz. Are you and your best friend similar?**

Josh: Hmm . . . what's this? "Are you and your best friend similar? Take this quiz and find out." Is this your magazine, Corey?

Corey: No, it's not. It's my sister's. It's silly.

Josh: No, it isn't. It's interesting. We're best friends. Let's take the quiz.

Corey: No thanks. I'm busy.

Josh: Oh, wow!

Corey: What is it?

Josh: Oh, my!

Corey: What? What is it? Tell me.

Josh: But you're busy.

Corey: Let me see that!

Are You Best Friends?

**Are you and your best friend similar? Are you different?
Are you really best friends?
Take this quiz and find out.**

Who is your best friend? _____

	YOU	Yes	No	YOUR BEST FRIEND	Yes	No
1.	Are you a social person?			Is your best friend a social person?		
2.	Are you a private person?			Is your best friend a private person?		
3.	Are you a good student?			Is your best friend a good student?		
4.	Are you cautious?			Is your best friend cautious?		
5.	Are you athletic?			Is your best friend athletic?		
6.	Are you active?			Is your best friend active?		
7.	Are you a spendthrift?			Is your best friend a spendthrift?		
8.	What is your favorite kind of music?			What is your best friend's favorite kind of music?		
9.	What are your hobbies?			What are your best friend's hobbies?		

active: busy
athletic: having a strong, healthy body
cautious: careful
find out: to learn or discover

private: not sharing feelings
social: having many friends
silly: not serious
spendthrift: a person who spends a lot of money

A3 **After You Read**

Work in small groups. Compare your answers to the magazine quiz.

B Yes/No Questions and Short Answers with *Be*

Examining Form

Read the sentences and complete the tasks below. Then discuss your answers and read the Form charts to check them.

a. It's silly.
b. Are you best friends?
c. Is she athletic?

d. Yes, they are.
e. We're best friends.
f. No, it isn't.

1. Which sentences are statements? Which are questions?

2. Circle the subjects and underline the verbs.

3. In statements, which is first, the subject or the verb? Which is first in questions?

Yes/No Questions with *Be*		
BE	**SUBJECT**	
Am	I	
Are	you	
Is	he	
	she	late?
	it	
Are	we	
	you	
	they	

Short Answers				
YES	**SUBJECT**	**BE**	**NO**	**SUBJECT + BE + NOT**
Yes,	you	are.	**No,**	you **aren't.** / you**'re not.**
	I	am.		I**'m not.**
	he	is.		he **isn't.** / he**'s not.**
	she	is.		she **isn't.** / she**'s not.**
	it	is.		it **isn't.** / it**'s not.**
	you	are.		you **aren't.** / you**'re not.**
	we	are.		we **aren't.** / we**'re not.**
	they	are.		they **aren't.** / they**'re not.**

Yes/No **Questions**

- In a question, *be* comes before the subject. A question ends with a question mark *(?)*.

Statement	Yes/No *Question*
They **are** late.	**Are they** late?

- Use a singular form of *be* with singular subjects. Use the plural form of *be* with plural subjects.

Singular	*Plural*
Is he late?	**Are** we late?

Short Answers

- We usually answer *Yes/No* questions with short answers.

- Do not use contractions in short answers with *yes*.

Yes, **I am**.	* Yes, I'm. (INCORRECT)

B1 **Listening for Form**

Listen to each sentence. Is it a question or a statement? Check (✓) the correct column.

	QUESTION	STATEMENT
1.	✓	
2.		
3.		
4.		
5.		
6.		
7.		
8.		
9.		
10.		

A. Form *Yes/No* questions. Use the words and phrases. Punctuate your sentences correctly.

1. from the United States/your best friend/is

   Is your best friend from the United States?

2. you/a smoker/are

   _____

3. your family/is/in the United States

   _____

4. your English/is/good

   _____

5. you/are/an active person

   _____

6. big/is/your home

   _____

B. Work with a partner. Take turns asking and answering the questions in part A.

A: Is your best friend from the United States?
B: No, she isn't.

B3 Changing Statements into Questions

Change the statements into *Yes/No* questions. Write them in your notebook. Use the correct pronoun in place of the subject noun.

1. Paul is from Saratoga Springs.

   Is he from Saratoga Springs?

2. Your English class is interesting.

3. Linda and Paul are friends.

4. Mrs. Miller is a Spanish teacher.

5. Juan and I are late for the party.

6. Emily is a spendthrift.

C Information Questions with *Be*

Examining Form

Read the sentences and complete the tasks below. Then discuss your answers and read the Form charts to check them.

1a. How is Marcia?   **2a.** Where are the classes?
1b. Is Marcia sick?   **2b.** Are the classes here?

1. Which questions are *Yes/No* questions? Which are information questions? What words do the information questions begin with?

2. Circle the subjects and underline the verbs in each question. Is the order of the subject and the verb the same in all of the questions?

Information Questions			Answers
WH- WORD	*BE*	**SUBJECT**	
Where	am	I?	On the second floor. You**'re** on the second floor.
How	are	you?	Fine, thanks. I**'m** fine, thanks.
Who	is	he?	My roommate. He**'s** my roommate.
		she?	My sister. She**'s** my sister.
When		it?	At noon. It**'s** at noon.
Where	are	we?	On Main Street. You**'re** on Main Street.
		you?	On campus. We**'re** on campus.
What		they?	Shoes. They**'re** shoes.

(Continued on page 34)

- Information questions are similar to *Yes/No* questions, but they begin with a question word (*wh-* word). The question word is before *be*.

Yes/No *Question*	Information *Question*
Is the manager outside?	**Where** is the manager?

- Use a singular form of *be* with singular subjects. Use a plural form of *be* with plural subjects.
- It is not necessary to answer an information question with a complete sentence.

C1 Listening for Form

Listen to each question in the conversation. Is it a *Yes/No* question or an information question? Check (✓) the correct column.

	YES/NO QUESTION	INFORMATION QUESTION
1.	✓	
2.		
3.		
4.		
5.		
6.		

C2 Changing Statements into Questions

Change the statements into information questions. Use the question word in parentheses. Punctuate your sentences correctly.

1. My name is Julie Bishop. (what) _What is your name?_

2. The apartment is very nice. (how) _____

3. The appointment is at 8:00. (when) _____

4. The apartment is on Carson Street. (where) _____

5. Mrs. Hewitt is the manager. (who) _____

6. Jada and Emily are the other roommates. (who) _____

Informally Speaking

Contractions with *Wh-* Word + *Be*

🎧 Look at the cartoon and listen to the conversation. How is the underlined form in the cartoon different from what you hear?

In informal speech, we often use contractions with question words + *is* or *are*.

STANDARD FORM	WHAT YOU MIGHT HEAR
When is the class?	"/wɛnz/ the class?"
How is your apartment?	"/haʊz/ your apartment?"
Who are your roommates?	"/huər/ your roommates?"
What are their jobs?	"/ˈwʌtər/ their jobs?"
Where are the students?	"/ˈwɛrər/ the students?"
How are your teachers?	"/ˈhaʊər/ your teachers?"
When are the tests?	"/ˈwɛnər/ the tests?"

C3 Understanding Informal Speech

🎧 Listen and write the standard form of the words you hear.

1. _Where are_ the children?

2. _____ their names?

3. _____ the meal?

4. _____ your friends?

5. _____ your class?

6. _____ your roommate?

7. _____ your grades?

8. _____ your books?

D Questions with *Be*

Examining Meaning and Use

Read the sentences and answer the questions below. Then discuss your answers and read the Meaning and Use Notes to check them.

1a. Bob: Is Fumiko from China? **2a. Jane:** Where is Fumiko from?
1b. Sara: No, she isn't. **2b. Dan:** She's from Japan.

1. Look at the questions and answers above. Which question asks if something is true or not?

2. Which question asks for specific information?

3. Which answer gives more information?

Meaning and Use Notes

Asking If Something Is True

1 Use *Yes/No* questions to find out if information is true or not.

A: **Are** you from Mexico?   A: **Is** your math class difficult?   A: **Is** Istanbul in Italy?
B: Yes, I am.   B: Yes, it is.   B: No, it's not.

A: **Is** Betty your friend?   A: **Is** breakfast at 8:00?
B: Yes, she is.   B: Yes, it is.

Asking for New Information

2A Use information questions when you want to learn specific information about someone or something.

A: **Where** are you from?   A: **How** is your math class?   A: **Where** is Istanbul?
B: Mexico.   B: It's very difficult!   B: In Turkey.

A: **Who** is your friend?   A: **When** is breakfast?
B: Betty Brown.   B: At 8:00.

2B Use *wh-* words to ask for specific information.

Who *for People*
A: **Who is** your teacher?
B: Mr. Brown.

Where *for Places*
A: **Where are** you from?
B: Argentina.

How *for Conditions*
A: **How are** you?
B: Fine, thanks.

What *for Things*
A: **What's** that?
B: It's my new phone.

When *for Time*
A: **When is** the test?
B: Tomorrow.

How *for Opinions*
A: **How are** your classes?
B: They're interesting.

Using Questions in Conversation

3 *Yes/No* questions and answers are usually short and direct. Ask an information question when you want to have a longer conversation with someone.

Yes/No *Question*
A: **Is** your roommate from Korea?
B: No.

Information Questions
A: **Where** is your roommate from?
B: She's from Taiwan. Her name's Jenny Wang.
A: My roommate is from Taiwan, too!
B: Really? **What's** his name?
A: David Wang. Maybe he's Jenny's brother!

D1 **Listening for Meaning and Use** ► Notes 1–2B

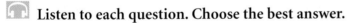 Listen to each question. Choose the best answer.

1. **a.** Yes, I am.
   b. I'm a student.

2. **a.** No, it isn't.
   b. Business.

3. **a.** Yes, it is.
   b. I'm at the university.

4. **a.** No, I'm not.
   b. It's beautiful.

5. **a.** Yes, I am.
   b. I'm from New York.

6. **a.** Yes, they are.
   b. They're in my class.

7. **a.** Yes, she is.
   b. Mrs. Jenkins.

8. **a.** Yes, she is.
   b. She's in her office.

9. **a.** I'm in the dorm.
   b. South Dorm.

10. **a.** No, it's not.
    b. It's small.

Work with a partner. Look at the picture. Ask and answer *Yes/No* **questions. Use the words and phrases.**

1. keys/on the floor

   A: *Are the keys on the floor?*
   B: *No, they aren't*

2. Julia/athletic

3. windows/open

4. Julia/happy

5. Julia/bad student

6. the shelf/neat

7. the ball/on the bed

8. the room/messy

D3 Asking for New Information ▶ Notes 2A, 2B

A. **Complete the form with your information.**

1. Name:

2. Address:

3. Country:

4. Hobbies:

5. Best Friend:

6. Birthday:

B. Write questions about the information on the form on the previous page. Use the *wh-* words below. Punctuate your sentences correctly.

1. What <u>is your name?</u>

2. What _____

3. Where _____

4. What _____

5. Who _____

6. When _____

C. Work with a partner. Use the information on your form to ask and answer questions.

A: What is your name?
B: My name is Elena Karanova.

D4 **Contrasting *Yes/No* and Information Questions** ▶ Notes 1–3

Complete the conversation with appropriate questions. Punctuate your sentences correctly.

Pete: Chris, meet Jorge Zapata. He's our new roommate.

Chris: Hi Jorge. <u>Where are you from?</u>
                                                1

Jorge: I'm from Mexico.

Chris: Wow! _____
                                              2

Jorge: No, I'm not from Mexico City. I'm from Monterrey.

Pete: _____
                                    3

Jorge: Yes, it is. It's very hot in Monterrey. . . . This apartment is very nice.

_____
                           4

Pete: No, it isn't. The neighborhood is very quiet.

Jorge: Great. _____
                                              5

Chris: The stores are on Freeman Street.

Jorge: _____
                                    6

Pete: The buses are great. They aren't crowded and they're on time.

Vocabulary Notes

Responses to *Yes/No* Questions

We use several different responses to *Yes/No* questions. These responses express different levels of certainty and formality.

	FORMAL	INFORMAL
Certainty	Yes. / No.	Yeah. / Yep. / Nope.
Some Certainty	I think so. / I don't think so.	I think so. / I don't think so.
	I'm not sure.	I'm not sure.
	Perhaps.	Maybe.
	Maybe.	
Uncertainty	I don't know.	Don't know.
		You got me.
		I have no idea.

D5) Responding to *Yes/No* Questions

A. Imagine a conversation with the following people. Write *F* if the situation is formal. Write *I* if it is informal.

__F__ **1.** your teacher   _____ **4.** a police officer

_____ **2.** your friend   _____ **5.** your new landlord

_____ **3.** your brother or sister   _____ **6.** your boss

B. Work with a partner. Imagine you are the people in each situation. Take turns asking and answering the questions. Use appropriate responses from the Vocabulary Notes.

1. Landlord: Is your heat broken?
   Tenant: _I think so._

2. Teacher: Is Lusaka the capital of Namibia?
   Student: _____

3. Guest: Is it cold in Jakarta?
   Hotel clerk: _____

4. Brother: Is your teacher nice?
   Sister: _____

5. Boss: Is the meeting in Room 5?
   Employee: _____

6. Friend: Is English class interesting?
   Friend: _____

Combining Form, Meaning, and Use

Thinking About Meaning and Use

Complete each conversation. Then discuss your answers in small groups.

1. **A:** _____

   B: No, it's in the library.
       a. How is the class?
       b. Is the class here?

2. **A:** Where is Linda?

   B: _____
       a. In class.
       b. An engineer.

3. **A:** When is dinner?

   B: _____
       a. Very nice.
       b. It's at 6:00.

4. **A:** _____

   B: A new student.
       a. Who is he?
       b. How is he?

5. **A:** Who are they?

   B: _____
       a. Alex and Naomi.
       b. They're fine.

6. **A:** _____

   B: No, they aren't.
       a. Where are they?
       b. Are they home?

7. **A:** _____

   B: It's interesting.
       a. How is the book?
       b. Where is the book?

8. **A:** _____

   B: It's at 9:30.
       a. Where is your appointment?
       b. When is your appointment?

9. **A:** _____

   B: She's from Japan.
       a. Where is Keiko from?
       b. Who is Keiko?

10. **A:** When is the class?

    B: _____
        a. Yes, it is.
        b. At 3:00.

Some of these sentences have errors. Find the errors and correct them.

1. Where ~~she is~~? *is she*

2. Is happy the teacher?

3. Where Dana is?

4. Who they?

5. When is the meeting?

6. How you are?

7. Yes, I'm.

8. She 19 years old.

▶ Beyond the Classroom

Searching for Authentic Examples

Watch an English-language movie or TV program. Listen for examples of *Yes/No* questions and information questions with *be*. Write three Y*es/No* questions and three information questions with answers in your notebook. Share them with your class.

Speaking

Follow the steps below to prepare an interview for a new roommate.

1. Write six interview questions. Use *Yes/No* and information questions.

2. Bring your questions to class. Work with a partner and ask your partner the interview questions. Write down your partner's answers.

   A: Are you a student?
   B: Yes, I am.

3. Change partners two more times and ask your new partners the same interview questions.

4. Tell the class which partner is the best roommate for you.

Imperatives

A The Adventures of an Office Assistant

A1 Before You Read

Discuss these questions.

What is an office assistant? Is it a good job? Why or why not?

A2 Read

Read these conversations. Is Rob busy at his new job?

Mr. Brooks: Rob, please bring this contract to Mr. Douglas. It's very important.

Ms. Lopez: Rob, take this to the mailroom immediately. Do not forget.

Mr. Green: Rob, call Snyder Supply Company for me, please.

Ms. Ryan: Rob, please copy this for me. Oh . . . and when is my appointment with Ms. Smith?

Rob: Oh no, Celia. The contract isn't here!

Celia: Don't panic. Look under these papers and files. Oh! It's here!

Rob: Great! OK. Where is Mr. Douglas's office?

Celia: Go to the third floor. Turn right. It's the first door on the left. Oh, and Rob . . . don't worry. Mr. Douglas is very nice!

contract: a legal paper
file: a collection of papers in a folder
immediately: right away; now

mailroom: a place in an office where people send letters and packages
panic: to feel fear and worry

A3 **After You Read**

Check (✓) the tasks that people ask Rob to do.

✓ **1.** take a package to the mailroom

____ **2.** make coffee

____ **3.** get lunch

____ **4.** make copies

____ **5.** write contracts

____ **6.** make phone calls

____ **7.** check appointments

____ **8.** file papers

B Imperatives

Examining Form

Read the sentences and complete the tasks below. Then discuss your answers and read the Form charts to check them.

    a. Do not forget.
    b. Call Mr. Snyder for me, please.
    c. Don't panic.
    d. Turn right.

1. The sentences above are imperatives. Which are affirmative imperatives? Which are negative imperatives?

2. How do we form affirmative imperatives? How do we form negative imperatives?

3. Look back at the conversations on pages 44–45. Find two more examples of affirmative imperatives, and one more example of a negative imperative.

Affirmative Imperatives	
BASE FORM OF VERB	
Take	the contract to Mr. Douglas.
Copy	this for me.
Call	the bank.

Negative Imperatives	
DO + NOT	**BASE FORM OF VERB**
Do not **Don't**	**worry.**
	smoke.
	forget.

- The subject of an imperative sentence is *you* (singular or plural), but we do not usually say or write the subject of the verb.
- Affirmative imperatives have only one form: the base form of the verb.
- Negative imperatives have two forms: *do not* + base form of verb and *don't* + base form of verb. We generally use *don't* + base form of verb in spoken English.

Listening for Form

🎧 Listen to each sentence. Do you hear an affirmative or a negative imperative? Check (✓) the correct column.

	AFFIRMATIVE	NEGATIVE
1.		✓
2.		
3.		
4.		
5.		
6.		
7.		
8.		
9.		
10.		

B2 **Working on Imperatives**

A. Complete the sentences with affirmative imperatives. Use the verbs below.

go	open	repeat	take out
listen	read	sit	talk

1. _Repeat_ the directions.

2. _____ to your partner.

3. _____ a pencil.

4. _____ to your partner's instructions.

5. _____ Chapter 4.

6. _____ the door.

7. _____ on the couch.

8. _____ home.

B. Change the affirmative imperatives in part A into negative imperatives.

Don't repeat the directions.

A. Write office rules with affirmative and negative imperatives. Use the words and phrases. Punctuate your sentences correctly.

1. play/loud music _Don't play loud music._

2. be/friendly to clients _____

3. call/your friends _____

4. be/polite _____

5. arrive/on time _____

6. lose/important files _____

7. be/messy _____

8. help/your co-workers _____

9. do/your work _____

10. forget/meetings _____

B. Work with a partner. Take turns saying the sentences in part A.

Don't play loud music.

C Imperatives

Examining Meaning and Use

Read the sentences and answer the questions below. Then discuss your answers and read the Meaning and Use Notes to check them.

a. Turn right at Grand Avenue.
b. Mix the sugar with the flour.
c. Watch out! The stove is hot.
d. Give me the book.

Which sentence gives:

_____ a command to do something?   _____ instructions about how to do something?

_____ a warning of danger?   _____ directions to a place?

Meaning and Use Notes

> ### Common Uses of Imperatives
>
> **1A** Use affirmative and negative imperatives to give commands, warnings, instructions, or directions.
>
> **1B** Commands express the authority of one person over another. Commands usually express strong feelings.
>
> | *Parent to Children* | *Boss to Employees* | *Teacher to Student* |
> |---|---|---|
> | **Sit down** and **be** quiet! | **Be** on time for the meeting. | **Don't run** in the hallways. |
>
> **1C** Warnings express danger.
>
> | *Bus Driver to Passenger* | *Two Strangers on the Street* |
> |---|---|
> | **Be** careful! The steps are wet. | **Look out**! A truck! |
>
> **1D** Instructions give information about what to do. Instructions are more neutral than commands and warnings.
>
> | *On a Test* | *On a Copy Machine* |
> |---|---|
> | **Underline** the negative sentences. | **Deposit** quarters. |

(Continued on page 50)

1E Directions are also neutral. Directions give information about how to go somewhere.

Turn right at the corner. The school is on the left.

Take Interstate 91 to Exit 3.

Polite Imperatives

2 *Please* makes an imperative more polite. We use *please* in commands and instructions. We do not use *please* in warnings and directions. *Please* comes at the beginning or at the end of an imperative sentence. Use a comma if *please* comes at the end.

Command

Please sit down and **be** quiet!

Instruction

Write your name on your paper, **please**.

Using *You* in Imperatives

3 Sometimes we use *you* at the beginning of an imperative sentence for emphasis or to talk to a specific person in a group we are talking to. You can also add the person's name.

Looking for Lost Car Keys

You look next to the sofa.

Gina, you look under the desk.

C1 Listening for Meaning and Use

▶ Notes 1A–3

Listen to each sentence. Choose the correct use of the imperative.

1. (instruction)   warning
2. warning   direction
3. command   instruction
4. warning   direction

5. instruction   command
6. command   warning
7. instruction   direction
8. direction   command

A. Read the commands and the situations. Match each situation to the appropriate command. In some cases, more than one answer may be possible.

Commands

Situations

___g___ **1.** Keep the change.

a. police officer to driver

_____ **2.** Follow me, please.

b. teacher to students

_____ **3.** Jack, you clean your room.

c. customs officer to tourist

_____ **4.** Don't be late.

d. librarian to students

_____ **5.** Please be quiet.

e. tour guide to tourists

_____ **6.** Do your homework.

f. boss to employee

_____ **7.** Do not park here.

g. customer to taxi driver

_____ **8.** Show me your passport.

h. father to son

B. Choose five of the situations from part A. Write a different command for each situation. Use *please* to make the commands more polite. Punctuate your sentences correctly.

1. **Situation:** *customer to taxi driver*

   Command: *Turn right at the next corner, please.*

2. **Situation:** _____

   Command: _____

3. **Situation:** _____

   Command: _____

4. **Situation:** _____

   Command: _____

5. **Situation:** _____

   Command: _____

6. **Situation:** _____

   Command: _____

Write an affirmative or negative imperative for each sign. Use the verbs below.

fasten   smoke   swim   take   turn   walk

1.

Fasten your seat belts.

3.

5.

2.

4.

6.

Vocabulary Notes

Prepositions of Location

Prepositions of location tell where someone or something is.

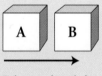

B is **on** the right.

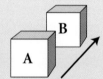

B is **behind** A.

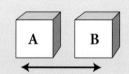

A is **next to** B.
B is **next to** A.

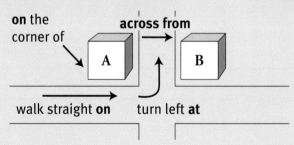

on the corner of   **across from**

walk straight **on**   turn left **at**

A is **on** the corner of High Street and Sherman Avenue.   A is **across from** B.
Walk straight **on** High Street.   Turn left **at** Sherman Avenue.

Look at the map. Complete each conversation with a preposition from the Vocabulary Notes. More than one preposition may be possible.

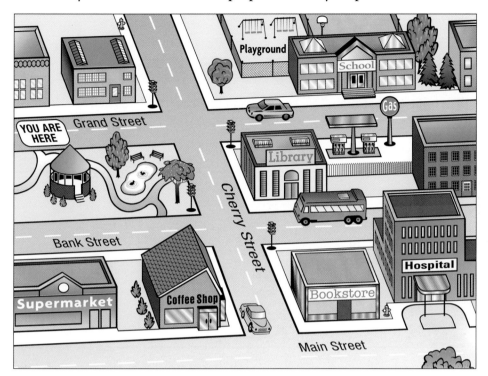

1. **A:** Is the school far?

   B: No, it's not. Walk straight ____on____ Grand Street.
                                          1

2. **A:** Where is the bookstore?

   B: It's _____ the corner of Cherry Street and Main Street, _____
                   1   2
   the hospital.

3. **A:** Is the gas station on Cherry Street?

   B: No, it isn't. It's _____ Grand Street, _____ the school.
                                 1   2

4. **A:** Where is the playground?

   B: Walk straight _____ Grand Street. It's _____ the school.
                             1   2

5. **A:** Where is the supermarket? Is it far?

   B: Yes, it is. Walk straight _____ Grand Street. Turn right _____
                                        1   2
   Cherry Street. Walk straight _____ Cherry Street. Turn right
                                     3
   _____ Main Street. It's _____ coffee shop.
        4   5

C5 **Identifying Imperatives** ► Note 1D

Read the instruction lines in this chapter. Find the imperative sentences. Write eight imperative sentences in your notebook. Compare your answers with a partner.

Discuss these questions.

C6 **Writing Instructions** ► Note 1D

A. Complete the recipe for oatmeal. Use the verbs below to complete each instruction.

add   boil   cook   lower   put   serve

1. Put _____ one cup of water into a pan.

3. _____ half a cup of oatmeal.

5. _____ for five minutes.

2. _____ the water.

4. _____ the heat.

6. _____ with butter, milk, and sugar.

B. Write instructions on how to do something. For example, how to cook rice, polish your shoes, or hang a picture.

Boil two cups of water.
Add one cup of rice. . . .

D Combining Form, Meaning, and Use

D1 Thinking About Meaning and Use

Complete each conversation. Then discuss your answers in small groups.

1. **A:** It's hot.

   B: _____
   - **a.** Open the window.
   - **b.** Put on a sweater.

2. **A:** The door is open.

   B: _____
   - **a.** Open it.
   - **b.** Close it.

3. **A:** It's Ana's birthday.

   B: _____
   - **a.** Don't be polite.
   - **b.** Buy her a present.

4. **A:** Is Jackie sick?

   B: Yes, she is. _____
   - **a.** Take her to the dance.
   - **b.** Please don't bother her.

5. **A:** It's dark in here.

   B: _____
   - **a.** Turn on the lights, please.
   - **b.** Don't turn off the lights.

6. **A:** Please don't sit on the table.

   B: _____
   - **a.** Oh, I'm sorry!
   - **b.** The chairs are comfortable.

7. **A:** The food is very hot!

   B: _____
   - **a.** Drink some water.
   - **b.** Put it in the oven.

8. **A:** It's sunny today.

   B: _____
   - **a.** Don't take your sunglasses.
   - **b.** Don't forget your sunglasses.

9. **A:** I'm late for work!

   B: _____
   - **a.** Take a taxi. Don't walk.
   - **b.** Walk. Don't take a taxi.

10. **A:** The mail is here.

    B: _____
    - **a.** Please get it.
    - **b.** Please send it.

Some of these sentences have errors. Find the errors and correct them.

1. ~~Not~~ Don't be noisy.

2. Brings a jacket.

3. Not go to the party.

4. Study tonight.

5. Be take a map.

6. No wear nice clothes.

7. Don't goes out.

8. Don't put the papers on the desk.

▶ Beyond the Classroom

Searching for Authentic Examples

Look for three imperatives on signs. Write them in your notebook and share them with your class. Copy the signs and exchange them with a partner. Compare your signs and imperatives with a partner.

Writing

Imagine that a friend is staying at your house while you are away. Follow the steps below to write a one-paragraph note to your friend.

1. Use these questions to make notes.
   - Does your friend need to feed your pets?
   - Does he or she need to water your plants?
   - Where do you keep the sheets and towels? Where are the keys?
   - Is there anything you want your friend to do or not to do?

2. Write a first draft. Use affirmative and negative imperatives.

3. Read your work carefully and circle grammar, spelling, and punctuation errors. Work with a partner to decide how to fix the errors and improve the content.

4. Rewrite your draft.

   Dear Carl,

   Welcome to my apartment. Please don't forget to feed my dog. Remember to change his water every day. The dog food is in the kitchen. . . .

Nouns

Introduction to Nouns

A A Nice Place to Live

A1 Before You Read

Discuss these questions.

Do you live in a house or an apartment? Do you like your neighborhood?

A2 Read

 Read these advertisements. What do they advertise?

Apartments for Rent

Two apartments in a good neighborhood, each with:

- a living room
- 2 bedrooms
- 1 1/2 bathrooms
- a large kitchen
- a garage
- a swimming pool
- a laundry room

- an elevator
- no pets

RENT
$750
per month
utilities included

Call Alan Marshall: 978-555-0921

Studio Apartments in Beautiful Downtown Danvers

Lovely studios in an old home on Grand Street

In each apartment: a kitchenette, a bathroom, and a balcony (great for plants!).

No smokers, please.

Call Larry Clark, manager: 978-555-5010

The Perfect House for a Family

- 2 bathrooms
- 3 bedrooms
- an elegant living room
- a sunny dining room
- a new kitchen

- a garage
- near Glenview Elementary School
- rent: $1,500 per month

Available March 1

Call Thompson Realty Today:
978-555-3285

---

kitchenette: a very small kitchen in an apartment

rent: money that people pay for the use of a house or an apartment

studio (apartment): a small apartment with only one room and a bathroom

utilities: electricity, water, and gas for heating and cooking

A3 After You Read

Work with a partner. Find a place to live for each person or family. Choose from the three ads.

RENTERS	CHILDREN	INCOME PER MONTH	OTHER INFORMATION
Derek Dobson	none	$1,200	Derek is a student.
Sally and John Freeman	Alex, 10 Amy, 8 Kim, 4	$5,500	Sally and John are teachers.
Paul and Jenny Rivera	Chris, 17	$4,000	Chris is a swimmer.

FORM 1

B Singular Count Nouns

Examining Form

Read the sentences and complete the tasks below. Then discuss your answers and read the Form charts to check them.

    a. Paul is an engineer.   **c.** Toronto is a city.
    b. John is a teacher.   **d.** Choose an apartment.

1. Underline three names for people or places.

2. Circle the other singular nouns in each sentence.

3. Look for the words *a* or *an* in the sentences. When do we use *a*? When do we use *an*?

Singular Count Nouns		
	A/AN	**NOUN**
Amy is	a	**child.**
Pinehurst is		**town.**
Mark is	an	**electrician.**
Call		**ambulance.**

Overview

- Nouns are words we use for people, places, or things.
  swimmer   park   car

- Some nouns have singular and plural forms. We call these nouns *count nouns*. (See Chapter 5 for more information on count and noncount nouns.)
  one **swimmer**   two/three/four **swimmers**

- *A, an,* or *the* can come before a singular count noun.

- Use *a* before a singular count noun that begins with a consonant sound. Use *an* before a singular count noun that begins with a vowel sound.

- If a noun begins with a silent *h* (the *h* is not pronounced), use *an*. If the *h* is pronounced, use *a*.
  an hour   **a** house

- The letter *u* sometimes has a consonant sound. (We pronounce it like the *y* in *yellow*.) Use *a* when the initial *u* is pronounced *y*.

  a utility   **an** umbrella

Proper Nouns and Common Nouns

- Proper nouns are names of specific people, places, or things. Proper nouns begin with a capital letter.

  John   Grand Street   Miami

- All other nouns are common nouns.

⚠ We do not usually use *a* or *an* before singular proper nouns.

B1 Listening for Form

🎧 Listen to each noun. Does it begin with a consonant sound or vowel sound? Check (✓) the correct column.

		CONSONANT SOUND	VOWEL SOUND
1.	hour		✓
2.	hospital		
3.	herb		
4.	hat		
5.	union		
6.	university		
7.	uncle		
8.	umpire		

B2 Identifying Nouns

A. Read the nouns. Write *P* for proper noun or *C* for common noun.

___P___ **1.** Toronto   _____ **4.** Julia Roberts

_____ **2.** building   _____ **5.** book

_____ **3.** Asia   _____ **6.** kitchen

B. Work with a partner. Write sentences with the nouns from part A. Use *a* or *an* with singular common nouns.

Toronto is my favorite city.

Complete the conversations with *a* or *an*. Write ✗ where it is not necessary to use *a* or *an*.

Conversation 1

Nesha: Is Soon-jun _a_ police officer?

Victor: No, he's _an_ ambulance driver.

Conversation 2

Sara: Is she ____ student?

Sam: No, she's ____ employee at the hospital. She's ____ receptionist.

Conversation 3

Reiko: Are you in ____ dorm?

Marta: No, I am in ____ house near campus.

Conversation 4

Celia: Where is ____ Yale University?

Hanna: It's in ____ town in ____ Connecticut.

Conversation 5

Lee: What is ____ umpire?

Sam: ____ umpire is ____ baseball official.

Conversation 6

Chris: ____ apartment is for rent in my building.

Stefan: Is it ____ studio?

Conversation 7

Jenny: Your neighborhood is ____ nice place to live.

Lisa: Yes, and it's near ____ Lyle Park.

C Plural Count Nouns

Examining Form

Read the sentences and complete the tasks below. Then discuss your answers and read the Form charts to check them.

    a. Sally and John are teachers.   **c.** Balconies are great for plants.
    b. Amy and Kim are children.   **d.** People are friendly in San Diego.

1. Underline the plural nouns that end in -*s* or -*es*.

2. Plural nouns that do not end in -*s* or -*es* are irregular. Circle the two irregular plural nouns.

Plural Count Nouns	
	NOUN
We are	**swimmers.**
Amy and Kim are	**children.**
They are	**women.**
Where are the	**balconies?**

Overview

- Add -*s* or -*es* to the singular form of a regular count noun to make it plural. See Appendix 1 for spelling rules for plural nouns.

- Plural nouns that do not end in -*s* or -*es* are irregular. Some common irregular nouns are:

    SINGULAR — PLURAL
    child — children   woman — women   man — men   person — people
    tooth — teeth   foot — feet   mouse — mice

- See Appendix 1 for a list of irregular plural nouns.

- *The* or no article can come before plural nouns. Do not use *a* or *an* before plural nouns.

Proper Nouns

- Use *the* + a plural proper noun for the family name of two or more people.
    the Riveras   the Sanchezes   the Kims

C1 Listening for Form

🎧 Listen to each noun. Is it singular or plural? Check (✓) the correct column.

	SINGULAR	PLURAL
1.	✓	
2.		
3.		
4.		
5.		
6.		
7.		
8.		

C2 Spelling Regular Plural Nouns

Write the plural forms of these nouns. Use Appendix 1 for help.

1. dictionary   _dictionaries_

2. balcony   _____

3. bedroom   _____

4. radio   _____

5. boy   _____

6. garage   _____

7. potato   _____

8. brush   _____

C3 Working with Irregular Plural Nouns

Complete each sentence with the correct irregular plural form of the noun in parentheses.

1. The _children_ (child) are in the park.

2. Two hundred _____ (person) are in line for the new Tom Cruise movie!

3. The _____ (man) are in my class.

4. Your smile is beautiful. Your _____ (tooth) are very white.

5. The _____ (woman) are from my hometown.

6. I'm not a good dancer. My _____ (foot) are too big!

Pronunciation Notes

Pronunciation of Regular Plural Nouns

We pronounce the final sound of regular plural nouns in three different ways.

1. As /s/ after the voiceless sounds /p/, /t/, /k/, /f/, and /θ/.

    caps   apartments   packs   cliffs   months

2. As /ɪz/ after the sounds /dʒ/, /tʃ/, /s/, /z/, /ʃ/, /ʒ/, and /ks/.

    bridges   watches   classes   quizzes   dishes   garages   boxes

3. As /z/ after all other sounds.

    doctors   employees   kitchens   words   lives

C4 Pronouncing Regular Plural Nouns

A. Listen to each plural noun. What ending do you hear? Check (✓) the correct column.

		/s/	/z/	/ɪz/
1.	cars		✓	
2.	pencils			
3.	wishes			
4.	roommates			
5.	nouns			
6.	maps			

B. Work with a partner. Take turns pronouncing the pairs of words below. Choose the correct sound for the plural ending.

1. road — roads   /s/ (/z/) /ɪz/

2. clock — clocks   /s/ /z/ /ɪz/

3. sentence — sentences   /s/ /z/ /ɪz/

4. room — rooms   /s/ /z/ /ɪz/

5. belief — beliefs   /s/ /z/ /ɪz/

6. excuse — excuses   /s/ /z/ /ɪz/

7. garage — garages   /s/ /z/ /ɪz/

8. apartment — apartments   /s/ /z/ /ɪz/

The Functions of Nouns

Examining Meaning and Use

Read the sentences and answer the questions below. Then discuss your answers and read the Meaning and Use Notes to check them.

   a. Flowers are expensive.
   b. Roses are flowers.
   c. The library is next to the bank.
   d. Open the door.

1. Which sentences have nouns used as subjects? Which sentence does not?

2. Which sentence has a noun after a verb other than *be*?

3. Which sentence has a noun after *be*?

4. Which sentence has a noun after a preposition?

Meaning and Use Notes

Nouns As Subjects

1 We can use a noun (or pronoun) as the subject of a sentence. The subject of a sentence with *be* tells who or what the sentence is about.

Barry King is the manager.
Computers are useful.
Teresa and **Pete** are children.

Nouns As Objects

2 We can use a noun as the object of a verb. The object usually receives the action of the verb.

Call the **manager**.   Please make the **sandwiches** now.

3 We can use a noun after the verb *be*. We use this noun to define or describe the subject of the sentence.

A studio <u>is</u> a small **apartment**.　　The Freemans <u>are</u> **teachers**.

Nouns After Prepositions

4 We can use a noun after a preposition. After many prepositions nouns refer to locations.

Mr. Clark is <u>on</u> the **telephone**.　　The school is <u>in</u> **town**.
Medford is <u>near</u> the **city**.　　　　Steve is from **Boston**.

D1 　Listening for Meaning and Use ▶ Notes 2, 3

Listen to the sentences. How do we use each noun? Check (✓) the correct column.

		RECEIVES THE ACTION	DESCRIBES THE SUBJECT
1.	vegetables	✓	
2.	building		
3.	apartments		
4.	newspaper		
5.	landlord		
6.	house		
7.	utilities		
8.	utensil		
9.	door		
10.	swimmer		

D2 　Writing an Ad ▶ Notes 1–4

Write an ad for a place to rent. The ad is for a college bulletin board. Is it a house or apartment? Describe it. Where is it? Who is the contact person?

Studio apartment for rent . . .

Read the messages. Then answer the questions.

To Do

Call a plumber
about the sink.
Buy hot dogs.
Do the laundry.

A.

Hi Jeff,
I am at the park.
The boys are at school.
Please make dinner.

Sheila

B.

Dear Sheila,
I'm in Tonga.
Tonga is a small
island. It's in the
Pacific Ocean. It's a
beautiful place.

C.

1. Look at message A. Which three nouns receive the action of the verb?

   plumber, . . .

2. Look at the underlined sentence in message B. Which noun is the sentence about?

3. Look at the underlined sentence in message C. Which noun defines Tonga?

4. Find four examples of prepositions + nouns used for locations.

Combining Form, Meaning, and Use

E1 Thinking About Meaning and Use

Complete each conversation. Then discuss your answers in small groups.

1. **A:** Call the children, please.

   B: Sure. _____
   - **a.** Where are they?
   - **b.** Where is she?

2. **A:** Is this apartment for rent?

   B: Yes. _____
   - **a.** It's available in June.
   - **b.** They are available in June.

3. **A:** When is the last day of classes?

   B: _____
   - **a.** They are in December.
   - **b.** It's in December.

4. **A:** Is your father a doctor?

   B: _____
   - **a.** No, teachers.
   - **b.** No, a teacher.

5. **A:** Is Albany near Los Angeles?

   B: No, _____
   - **a.** they aren't.
   - **b.** it isn't.

6. **A:** Where are the women?

   B: _____
   - **a.** They're at work.
   - **b.** She's at work.

E2 Editing

Some of these sentences have errors. Find the errors and correct them.

1. Dustin hoffman is a famous actor.

2. When is a Christmas?

3. The Watson are here.

4. The childs are happy.

5. They are employees at Microsoft.

6. Eat a apple every day.

7. Kenya is country in Africa.

8. Don't write in the books.

9. A Spain is a beautiful country.

10. The pen is in my bag.

11. Marta and Stefan are student in my class.

12. The books are on the shelves.

Beyond the Classroom

Searching for Authentic Examples

Look in an English-language newspaper or on the Internet for advertisements for apartments. Find three singular nouns and three plural nouns. Write them in your notebook and share them with your class.

Speaking

A scavenger hunt is a game for teams. Follow these steps to organize and participate in a scavenger hunt.

1. In teams, make a list of 15 objects for a scavenger hunt. Make the objects small or easy to bring to class.

2. Use *a/an* or a number before each noun in your list.

3. Exchange lists with another team. Find the objects from the list and bring them to class. The team with the most things on the list is the winner.

Scavenger Hunt List

an athletic shoe
an English dictionary
an earring
two pencils
a postcard from a different country . . .

Introduction to Count and Noncount Nouns

A Protect Our Environment

A1 Before You Read

Discuss these questions.

Is the environment important to you? Is it important to protect the environment? Why?

A2 Read

🎧 Read the flyer from an environmental organization on the following page. What are some ways to protect the environment?

A3 After You Read

Match the first half of each sentence to the second half.

_e_ **1.** Turn off . . .   **a.** energy-efficient office machines.

____ **2.** Use . . .   **b.** paper and plastic.

____ **3.** Reuse . . .   **c.** the curtains.

____ **4.** Recycle . . .   **d.** old furniture.

____ **5.** Donate . . .   **e.** the lights.

____ **6.** Close . . .   **f.** the heat.

____ **7.** Wash . . .   **g.** glass bottles.

____ **8.** Lower . . .   **h.** clothes in cold water.

PROTECT OUR ENVIRONMENT
Here are tips for home and office:

CONSERVE ENERGY

At Home
- Turn off the lights.
- Use energy-efficient light bulbs.
- Use appliances efficiently. For example, wash clothes in cold water.
- Lower the heat.
- Close the curtains on hot days.

In the Office
- Turn off all equipment at night.
- Use energy-efficient photocopying machines, computers, and printers.

RECYCLE

At Home
- Recycle cans, glass, plastic, and newspapers.
- Reuse glass bottles.

In the Office
- Recycle paper.
- Donate old computers and equipment to schools.
- Donate old office furniture.

---

appliances: machines we use at home
conserve: not to waste
donate: to give something for free to an organization or group
energy-efficient: not using much energy

equipment: things that we need to perform a particular activity
protect: to keep safe
tips: pieces of useful advice

B Count and Noncount Nouns

Examining Form

Read the sentences and complete the task below. Then discuss your answers and read the Form charts to check them.

1a. The <u>bottle</u> is in the <u>garbage</u>.
1b. The <u>bottles</u> are in the <u>garbage</u>.
2a. Turn off the <u>computer</u>. Save <u>electricity</u>.
2b. Turn off the <u>computers</u>. Save <u>electricity</u>.

Look at the underlined nouns. Which nouns have both singular and plural forms? Which nouns have only one form?

Singular Count Nouns

	NOUN	VERB	
A	computer	is	expensive.
The	umbrella		inexpensive.

Plural Count Nouns

	NOUN	VERB	
	Computers	are	expensive.
The	umbrellas		inexpensive.

Noncount Nouns

	NOUN	VERB	
	Pollution	is	unhealthy.
The	air		clean.

Count Nouns

- We use count nouns for people, places, or things we can count. Count nouns usually have singular and plural forms.
- Some count nouns have only a plural form.
    The **jeans** are dirty.　　The **clothes** are new.　　The **sunglasses** are on the table.
- Some count nouns have the same singular and plural form.
    one **fish**　　three **fish**　　one **sheep**　　two **sheep**
- Singular count nouns occur with *a/an* or *the*. Plural count nouns occur with *the* or no article.

Noncount Nouns

- We use noncount nouns for things we cannot count, for example, substances (*gold, paper*) and abstract nouns (*love, beauty, help*). These nouns are also noncount:

air	equipment	information	music	transportation
energy	furniture	money	pollution	water

- Some noncount nouns end in -*s*, but they also take singular verbs.

  Economics is an interesting subject.   The **news** is not good.

- Use a singular verb when a noncount noun is the subject of a sentence.

⚠ Use *the* or no article with noncount nouns. Do not use *a* or *an*.

B1 Listening for Form

🎧 Listen to each sentence. Is the noun count or noncount? Check (✓) the correct column.

	COUNT NOUN	NONCOUNT NOUN
1.	✓	
2.		
3.		
4.		
5.		
6.		

B2 Identifying Count and Noncount Nouns

Work with a partner. Underline the nouns in each sentence. Write *C* for count or *NC* for noncount above each noun.

      NC   C

1. <u>Transportation</u> is expensive in a big <u>city</u>.

2. Pollution is not a problem in my country.

3. Buy a bicycle. Reduce pollution.

4. Close the curtains, please. The room is hot.

5. You are the last person in the office. Turn off the equipment, please.

6. Please don't put newspapers in the garbage. Recycle them.

Form sentences with count and noncount nouns. Use the words and phrases. Make all necessary changes. Punctuate your sentences correctly.

1. The environment/be/important

   The environment is important.

2. Energy/not/be/cheap

   _____

3. The computers/not/be/on

   _____

4. The refrigerator door/be/open

   _____

5. Our air conditioner/be/not/energy efficient

   _____

6. New furniture/be/expensive

   _____

B4) **Working on Count and Noncount Nouns**

Complete the advertisement with *is* or *are*.

_____*Are*_____ clean clothes important to you? Then
   1
use Oxybright! Wash your clothes with Oxybright!

Oxybright _____ a powerful detergent. Dirt on
            2
your jeans? Don't worry. Dirty jeans _____
                                      3
not a problem with Oxybright. _____ your
                               4
windows dirty? Use Oxybright! That's right. This

amazing product _____ a detergent and a
                 5
cleaner! _____ Oxybright expensive? Great news!
          6
It's only $5.99!

BUY OXYBRIGHT!
IT'S ONLY $5.99!

OXYBRIGHT

Count and Noncount Nouns

Examining Meaning and Use

Read the sentences and answer the questions below. Then discuss your answers and read the Meaning and Use Notes to check them.

1a. Oh no! A gray hair!
1b. Long hair is beautiful.

2a. Chocolate is delicious.
2b. The chocolates are from Jim.

1. Underline the noncount nouns and circle the count nouns in each pair of sentences.

2. Which sentences are about individual items? Which are more general statements about a category or a kind of thing?

Meaning and Use Notes

> ### Count Nouns vs. Noncount Nouns
>
> **1A** Count nouns are people, places, or things that we can count as individual items. Noncount nouns are things we cannot count or think about as individual items.
>
> **1B** Count and noncount nouns are sometimes related in meaning. Noncount nouns sometimes refer to a class of objects. Count nouns refer to a particular example of something. Compare the nouns in the two columns. See Appendix 2 for a list of common noncount nouns.
>
> | *Count Nouns* | *Noncount Nouns* |
> |---|---|
> | an apple | fruit |
> | a job | work |
> | a trip | travel |
> | a dollar bill | money |
> | a suitcase | luggage |
> | a necklace | jewelry |

(Continued on page 80)

Noncount Nouns

2A Many noncount nouns are substances and materials. See Appendix 2 for a list of common noncount nouns.

Solids	*Gases*	*Materials*
chalk, glass	oxygen, air	wood, plastic

Liquids	*Grains and Powders*
shampoo, water	sugar, flour

2B Noncount nouns also refer to feelings and ideas, school subjects, and activities.

Feelings and Ideas	*School Subjects*	*Activities*
love, knowledge	biology, mathematics	basketball, swimming

General vs. Individual

3 Some nouns are both count and noncount. However, their meanings are different. Count nouns refer to individual things. Noncount nouns are usually more general.

Count (Individual)	*Noncount (General)*
Two large **coffees**, please. (two cups of coffee)	Don't drink **coffee**. (the drink)
Give me the **basketball**. (the ball)	**Basketball** is exciting. (the sport)
A **lamb** is a young sheep. (the animal)	**Lamb** is good in stew. (the meat)
Hand in your **paper**. (a piece of paper)	Recycle **paper**. (the material)

C1 Listening for Meaning and Use ▶ Notes 1A–3

🎧 Listen to each sentence and look at the noun. Does the speaker use it as a count noun or a noncount noun? Check (✓) the correct column.

		COUNT	NONCOUNT
1.	education		✓
2.	coffee		
3.	glass		
4.	chocolate		
5.	glass		
6.	hair		
7.	basketball		
8.	paper		

Find six objects in your classroom. What material are they made of? Write the name of the object and the material in your notebook. Label the nouns count or noncount.

desk = count
wood = noncount

C3 Thinking About Count and Noncount Nouns ► Notes 1A, 2A, 2B

A. Write the nouns in the correct categories below.

books	cars	feet	jewelry	pencil	teeth
boxes	children	flowers	mathematics	people	telephone
bracelet	computers	furniture	mice	radios	weather
building	equipment	jacket	music	sofa	women

COUNT NOUNS

SINGULAR   PLURAL
                Regular   Irregular

<u>bracelet</u>   <u>books</u>   <u>children</u>

_____   _____   _____

_____   _____   _____

_____   _____   _____

_____   _____   _____

_____   _____   _____

NONCOUNT NOUNS

<u>equipment</u>

_____

_____

_____

_____

_____

B. Choose four count nouns and four noncount nouns from the list in part A. Use each word in a sentence.

Don't buy the expensive bracelet.

A. Read each pair of sentences. One sentence uses the count form of a noun. The other uses the noncount form of the same noun. Is the underlined noun used as a count noun or a noncount noun? Write *C* for count noun or *N* for noncount noun.

1. _C_ a. A <u>baseball</u> is round and white.

   _N_ b. <u>Baseball</u> is a popular sport in Japan.

2. ____ a. Recycle <u>glass</u>.

   ____ b. Give me a <u>glass</u>, please.

3. ____ a. <u>Business</u> is slow now. The economy is bad.

   ____ b. Don't start a <u>business</u>! Go to college.

4. ____ a. Don't make a <u>change</u> in your life now.

   ____ b. Give me <u>change</u> for the telephone, please

5. ____ a. Eat more <u>fish</u>. It is good for your health.

   ____ b. Three <u>fish</u> are in the aquarium.

6. ____ a. A good <u>education</u> is expensive in the United States.

   ____ b. <u>Education</u> is important.

B. Each noun below has a count and a noncount meaning. Write one sentence using the count form of the noun and one sentence using the noncount form. Use a dictionary if you need help.

1. hair

   Waiter, there's a hair in my soup.
   Her hair is red.

2. glass

3. chicken

4. football

5. coffee

6. cake

Customer: *Waiter, there is a hair in my soup.*
Waiter: *Don't worry, sir. It's free.*

D Combining Form, Meaning, and Use

D1 Thinking About Meaning and Use

Complete each conversation. Then discuss your answers in small groups.

1. **A:** Wash the clothes.

   B: _____

      a. OK. Where are they?

      b. Sure. Where is it?

2. **A:** Where's the meat?

   B: _____

      a. It's on the table.

      b. They're in the refrigerator.

3. **A:** Is this plastic?

   B: No, _____

      a. it's a glass.

      b. it's glass.

4. **A:** Get me a coffee, please.

   B: _____

      a. One pound or two?

      b. With cream or sugar?

5. **A:** What is your favorite sport?

   B: _____

      a. A football.

      b. Football.

6. **A:** Buy your mother a present for her birthday.

   B: Okay. Is _____ a good gift?

      a. earrings

      b. jewelry

D2 Editing

Some of these sentences have errors. Find the errors and correct them.

1. Don't drink the *water* ~~waters~~.

2. Comb your hairs.

3. Your new clothes are beautiful.

4. Mathematics are easy.

5. The money is in the bank.

6. The furniture are new.

7. A football is an exciting sport.

8. Give me a coffee, please.

▶ Beyond the Classroom

Searching for Authentic Examples

Collect English-language take-out restaurant menus or look for them on the Internet. Find five count nouns and five noncount nouns. Write them in your notebook. Share the menus and your findings with your class.

Speaking

Think about your school or your job. Make a list of at least ten nouns that you use when you talk about your school or job. Use a dictionary if you need help. Then show your list to a partner.

My job: groceries, manager, cash register . . .

Choose five words from your list and make a sentence for each to explain its importance. Make sure you use the noun correctly as a singular or plural count noun or as a noncount noun.

Groceries are expensive at my supermarket.

Adjectives and Pronouns

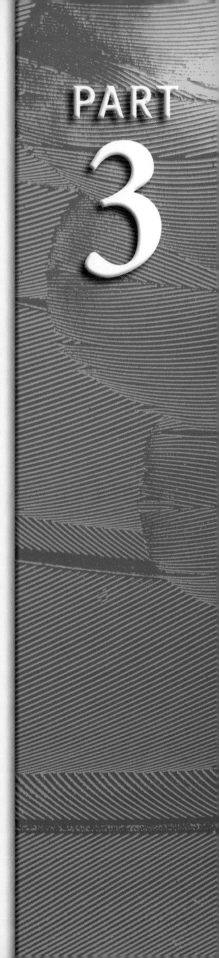

PART

3

Descriptive Adjectives

Westbrook College News

Before You Read

Discuss these questions.

What are classified advertisements? Does your college newspaper have classified advertisements? What do people advertise?

A2 **Read**

Read these classified ads from an on-line college newspaper. What do students at Westbrook College advertise?

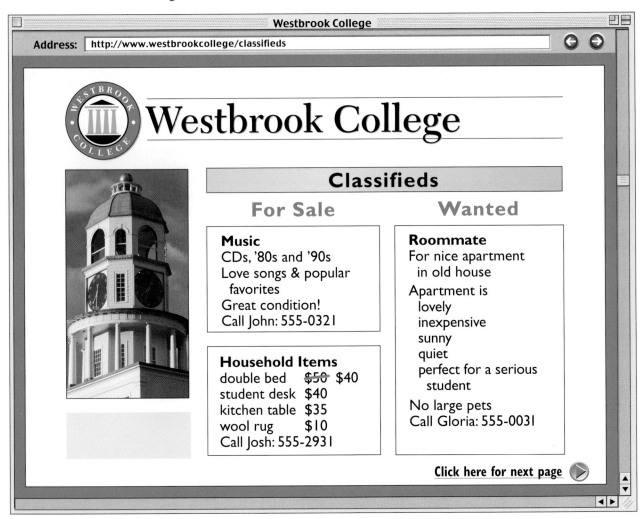

Westbrook College

Address: http://www.westbrookcollege/classifieds

Westbrook College

Classifieds

For Sale

Music
CDs, '80s and '90s
Love songs & popular
 favorites
Great condition!
Call John: 555-0321

Household Items
double bed   ~~$50~~ $40
student desk $40
kitchen table $35
wool rug $10
Call Josh: 555-2931

Wanted

Roommate
For nice apartment
 in old house
Apartment is
 lovely
 inexpensive
 sunny
 quiet
 perfect for a serious
  student

No large pets
Call Gloria: 555-0031

Click here for next page ▶

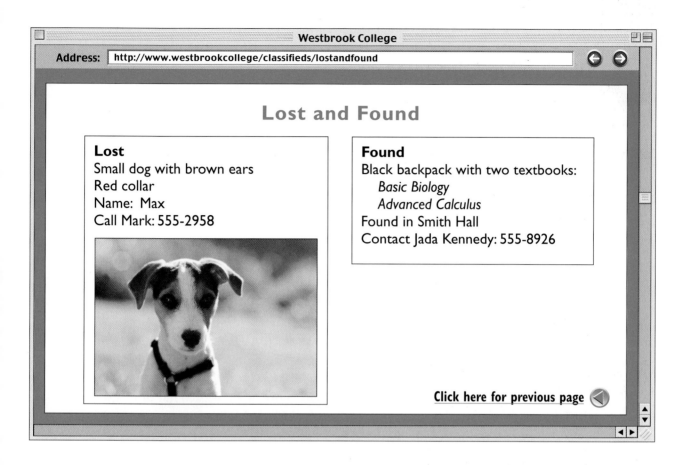

Lost and Found

Lost
Small dog with brown ears
Red collar
Name: Max
Call Mark: 555-2958

Found
Black backpack with two textbooks:
 Basic Biology
 Advanced Calculus
Found in Smith Hall
Contact Jada Kennedy: 555-8926

Click here for previous page

---

collar: a band around the neck of a dog or cat
condition: how well something works; how it looks

pet: an animal that you keep in your home
wool: material from sheep's hair used to make clothes

A3 After You Read

Check (✓) the things in the classified ads.

__✓__ **1.** a lost dog

_____ **2.** CDs from the '80s and '90s

_____ **3.** a diamond ring

_____ **4.** a student desk

_____ **5.** a new dress

_____ **6.** a black backpack

Descriptive Adjectives

Examining Form

Complete the tasks below. Then discuss your answers and read the Form charts to check them.

1. Adjectives describe nouns. Underline the nouns in the phrases below. Circle the adjectives.

   large pets   red collar   serious student   nice apartment

2. Look at the sentences below. Underline the nouns and circle the adjectives in each sentence. Which nouns are singular? Which nouns are plural? Does the form of the adjective change with singular and plural nouns?

   a. It is a small dog with a red collar.

   b. They are small dogs with red collars.

3. Look back at the ads on pages 88–89. Find four more adjectives. What nouns do they describe?

Adjectives After *Be*			
	NOUN	*BE*	ADJECTIVE
The	dog	is	**black.**
	dogs	are	

Adjectives Before Nouns			
	ADJECTIVE	NOUN	
The	**new**	teacher	is here.
They are	**friendly**	students.	

Overview
- Adjectives describe nouns.
- Adjectives have only one form. Use the same adjective with singular and plural nouns.
  a **friendly** student   **friendly** students

Adjectives After *Be*
- An adjective can occur alone after *be*. When two adjectives come after *be*, separate them with *and*.
  The apartment is bright **and** quiet.
- ⚠Do not use *a*, *an*, or *the* with adjectives that occur alone after *be*.
  *The dog is a black. (INCORRECT)

Adjectives Before Nouns
- An adjective can come before a noun.

> • When an adjective comes before a singular noun, use *a* before the adjective if it begins with a consonant sound. Use *an* before the adjective if it begins with a vowel sound.
>   <u>a</u> **new** apartment   <u>an</u> **old** apartment
> • Some nouns can function as adjectives when they describe other nouns.
>   a **wedding** dress   a **leather** collar

B1 Listening for Form

🎧 Listen to the sentences. Do the sentences have adjectives or not? Check (✓) the correct column.

	ADJECTIVE	NO ADJECTIVE
1.	✓	
2.		
3.		
4.		
5.		
6.		
7.		
8.		

B2 Identifying Adjectives

Circle the adjectives in the sentences. Then draw an arrow to show the noun they describe.

1. The tea is (hot.)

2. The oatmeal cookies are delicious.

3. The students are intelligent.

4. Amsterdam is a pretty city.

5. The weather is cloudy and rainy.

6. He is a strong athlete.

7. Chocolate cake is on the menu.

8. We are tired and hungry.

A. Form sentences with adjectives. Use the words. Punctuate your sentences correctly.

1. drive/don't/an/car/old

   Don't drive an old car.

2. is/an/he/student/excellent

   _____

3. new/dress/buy/a

   _____

4. famous/a/writer/Hiro/is

   _____

5. is/small/a/apartment/it

   _____

6. ink/red/use/don't

   _____

B. Add the word in parentheses to each sentence. Write your sentences in your notebook. Make any necessary changes.

1. Jack Nicholson is an actor. (famous)

   Jack Nicholson is a famous actor.

2. Don't buy a car. (expensive)

3. Send them an invitation. (wedding)

4. Tell us a story. (interesting)

5. She's a student. (university)

6. It's a mistake. (unusual)

Descriptions with Adjectives

Examining Meaning and Use

Read the sentences and complete the tasks below. Then discuss your answers and read the Meaning and Use Notes to check them.

a. His hair is red.

b. He is Korean.

c. She is a young woman.

d. The book is interesting.

e. The building is small.

f. The tables are round.

1. Underline the adjectives.

2. Write the adjectives next to the correct categories below.

quality/opinion: _____   age: _____   origin: _____

size: _____   color: _____   shape: _____

Meaning and Use Notes

> ### Categories of Adjectives
>
> **1A** Adjectives describe nouns in many ways.
>
> *Quality/Opinion:* It's a **nice** ring.　　*Color:* My **brown** belt is lost.
>
> *Size:* Where's the **little** dog?　　*Origin:* My aunt is **Brazilian**.
>
> *Age:* It's an **old** dress.　　*Shape:* The table is **round**.
>
> **1B** Below are some common adjectives. See Appendix 9 for a list of common adjectives by categories.
>
> | Quality/Opinion | Size | Age | Color | Origin | Shape |
> |---|---|---|---|---|---|
> | beautiful | big | new | blue | Chinese | oval |
> | expensive | large | old | brown | European | round |
> | happy | little | young | green | French | square |
> | hard | short | | red | Italian | |
> | ugly | small | | white | Japanese | |

(Continued on page 94)

> ## Using Nouns as Adjectives
>
> **2** We often use a noun to describe another noun. In this case, the first noun always describes the second noun.
>
> a **table** lamp = a lamp that you put on a table   a **wool** hat = a hat made of wool
> a **wedding** dress = a dress for a wedding   a **winter** coat = a coat for winter

C1 Listening for Meaning and Use

▶ Notes 1A, 1B

Listen to these sentences about a restaurant. Choose the correct answer.

1. **a.** Tony's isn't new.
   b. Tony's isn't old.

2. **a.** The owner is famous.
   b. The restaurant is famous.

3. **a.** The chef is from Italy.
   b. The chef is in Italy.

4. **a.** The chef is good.
   b. The chef isn't good.

5. **a.** It's a cheap restaurant.
   b. It's an expensive restaurant.

6. **a.** The food at Tony's is good.
   b. The food at Tony's isn't good.

C2 Asking About Qualities and Opinions

▶ Notes 1A, 1B

Work with a partner. Think about your school. Take turns asking and answering questions about these topics. Use adjectives of quality or opinion. See Appendix 9 for a list of common adjectives.

1. cafeteria food

   A: How is the cafeteria food?
   B: It's terrible.
   OR
   A: What is the cafeteria food like?
   B: It's great.

2. library

3. teachers

4. sports teams

5. students

6. computer lab

A. Put each adjective into the correct category in the chart.

beautiful	large	old	red	small	tall
Brazilian	new	orange	round	Spanish	yellow
Italian	noisy	oval	slow	square	young

QUALITY/OPINION	SIZE	AGE	COLOR	ORIGIN	SHAPE
beautiful					

B. Write six sentences in your notebook. Use some of the adjectives from the chart in part A.

Nepal is a beautiful country.

A. Complete the definitions with the correct words.

1. An airport bus is a kind of ((bus)/ airport).

2. A ticket office is a kind of (office / ticket).

3. Milk chocolate is a kind of (milk / chocolate).

4. Chocolate milk is a kind of (milk / chocolate).

5. A pocket calculator is a kind of (calculator / pocket)

6. A car seat is a kind of (car / seat)

B. Complete the definitions. Use nouns as adjectives.

1. A _school library_ is a library in a school.

2. A _____ is an earring made of gold.

3. A _____ is a ticket for a theater.

4. A _____ is a plate made of paper.

5. A _____ is a student at a university.

6. A _____ is a cup used for coffee.

A. These ads are from a college bulletin board. Complete each one. Use some of the adjectives below. More than one answer may be possible.

A __small__ cat with a

_____ collar. His eyes

are _____. Name: Max

Call Naomi: 555-3366

Furniture for Sale

_____ sofa

_____ table

_____ chairs

_____ prices

Call 555-4545

1. white, grey, large, small

3. antique, European, low, new

WANTED

A _____ apartment

with two _____ bedrooms

for _____ students.

Call 555-4291. Ask for Kim.

FOUND

Call Gloria: 555-9292

A _____ sweater with

_____ buttons and

_____ sleeves.

2. bright, cheap, quiet, big

4. long, round, yellow, green

B. Show your advertisements to a partner. How are they different?

C. In your notebook write a three-line ad about a lost object. Use adjectives or nouns as adjectives to describe the object.

Lost: a baseball hat . . .

D Combining Form, Meaning, and Use

D1 Thinking About Meaning and Use

Complete each conversation. Then discuss your answers in small groups.

1. **A:** What's your apartment like?

   B: _____
   a. I'm glad.
   b. It's small.

2. **A:** How's your homework?

   B: _____
   a. It's hard.
   b. It's pretty.

3. **A:** Who's that?

   B: _____
   a. A student newspaper.
   b. A new student.

4. **A:** Where is your brother?

   B: On the _____
   a. school bus.
   b. bus schedule.

5. **A:** Is your school large?

   B: No, it's _____
   a. small
   b. old

6. **A:** Twenty people for dinner! Think about all the dirty dishes!

   B: _____
   a. Try expensive dishes.
   b. Try paper plates.

D2 Editing

Some of these sentences have errors. Find the errors and correct them.

1. She's a tall.

2. Baseball is a fantastic game.

3. Buy me a expensive ring.

4. His roommate is smart and handsome.

5. The girl short is my friend.

6. Eva and Amy are great runners.

7. Bring the bigs books.

8. Buy him a sweater wool.

Beyond the Classroom

Searching for Authentic Examples

Look for ads in an English-language newspaper or on the Internet. Find five adjectives that are new to you. Find their meanings in the dictionary. Write the meanings in your notebook and share them with your class. What noun does each adjective describe?

Writing

Imagine you want to sell some things in your house or apartment. Follow the steps below to write an ad for a bulletin board.

1. Use these notes to plan your writing.
   - Make a list of the objects for sale.
   - Think of some adjectives to describe the objects.
   - Remember to include the name of a contact person and a phone number.

2. Write your draft. Use a variety of adjectives.

3. Read your work carefully and circle grammar, spelling, and punctuation errors. Work with a partner to decide how to fix the errors and improve the content.

4. Rewrite your draft. Draw pictures or add photographs to your ad. Put the advertisement on the wall of your classroom.

Possessives and Demonstratives

A | Keeping in Touch

A1 | Before You Read

Discuss these questions.

How do you communicate with your friends? Do you e-mail? Do you write letters? Which do you prefer?

A2 | Read

Read these e-mail messages. How is Koji's life different from Alan's?

Mail

Hi Koji,

Thanks for the pictures from our graduation party. They're up on my wall already. School is OK, but I'm a little lonely. Jack, my roommate, is lucky! A lot of Jack's high school friends are here too. Mine are 1,000 miles away!

My classes are OK. Bio is interesting and the other classes aren't difficult except for Spanish. Señorita Vazquez, my teacher, is fine. It isn't her fault. It's probably mine. My accent is terrible, and I'm embarrassed to speak in class. My grades are OK in other subjects—an A and two B's, but a C in Spanish.

How is your new job?

Alan

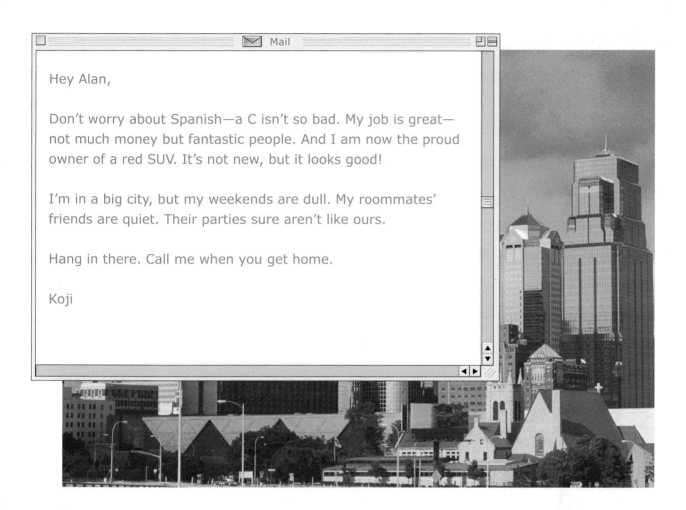

Hey Alan,

Don't worry about Spanish—a C isn't so bad. My job is great—not much money but fantastic people. And I am now the proud owner of a red SUV. It's not new, but it looks good!

I'm in a big city, but my weekends are dull. My roommates' friends are quiet. Their parties sure aren't like ours.

Hang in there. Call me when you get home.

Koji

Bio: abbreviation for Biology

embarrassed: uncomfortable or ashamed

fault: responsibility for a mistake

hang in there: be patient

subjects: areas of study, e.g., math, history

SUV (sport utility vehicle): a large vehicle similar to a van

A3 After You Read

Write *T* for true or *F* for false for each statement.

___T___ **1.** Alan is lonely.

_____ **2.** Jack is Alan's roommate.

_____ **3.** Spanish is hard for Alan.

_____ **4.** Koji doesn't like his new job.

_____ **5.** Koji enjoys his weekends.

_____ **6.** Koji has a red SUV.

B Possessive Nouns, Possessive Adjectives, and *Whose*

Examining Form

Read the sentences and complete the tasks below. Then discuss your answers and read the Form charts to check them.

1a. My <u>roommate's</u> friends are quiet. He's noisy.
1b. My <u>roommates'</u> friends are quiet. They're noisy.

2a. My brother is tall. I'm short.
2b. Their brother is tall. They are short.

1. Look at sentences 1a and 1b. Look at the underlined possessive nouns. Which noun is singular? Which is plural? How do you know?

2. Look at sentences 2a and 2b. Possessive adjectives come directly before nouns. Underline the nouns. Circle the possessive adjectives.

POSSESSIVE NOUNS

Singular		
NOUN + *'S*		
Karen's	friend	is nice.
My sister's		

Plural			
	REGULAR NOUN + *'*		
The	**students'**	classroom	is small.
	teachers'	classrooms	are small.
	IRREGULAR NOUN + *'S*		
The	**women's**	apartment	is bright and sunny.
	children's	classes	are interesting.

- Use an apostrophe + -s (*'s*) after singular nouns to form the possessive.
- For singular nouns that end in -s, add an apostrophe alone or *'s*. Either one is correct.
  Marcus' roommate   Marcus**'s** roommate
- For regular plural nouns, add an apostrophe alone to form the possessive.
- For irregular plural nouns, add *'s*.
- For two or more nouns together, add *'s* to the last noun.
  Dan and Karen**'s** mother
- Possessive nouns usually come before another noun.

- Possessive nouns can occur alone if the reference to a noun is clear.

    Is she the boy's mother or the girl's (mother)?

⚠️ In informal writing, we sometimes see contractions with a noun + *is*. Do not confuse a possessive *'s* with a contraction.

    John's last name is Vazquez.   "John's here." (John is here.)

POSSESSIVE ADJECTIVES AND *WHOSE*

Possessive Adjectives

SUBJECT PRONOUN	POSSESSIVE ADJECTIVE	EXAMPLES
I	**my**	I'm a hard worker. **My** job is important.
you	**your**	You're a good teacher. **Your** class is fun.
he	**his**	He's an artist. **His** paintings are beautiful.
she	**her**	She's smart. **Her** parents are proud.
it	**its**	It's Emily's cat. **Its** fur is white.
we	**our**	We're excited. **Our** football team is in first place.
you	**your**	You're late. **Your** teachers are angry.
they	**their**	They're sad. **Their** friend is sick.

Questions with *Whose*

WHOSE	NOUN	
Whose	car	is new?
	grades	are good?

Answers

Joe's.   **Joe's** car is new.
Tom's are.

Possessive Adjectives

- Possessive adjectives always come before nouns. They do not change form.
    His friend   **His** friends
- Possessive adjectives replace possessive nouns. They agree with the noun they replace.
    Juan's sister is in New York. = **His** sister is in New York.
                    *Her sister is in New York. (INCORRECT)

⚠️ Do not confuse the possessive adjective *its* with the contraction *it's*.
    Its fur is white.   **It's** friendly. (It is friendly.)

(Continued on page 104)

Questions with *Whose*

- Use *whose* in information questions to ask about possession.
- We can use *whose* without a noun if the meaning is clear.

    Whose pen is this?   **Whose** is it?

⚠️ Do not confuse *whose* with the contraction *who's*. They sound exactly the same.

    Whose boyfriend is away at college?   **Who's** from Costa Rica? (Who is from Costa Rica?)

B1 Listening for Form

🎧 Listen to each sentence. Do you hear a possessive noun, a possessive adjective, or *whose*? Check (✓) the correct column.

	POSSESSIVE NOUN	POSSESSIVE ADJECTIVE	*WHOSE*
1.	✓		
2.			
3.			
4.			
5.			
6.			
7.			
8.			

B2 Working on Possessive Nouns

Complete the sentences with possessive nouns. Use the nouns in parentheses.

1. _____Carol's_____ (Carol) book is on the table.

2. _____ (Brad and Jack) room is messy.

3. _____ (Mr. Miller) desk is in the corner.

4. The _____ (teachers) office is Room 432.

5. The _____ (Smiths) car is red.

6. The _____ (children) toy is broken.

7. _____ (Tamika) artwork is beautiful.

8. _____ (Sasha) garden is huge!

Forming Questions with *Whose*

A. Form pairs of questions with *whose*. In the first question of each pair, use *whose* + noun. In the second question, use *whose* alone. Punctuate your sentences correctly.

1. **a.** major/whose/engineering/is <u>Whose major is engineering?</u>

    b. biology/whose/is <u>Whose is biology?</u>

2. **a.** car/whose/is/new _____

    b. old/whose/is _____

3. **a.** this month/whose/is/birthday _____

    b. next month/is/whose _____

4. **a.** whose/large/family/is _____

    b. is/whose/small _____

5. **a.** apartment/is/near school/whose _____

    b. far/is/whose _____

B. Work with a small group. Take turns asking and answering the questions in part A.

B4 **Working on Possessive Adjectives**

Complete the letter with the correct possessive adjective. Use the subject pronoun in parentheses to help you. Compare your answers with a partner.

Dear Keiko,

Good news! Jenny and I are finally in ___<u>our</u>___ (we) new house. The house
                                         1

isn't big but it's pretty. My best friend and _____ (he) wife are next door.
                                                2

_____ (they) son is in the same school as _____ (we) son.
3   4

Jenny is happy because the house is near _____ (she) new office. John
                                          5

Bentley, _____ (she) boss, is a really nice guy. And guess what! _____
         6   7

(he) wife is the principal of _____ (we) daughter's new school!
                              8

How are you and _____ (you) family? Write soon!
                9

Paulo

C Possessive Pronouns

Examining Form

Read the sentences and complete the tasks below. Then discuss your answers and read the Form charts to check them.

  a. My book isn't here. Mine is there.
  b. It isn't their dog. Theirs is black.

1. Underline the possessive adjectives + nouns.

2. A possessive pronoun replaces a possessive adjective + noun. Circle the possessive pronouns. What words do they replace?

Possessive Pronouns		
POSSESSIVE ADJECTIVE	POSSESSIVE PRONOUN	EXAMPLES
my	**mine**	My car isn't new. **Mine** is old.
your	**yours**	Your house isn't far. **Yours** is near.
his	**his**	His major isn't English. **His** is business.
her	**hers**	Her parents aren't Italian. **Hers** are Mexican.
Its		Its tail is short.
our	**ours**	Our class isn't difficult. **Ours** is easy.
your	**yours**	Your books aren't new. **Yours** are old.
their	**theirs**	Their families aren't in the United States. **Theirs** are in Mexico.

- A possessive pronoun replaces a possessive adjective + noun. Possessive pronouns are never followed by a noun.
    It's **my car.**   It's **mine.**   *It's **mine car.** (INCORRECT)
- A possessive pronoun agrees with the possessive adjective that it replaces. Possessive pronouns have only one form.
    My book is red. — **Mine** is red.
    My books are red. — **Mine** are red.

Listen to each sentence. Choose the word you hear.

1. **a.** your
   b. yours

2. **a.** his
   b. hers

3. **a.** our
   b. ours

4. **a.** yours
   b. your

5. **a.** your
   b. yours

6. **a.** their
   b. theirs

C2 **Forming Sentences with Possessive Pronouns**

Form sentences with possessive pronouns. Use the words and phrases. Punctuate your sentences correctly.

1. mine/the geology/book/is

   The geology book is mine.

2. the red/coat/yours/is

   _____

3. the tickets/his/are

   _____

4. the chocolate/theirs/is

   _____

5. is/the letter/ours

   _____

6. hers/are/the old/newspapers

   _____

C3 **Contrasting Possessive Pronouns and Possessive Adjectives**

Complete the conversation. Choose the correct word in parentheses.

Irina: Whose books are on my desk? Are they (our / ours) new books?

Robin: No, they're not (our / ours). They're Kim's.

Irina: Why are they on (my / mine) desk?

Robin: (Her / Hers) desk is too crowded.

Irina: And the calculator? Is it (her / hers)?

Robin: No, it isn't. It's (my / mine). Is the dictionary (your / yours)?

Irina: No, Robin. I think it's (your / yours)!

D   Possessives

Examining Meaning and Use

Read the sentences and answer the questions below. Then discuss your answers and read the Meaning and Use Notes to check them.

   a. My sister is a doctor. Keiko's sister is a teacher.
   b. Their car is in the street. Mine is in the garage.
   c. Mary's eyes are blue. Her brother's are green.

1. Underline the possessive forms.

2. Which sentence shows . . .

   _____ ownership?

   _____ a human relationship?

   _____ a physical characteristic?

Meaning and Use Notes

Ownership and Possession

1   Possessive nouns, adjectives, and pronouns show that someone owns or possesses something.

   Erica's car is old.   **Her** car is old.   **Hers** is old.

   John's homework is complete.   **His** homework is complete.   **His** is complete.

Human Relationships

2   Possessives show human relationships.

   Yuki's mother is a doctor.   **Their** mother is a teacher.   **Mine** is a nurse.

Physical Characteristics

3   Possessives show physical characteristics.

   Paul's hair is wavy.   **My** hair is black.   **Hers** is brown.

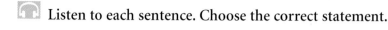
Listen to each sentence. Choose the correct statement.

1. **a.** Dan is 16 years old.
   b. Dan has a cat.
   c. I have a cat.

2. **a.** Karen is a doctor.
   b. Karen is in the hospital.
   c. Mr. Foster is sick.

3. **a.** Josh's grades are bad.
   b. Bob's and Josh's grades are good.
   c. Bob's grades aren't good.

4. **a.** Lynn is Robin's mother.
   b. Lynn is Larry's daughter.
   c. Larry is Robin's father.

5. **a.** I am in her house.
   b. She is in my house.
   c. He is in our house.

6. **a.** His car is new.
   b. Their car is new.
   c. Her car is new.

7. **a.** Paul's hair is black.
   b. Rick's hair is brown.
   c. Paul's hair is brown.

8. **a.** Irina's apartment is on Elm Street.
   b. My apartment is on Elm Street.
   c. My apartment is on Main Street.

D2 **Describing Physical Characteristics** ▶ Note 3

A. Work in pairs or small groups. Think of a person that everyone in your class knows, for example, a celebrity, a teacher, or a member of your class. Write three clues in your notebook to help your classmates guess the person's name. Use possessives.

1. His eyes are blue.
2. His hair is brown.
3. His hair is short.

B. Work with another group. Take turns reading your clues. Ask your classmates to guess the person's name.

A: His hair is short.
B: Is it our teacher?

A. Complete the conversation. Use possessive forms of the words in parentheses. Think about the relationships between the family members.

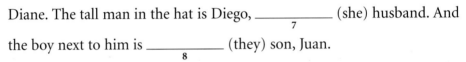

Betty: What a nice photograph! Robin, is it

_____yours_____ (you)?
     1

Robin: Yes, it's _____ (me).
         2

Betty: Is this _____ (you) family?
        3

Robin: Well, it's _____ (Jim) family. This
        4

is Jim. He's _____ (I) husband.
      5

He's the man on the left. The woman

next to him is _____ (he) sister,
      6

Diane. The tall man in the hat is Diego, _____ (she) husband. And
          7

the boy next to him is _____ (they) son, Juan.
        8

Betty: Is the woman in the white dress _____ (Jim and Diane) mother?
         9

Robin: No, she's _____ (they) aunt Linda.
      10

Betty: What a beautiful house! Is it _____ (she) house?
        11

Robin: No, it's _____ (we) house . . . but thank you for the compliment!
    12

B. Read the conversation in part A again. Complete the sentences to express the relationships. Use possessive nouns.

1. Robin is _____Jim's_____ wife.

2. Diane is _____ sister.

3. Diego is _____ husband.

4. Juan is _____ son.

5. Linda is _____ aunt.

6. Diane is _____ mother.

E Demonstrative Adjectives and Demonstrative Pronouns

Examining Form

Read the sentences and complete the tasks below. Then discuss your answers and read the Form charts to check them.

1a. <u>This</u> desk is old. <u>That</u> desk is new.
1b. <u>These</u> pens are blue. <u>Those</u> pens are red.

2a. <u>This</u> book is mine. <u>That</u> is yours.
2b. <u>These</u> shoes are new. <u>Those</u> are old.

1. Look at the underlined adjectives in 1a and 1b. Which are singular? Which are plural? How do you know?

2. Look at the underlined words in 2a and 2b. Which are adjectives? Which are pronouns? How do you know?

DEMONSTRATIVE ADJECTIVES

Singular			
THIS/THAT	NOUN	VERB	
This	desk	is	new.
That			

Plural			
THESE/THOSE	NOUN	VERB	
These	desks	are	new.
Those			

DEMONSTRATIVE PRONOUNS

Singular		
THIS/THAT	VERB	
This	is	new.
That		

Plural		
THESE/THOSE	VERB	
These	are	new.
Those		

Demonstrative Adjectives and Pronouns

- *This, that, these,* and *those* are adjectives and pronouns.
- When they come before singular and plural nouns, they are demonstrative adjectives.
    This sports equipment is new.   **Those** books are old.

(Continued on page 112)

- When we use demonstratives without a noun, they are demonstrative pronouns.

  This is new.   **Those** are old.

- We usually use *it* or *they* in answers to *Yes/No* questions with demonstratives. We do not use *this, that, these,* or *those.*

  A: Is **that** shirt new?   A: Are **these** yours?

  B: No, **it** isn't.   B: Yes, **they** are.

- We often use demonstratives in questions with *whose.*

  Whose book bag is **this**?   Whose are **these**?

E1) Listening for Form

A. Listen to each sentence. Write the demonstrative (*this, that, these, those*) you hear.

1. _These_ socks are not mine. ((adjective) / pronoun)

2. _____ books are interesting. (adjective / pronoun)

3. _____ tie is Alan's. (adjective / pronoun)

4. _____ is a beautiful painting. (adjective / pronoun)

5. _____ is my sister Wendy. (adjective / pronoun)

6. _____ are Jack's books, not mine. (adjective / pronoun)

B. Look at your answers in part A. Are they adjectives or pronouns? Choose the correct answer.

E2) Building Sentences

Build six logical sentences with demonstrative adjectives. Choose one word from each column, and write the sentences in your notebook. Punctuate your sentences correctly.

This dog is young.

this	children		young
that	dog	is	yours
these	pictures	are	a dormitory
those	building		small

Demonstratives

Examining Meaning and Use

Read the conversation and answer the questions below. Then discuss your answers and read the Meaning and Use Notes to check them.

Sally: This is my telescope, and these are my astronomy books.
Brad: What planet is that?
Sally: That's Saturn. And those stars are the Pleiades.

1. Underline the demonstrative in each sentence.

2. Which demonstratives refer to objects near the speaker? Which refer to objects far from the speaker?

Meaning and Use Notes

People and Things

1 Demonstratives help a speaker identify people and things for a listener. We usually use them when both the speaker and the listener can see the people or objects. The speaker often points or gestures toward the object.

This house is cheap.

That house across the street is expensive.

These shoes are too small.

Those shoes next to the chair are fine.

Near and Far

2 *This* and *these* refer to people or things that are near the speaker. *That* and *those* refer to people or things that are far away.

Looking in a Mirror
This shirt is fine, but **these** pants are dirty.

Looking at the Sky
A: Look at **that** star!
B: **That's** not a star. It's the planet Venus.
A: Are **those** planets too?

Two Roommates Talking
A: Are **these** shoes OK?
B: No, don't wear **those**. Try **these**.

Listening for Meaning and Use ▶ Notes 1, 2

🎧 Listen to each sentence. Is the noun near the speaker or far from the speaker? Check (✓) the correct column.

	NEAR	FAR
1.		✓
2.		
3.		
4.		
5.		
6.		

F2 **Talking About Near and Far Objects** ▶ Notes 1, 2

A. Look at the objects. Write one true statement about each in your notebook. Use a demonstrative in each statement.

1.

These plants are healthy.

3.

5.

2.

4.

6.

B. Work with a partner. Find some of the objects in part A in your classroom. Make sentences about the objects. Use demonstratives.

Those plants are not healthy.

G Combining Form, Meaning, and Use

G1 Thinking About Meaning and Use

Complete each conversation. Then discuss your answers in small groups.

1. **A:** Is this my book?

   B: _____

   a. No, it's mine.
   b. Yes, it's mine.
   c. No, it's yours.

2. **A:** Is your aunt old?

   B: _____

   a. No, you're young.
   b. Yes, she is.
   c. Yes, it is.

3. **A:** _____

   B: Mark's.
   a. Who is Mark's teacher?
   b. Whose teacher is that?
   c. Who is that?

4. **A:** Is that dog yours?

   B: _____

   a. No, it's Carl.
   b. Yes, it's his.
   c. No, it's not.

5. **A:** Is that your glass?

   B: _____

   a. No, it's mine.
   b. No, it's yours.
   c. Yes, it's yours.

6. **A:** Is that their apartment?

   B: _____

   a. No, it's theirs.
   b. Yes, they are.
   c. Yes, it is.

G2 Editing

Some of these sentences have errors. Find the errors and correct them.

1. ~~Mine~~ My house is white.

2. Her professors' family is from Mexico.

3. These are for you.

4. The records are mines.

5. Is this your or hers?

6. The university's library is very good.

7. Who's house is this?

8. Wash these dish.

▶ Beyond the Classroom

Searching for Authentic Examples

Look for advice columns in English-language newspapers and magazines, or on the Internet. Find at least three examples of possessive forms and three examples of demonstrative forms. Write them in your notebook. Explain to a partner why each one is a possessive or a demonstrative.

Speaking

Bring a photograph of your family or friends to class. Work in small groups. Take turns talking about the people in the photo. Describe their relationship to you. Ask questions about the people in the other students' photos.

A: *This is my family. This is my sister, Hanna, and this is my brother, Joon-ho. These are my parents.*
B: *Who is this woman?*
A: *That's my aunt. She's my father's sister.*

The Present

PART

4

The Present Continuous

People Watching

A1 Before You Read

Discuss these questions.

What is a journal? Do you write in a journal? What do you write about?

A2 Read

  Read this journal entry. What is the writer doing?

It's morning—my favorite time of day in Seattle. The city is waking up and I am too. I'm sitting in a small coffee shop. Outside, the weather is gloomy. It's cloudy, but it isn't raining. Two people are waiting at the bus stop. The woman is angry. She is pointing to her watch. She's complaining to the

5 man next to her. He isn't listening. He's reading his newspaper. A couple is sitting on a bench. They're about 25. The woman is wearing a waitress's uniform. The man is wearing a bus driver's uniform. They aren't talking. They are just holding hands and smiling at each other. I'm sure they are in love. Another couple is standing near them. They're both about 40.

10 They are carrying briefcases and wearing expensive clothes. They aren't talking; they aren't holding hands; and they aren't smiling. They are married—I'm sure. Are they fighting? Maybe. The woman is looking at the young couple. Perhaps she is thinking about happier times.

bench: a long seat for two or more people

complaining: expressing negative feelings about someone or something

couple: two people who have a romantic relationship

gloomy: dark and depressing

perhaps: maybe

A3 **After You Read**

Write *T* for true or *F* for false for each statement.

__F__ **1.** The writer is waiting for the bus.

_____ **2.** The sun is shining.

_____ **3.** A woman is complaining.

_____ **4.** A woman is reading the newspaper.

_____ **5.** A man and a woman are sitting on a bench.

_____ **6.** Another couple is standing near the bench.

B The Present Continuous

Examining Form

Look back at the journal entry on page 120 and complete the tasks below. Then discuss your answers and read the Form charts to check them.

1. Look at the two underlined examples of the affirmative form of the present continuous. Each has two words. What are they?

2. Find three more affirmative examples of the present continuous.

3. Look at the circled examples of the negative form of the present continuous. Find three more negative examples.

Affirmative Statements		
SUBJECT	BE	BASE FORM OF VERB + -ING
I	am	
You	are	
He She It	is	waiting.
We		
You	are	
They		

CONTRACTIONS	
I'm	
You're	
He's	waiting.
They're	

Negative Statements			
SUBJECT	BE	NOT	BASE FORM OF VERB + -ING
I	am		
You	are		
He She It	is	not	waiting.
We			
You	are		
They			

CONTRACTIONS	
I'm not	
You're not You aren't	
He's not He isn't	waiting.
They're not They aren't	

- The contraction of *I* + *am* + *not* has only one form (**I'm not**).
- The contractions of all other subject pronouns + *be* + *not* have two possible forms. The meaning of these forms is the same.

    you **aren't** = you**'re** not   he **isn't** = he**'s** not

- See Appendix 3 for spelling rules for verbs ending in *-ing*.

Yes/No Questions

BE	SUBJECT	BASE FORM OF VERB + *-ING*
Am	I	
Are	you	
Is	she	**waiting?**
	we	
Are	you	
	they	

Short Answers

YES	SUBJECT	BE	NO	SUBJECT + BE + NOT
	you	are.		you **aren't**. you**'re** not.
	I	am.		I'm not.
Yes,	she	is.	No,	she **isn't**. she**'s** not.
	you			you **aren't**. you**'re** not.
	we	are.		we **aren't**. we**'re** not.
	they			they **aren't**. they**'re** not.

Information Questions

WH- WORD	BE	SUBJECT	BASE FORM OF VERB + *-ING*
How	am	I	**doing?**
What	are	you	
Who	is	he	**calling?**
Why	are	you	**waiting?**
Where		they	

WH- WORD (SUBJECT)	BE		BASE FORM OF VERB + *-ING*
Who	is		**talking?**
What			**cooking?**

Answers

Great.
I'm cooking dinner.
He**'s calling** David.
Because we missed the bus.
In the cafeteria.

Sasha.
Your dinner **is cooking**.

(Continued on page 124)

B1 **Listening for Form**

🎧 **Listen to Mark and Gloria's telephone conversation. Choose the short answer you hear.**

1. a. No, he's not
   b. No, I'm not. *(circled)*
   c. No, we aren't.

2. a. Yes, I am.
   b. Yes, it is.
   c. Yes, she is.

3. a. Yes, he is.
   b. Yes, it is.
   c. Yes, she is.

4. a. Yes, she is.
   b. Yes, he is.
   c. Yes, it is.

5. a. No, it's not.
   b. No, they're not.
   c. No, he's not.

6. a. Yes, he is.
   b. Yes, she is.
   c. Yes, it is.

7. a. No, it isn't.
   b. No, he isn't.
   c. No, it's not.

8. a. Yes, I am.
   b. Yes, we are.
   c. Yes, they are.

B2) Spelling the Present Continuous

Complete each sentence with the present continuous form of the verb in parentheses.

1. He _is losing_ (lose) the game.

2. I _____ (stop) for lunch.

3. She _____ (hug) her child.

4. We _____ (sit) on the couch.

5. They _____ (come) up the street.

6. You _____ (study) hard.

7. Paul and Susan _____ (exercise) at the gym.

8. Lee _____ (argue) with her sister.

B3) Working with Affirmative and Negative Statements

Change the affirmative statements to negative statements. Rewrite the sentences in two different ways when possible.

1. It's raining right now.

   It's not raining right now. It isn't raining right now.

2. It's snowing in Maine.

   _____

3. The children are playing outside.

   _____

4. Celia is exercising at the gym.

   _____

5. I am fixing the car.

   _____

6. We are studying.

   _____

B4 Writing *Yes/No* Questions

Complete the conversations with *Yes/No* questions. Use the words and phrases in parentheses and the present continuous. Punctuate your sentences correctly.

1. **A:** Excuse me. _Are you looking for something?_ (you/look for something)
   B: Yes. Where's the shampoo?

2. **A:** _____ (it/rain)
   B: No. The sun is shining.

3. **A:** _____ (I/pass the course)
   B: Yes, you are. In fact you are doing very well!

4. **A:** _____ (the kids/play outside)
   B: No, they're at the movies.

5. **A:** _____ (she/listen to a CD)
   B: No. She is playing the piano.

6. **A:** _____ (you/study Japanese)
   B: Yes. I'm taking classes at the community college.

B5 Writing Information Questions

Write information questions in your notebook about the underlined words in the statements. Punctuate your sentences correctly.

1. Reiko is reading <u>a magazine</u>.

   What is Reiko reading?

2. <u>Eva</u> is studying French.

3. Naomi is sitting <u>in the kitchen</u>.

4. Celia is drinking <u>coffee</u>.

5. Tom is feeling <u>fine</u>.

6. John's father is watching <u>television</u>.

The Present Continuous

Examining Meaning and Use

Read the sentences and answer the questions below. Then discuss your answers and read the Meaning and Use Notes to check them.

    a.   **Julie:** Here, take your umbrella. <u>It's raining.</u>
         Paulo: Thanks. That's a good idea.

    b.   **Steve:** Hi Carol. How are you?
         Carol: I'm very busy this week. <u>I'm writing a long research paper.</u>

1. Which underlined sentence talks about an activity that is in progress (happening) at the moment the speaker is talking?

2. Which underlined sentence talks about an activity that is in not happening at the moment the speaker is talking?

Activities in Progress

1A Use the present continuous to talk about activities that are in progress (happening) at the exact moment of speaking. Time expressions such as *now, right now,* and *at the moment* make the meaning clearer.

    A: What **are** you **doing**?
    B: **I'm studying** for my chemistry test.

    A: How is the weather there in Michigan?
    B: **It's snowing** <u>right now</u>.

1B Use the present continuous for activities that are in progress, but are not happening at the exact moment of speaking. Time expressions such as *still, these days, this week,* and *this semester* make the meaning clearer.

Two Former Classmates Meet on the Street
    A: So, Rick, what **are** you **doing** <u>these days</u>?
    B: **I'm** <u>still</u> **working** for my dad.

C1) Listening for Meaning and Use

▶ Notes 1A, 1B

🎧 Listen to the conversations. Which activities in progress are happening right now? Which are not happening right now? Check (✓) the correct column.

	HAPPENING RIGHT NOW	NOT HAPPENING RIGHT NOW
1.	✓	
2.		
3.		
4.		
5.		
6.		
7.		
8.		

C2) Describing Activities in Progress

▶ Note 1A

Look at the pictures. Then write a sentence in your notebook to describe each picture. Use contractions when possible.

1.

He's reading a newspaper.

3.

5.

2.

4.

6.

A. Read the list of activities. Put a check (✓) in the box for activities that you are doing these days. Put an ✗ in the box for activities that you are not doing these days.

	ACTIVITIES	✓/✗
1.	studying hard	
2.	working	
3.	playing a sport	
4.	dating someone	
5.	cooking dinner at home	
6.	planning a trip	
7.	dieting	
8.	learning to play an instrument	

B. Work with a partner. Ask and answer *Yes/No* questions and information questions about the information in part A.

A: What are you doing these days?
B: I'm studying hard.
A: Are you working, too?

C4 Guessing Activities in Progress ► Note 1A

Work in groups. Think of an activity, or use a suggestion from the list below. Act out the activity for the group, but don't say what activity you are doing. Your group asks *Yes/No* questions to guess what you are doing.

SUGGESTED ACTIVITIES	
riding a bicycle	arguing with your roommate
shopping	playing basketball
driving a truck	running a race

A: Are you riding a horse?
B: No, I'm not.

A: You are riding a bicycle!
B: Yes, I am.

Combining Sentences with *And*

We can use *and* to combine sentences. Use a comma when you combine two complete sentences.

> I am taking a shower. Alex is making dinner.
>
> I am taking a shower, **and** Alex is making dinner.

When two affirmative present continuous sentences have the same subject, we usually don't repeat the subject or *am/is/are*. In this case, we do not use a comma.

> **He** <u>is doing</u> his homework. **He** <u>is watching</u> television.
>
> **He** <u>is doing</u> his homework **and** <u>watching</u> television.

When we write, we combine sentences because it makes our writing sound more natural. Compare these two paragraphs.

A.

Everyone in my family is very busy. My father is working out of town during the week. My father is coaching a soccer team on the weekends. My mother is teaching at the university. My mother is trying to start her own business. My brother Josh is going to law school. My brother Josh is working at a law firm.

B.

Everyone in my family is very busy. My father is working out of town during the week **and** coaching a soccer team on the weekends. My mother is teaching at the university **and** trying to start her own business. My brother Josh is going to law school **and** working at a law firm.

C5 Combining Sentences with *And*

Rewrite the paragraph in your notebook. Use *and* to combine the underlined sentences. Punctuate your sentences correctly.

Dear Luisa,

Thanks for your letter. We're very busy, too. <u>We're working hard. We're saving money.</u> <u>Celia is teaching piano at the local high school. She's giving private lessons on the weekends.</u> <u>I'm finishing my Ph.D. I'm writing my dissertation.</u> <u>At the moment, Celia is making dinner. Our daughter Lucy is helping her.</u> . . .

Thanks for your letter. We're very busy, too. We're working hard and saving money. Celia . . .

D Combining Form, Meaning, and Use

D1 Thinking About Meaning and Use

Complete each conversation. Then discuss your answers in small groups.

1. **A:** Where is she going?

   B: _____

   a. Now.

   b. To the library.

2. **A:** Are you sleeping?

   B: _____

   a. Yes, I'm studying.

   b. No, I'm not.

3. **A:** Who is working with you?

   B: _____

   a. Sara.

   b. Now.

4. **A:** What are you looking at?

   B: _____

   a. It's snowing.

   b. It's snowing these days.

5. **A:** What are you doing these days?

   B: _____

   a. I'm taking a bath.

   b. I'm looking for a new job.

6. **A:** Is the baby crying?

   B: _____.

   a. No, not now.

   b. Yes, this week.

D2 Editing

Find the errors in this letter and correct them.

Dear Gina,

    standing

I'm stand in front of your apartment. Unfortunately, you're not at home, so

I writing you this note. Dan and I are visiting our families. We're live in San Diego

now. Dan working for a telecommunications company, and I'm looking for a job.

What you are doing these days? Are you still write for the newspaper? Call me at

my mother's house and please visit us!

                Miss you,

                Holly

Beyond the Classroom

Searching for Authentic Examples

Watch an English-language movie or TV program. Listen for the present continuous. Write six examples in your notebook and share them with your class. Why do you think the sentences are in the present continuous?

Writing

Follow the steps below to write a paragraph about activities and events that you see at a public place.

1. Go to a restaurant, a coffee shop, a shopping center, a park, or somewhere where you can watch people. Use these questions to make notes.

   - Where are you?
   - What are you doing?
   - What are other people doing?
   - Where are they going?

2. Write a first draft. Use the present continuous to describe the activities you see.

3. Read your work carefully and circle grammar, spelling, and punctuation errors. Work with a partner to decide how to fix the errors and improve the content.

4. Rewrite your draft.

   I'm sitting in a park. A man is reading the newspaper and eating a sandwich. . . .

The Simple Present

A *Career Path* Asks: "What Do You Do?"

A1 Before You Read

Discuss these questions.

Do you work and go to school? Do you know anyone who works and goes to school? Is it easy or difficult to work and go to school? Why?

A2 Read

Read this magazine interview with Kyla Adams. What makes Kyla an unusual student?

CAREER PATH

Career Path Asks "What Do You Do?"
Interviews with students with unusual lives

Every month *Career Path* magazine interviews a student with an unusual life. This month Kyla Adams is our unusual student. Kyla is a very busy young woman. She is a student, and she dances for the Ballet Tech Company in New York City. Read what Kyla says to our interviewer.

5 **Career Path:** How many hours a day do you dance?

Kyla: A lot. I have ballet class from 10:30 to 12:00. Then we rehearse from 10 12:00 to 3:30 and 4:30 to 6:00.

Career Path: What do you do after rehearsal?

Kyla: I'm usually very 15 tired. I go home and make dinner. Then I study or read and go to bed.

Career Path: Who do you live with?

20 **Kyla:** I live alone. I have a tiny apartment in Manhattan.

Career Path: Where does your family live?

25 **Kyla:** They're about four hours away in Vermont.

Career Path: Do you get lonely?

Kyla: No. I have a lot of 30 friends. They call or visit a lot.

Career Path: Does your family visit you?

Kyla: Oh yes. They come 35 here, or I go home twice a month.

Career Path: You are still in high school. Who teaches you?

40 **Kyla:** I have a tutor for a couple of classes. For my other classes, I work by myself. But I communicate with 45 students in my home high school on the telephone and the computer.

Career Path: When do 50 you study?

Kyla: On Sundays. That's my day off. We have three weeks of vacation a year. I study a lot then, too.

55 **Career Path:** How are you doing in school?

Kyla: Very well. I'm actually the valedictorian of my high school class.

60 **Career Path:** What do you do in your free time?

Kyla: I don't have much free time. But I live in New York City, so it's not 65 hard to find things to do.

---

rehearse: to practice
rehearsal: a practice for a show or performance

tutor: a private teacher who teaches one person
valedictorian: the student who receives the best grades in his or her high school class

A3 After You Read

Write *T* for true or *F* for false for each statement. Change the false statements to true ones.

__F__ **1.** Kyla rehearses from 10:30 to 12:00.

Kyla rehearses from 12:00 to 3:30 and 4:30 to 6:00.

_____ **2.** Kyla lives with a friend.

_____ **3.** Kyla's family lives in New York.

_____ **4.** Kyla doesn't get lonely.

_____ **5.** Kyla communicates with other students by phone.

_____ **6.** Kyla doesn't have a lot of free time.

B Simple Present Statements

Examining Form

Read the sentences and complete the tasks below. Then discuss your answers and read the Form charts to check them.

1a. I come home at six o'clock.   **2a.** I do not walk to work.
1b. She comes home at three o'clock.   **2b.** He does not walk to work
1c. They come home at eight o'clock.   **2c.** They do not walk to work.

1. Sentences 1a–1c are affirmative. Circle the subjects and underline the verbs. What is different about the form of the verb in 1b?

2. Sentences 2a–2c are negative. Circle the subjects. What three words come after each subject? What is different about the form of the negative verb in 2b?

3. Look back at the interview on pages 134–135. Find three affirmative sentences and one negative sentence.

Affirmative Statements		
SUBJECT	BASE FORM OF VERB or BASE FORM OF VERB + -S/-ES	
I	**live**	
You		
He She It	**lives**	in Texas.
We		
You	**live**	
They		

Negative Statements			
SUBJECT	*DO/DOES* + *NOT*	BASE FORM OF VERB	
I	**do not don't**		
You			
He She It	**does not doesn't**	**live**	in Texas.
We	**do not don't**		
You			
They			

- To form the simple present, use the base form of the verb. In the third-person singular (*he, she,* or *it*), add *-s* or *-es* to the base form.

    He **works** hard.   She **teaches** math.

- See Appendix 4 for spelling rules for verbs ending in *-s* or *-es.*
- *Have* is an irregular verb. The third-person singular form of *have* is *has.*

    I **have** a new car.   He **has** a new car.

- To form negative statements, use *do/does + not +* the base form of the verb. Only use *does not (doesn't)* in the third-person singular *(he, she,* or *it).*

    He **does not work** hard.   She **doesn't teach** math.

- We usually use the contractions *don't* and *doesn't* in speaking and informal writing.
- ⚠ In negative statements, do not add *-s* or *-es* to the base form of the verb in the third-person singular.

    He **does not play** golf.
    *He does not plays golf. (INCORRECT)

B1) Listening for Form

🎧 Listen to each sentence about Kyla Adams. Choose the affirmative or negative form of the verb you hear.

1. **a.** live
   b. lives
   c. doesn't live

2. **a.** has
   b. have
   c. doesn't have

3. **a.** has
   b. have
   c. doesn't have

4. **a.** dance
   b. dances
   c. doesn't dance

5. **a.** study
   b. studies
   c. doesn't study

6. **a.** worry
   b. worries
   c. doesn't worry

7. **a.** miss
   b. misses
   c. doesn't miss

8. **a.** work
   b. works
   c. doesn't work

B2) Working on Simple Present Affirmative Statements

Complete the paragraph. Use the correct simple present form of the verb in parentheses.

Lisa and Alan ___work___ (work) in a bank. Lisa _____ (live) with her
1   2

parents. Alan _____ (share) an apartment with his brother. Lisa and Alan
3

are good friends. They _____ (drive) to work together in Alan's car. Lisa
4

_____ (have) a job in the bank's loan department, and Alan _____ (fix)
5   6

the bank's computers. They _____ (finish) work at 5:00 P.M. After work, Lisa
7

_____ (go) to the gym and _____ (exercise). Alan _____ (drive)
8   9   10

home alone. He and his brother _____ (watch) the six o'clock news. Then they
11

_____ (make) dinner.
12

B3) Contrasting Simple Present Affirmative and Negative Statements

Make the false statements true by changing them to negative statements. Then
write a true affirmative statement. Use the words in parentheses in place of the
underlined words.

1. Tigers have spots. (stripes)

   Tigers don't have spots. They have stripes.

2. Trees lose their leaves in the summer. (fall)

   _____

3. The moon goes around the sun. (earth)

   _____

4. Panda bears eat bananas. (bamboo)

   _____

5. An astronomer studies the ocean. (stars)

   _____

6. Water boils at 100°F. (212°F)

   _____

Pronunciation Notes

Pronunciation of Verbs Ending in -s and -es

The final -s or -es of third-person singular verbs has three pronunciations: /s/, /z/, and /ɪz/. The pronunciation depends on the final sound of the base form of the verb.

1. If the base form of the verb ends with the sound /p/, /t/, /k/, or /f/, pronounce -s or -es as /s/.

stop — stops /stɑps/	like — likes /laɪks/
meet — meets /mits/	laugh — laughs /læfs/

2. If the base form of the verb ends with the sound /b/, /d/, /g/, /v/, /ð/, /m/, /n/, /ŋ/, /l/, or /r/, pronounce -s or -es as /z/.

build — builds /bɪldz/	ring — rings /rɪŋz/
leave — leaves /livz/	tell — tells /tɛlz/

3. If the base form of the verb ends in a vowel sound, pronounce -s or -es as /z/.

stay — stays /steɪz/	go — goes /goʊz/
see — sees /siz/	fly — flies /flaɪz/

4. If the base form of the verb ends with the sound /s/, /z/, /ʃ/, /ʒ/, /tʃ/, /dʒ/, or /ks/, pronounce -es as /ɪz/. This adds an extra syllable to the word.

wash — washes /ˈwaʃɪz/	judge — judges /ˈdʒʌdʒɪz/
catch — catches /ˈkætʃɪz/	fix — fixes /ˈfɪksɪz/

B4) Pronouncing the Third-Person -s and -es

Listen to each verb alone and in a sentence. What final sound do you hear? Check (✓) the correct column.

		/s/	/z/	/ɪz/
1.	speaks	✓		
2.	smells			
3.	washes			
4.	leaves			
5.	notices			
6.	stops			
7.	pays			
8.	teaches			

C

Simple Present *Yes/No* Questions and Short Answers

Examining Form

Read these sentences and complete the tasks below. Then discuss your answers and read the Form charts to check them.

    a. Do you like spinach?
    b. Does she watch TV every day?
    c. Do they have a lot of homework?

1. Circle the subject in each question. What word comes before each subject?

2. What is different about sentence b?

3. Underline the verb form that follows each subject. Do we add an ending to the verb?

Yes/No Questions				Short Answers					
DO/DOES	SUBJECT	BASE FORM OF VERB	*YES*	SUBJECT	*DO/DOES*	*NO*	SUBJECT	*DO/DOES + NOT*
Do	I			you	**do.**		you	**don't.**
	you			I			I	
Does	he she it	**work?**	**Yes,**	he she it	**does.**	**No,**	he she it	**doesn't.**
Do	we			you	**do.**		you	**don't.**
	you			we			we	
	they			they			they	

    • Use *does* for the third-person singular.

    ⚠ In *Yes/No* questions, do not add *-s* or *-es* to the base form in the third-person singular.

        Does he **work** here?

        * Does he **works** here? (INCORRECT)

Listen to the conversation between Sally and her father. Choose the answer you hear.

1. a. Yes, she does.
   b. Yes, it does.
   c. No, I don't. *(circled)*

2. a. Yes, I do.
   b. Yes, he does.
   c. No, it doesn't.

3. a. Yes, I do.
   b. Yes, it does.
   c. No, it doesn't.

4. a. No, she doesn't.
   b. Yes, they do.
   c. Yes, we do.

5. a. Yes, you do.
   b. Yes, we do.
   c. No, I don't.

6. a. No, she doesn't.
   b. No, he doesn't.
   c. No, I don't.

7. a. Yes, we do.
   b. No, they don't.
   c. No, we don't.

8. a. Yes, I do.
   b. Yes, they do.
   c. No, I don't.

C2) Working on Simple Present *Yes/No* Questions

A. Complete the questions with *do* or *does*.

1. __Do__ you like ethnic food?

2. _____ you go to jazz clubs?

3. _____ you exercise?

4. _____ you dislike violence on television?

5. _____ classical music relax you?

6. _____ you read many books?

7. _____ science interest you?

8. _____ your best friend live with you?

B. Work with two other students. Take turns asking and answering the questions in part A.

A: Do you like ethnic food?
B: Yes, I do.

A. Look at the class schedules and complete the *Yes/No* questions below. Use *do* or *does*.

Lightman College Winter Term

Name: Diego Florez
Address: Cherry Hill Dorm
          Lightman College

Schedule

Biology 101	M-F 9:00-11:00
Chemistry 1	Tu, Thu 2:30-5:00
Italian 101	M-F 12:45-1:30
Basketball	Sat 9:00-11:00

Lightman College Winter Term

Name: Amy Lim
Address: Grandview Dorm
          Lightman College

Schedule

Biology 101	M-F 9:00-11:00
Chemistry 1	Tu, Thu 2:30-5:00
German 101	M-F 12:45-1:30

1. _Does_ Diego study biology?

2. _____ Amy go to Chemistry 1 on Fridays?

3. _____ Diego and Amy live on campus?

4. _____ German 101 meet on Wednesdays?

5. _____ Biology 101 start at 10:00?

6. _____ Diego play football?

7. _____ Diego and Amy study accounting?

8. _____ Amy have a class on Tuesday morning?

B. Look at the class schedules again, and answer the questions in part A. Use short answers.

1. _Yes, he does._   5. _____

2. _____   6. _____

3. _____   7. _____

4. _____   8. _____

D Simple Present Information Questions

Examining Form

Read the sentences and complete the tasks below. Then discuss your answers and read the Form charts to check them.

1a. Do you live here?   **2a.** Does she study in the evening?
1b. Where do you live?   **2b.** When does she study?

1. Which sentences are *Yes/No* questions? Which are information questions?

2. How do *Yes/No* questions begin? How do information questions begin?

Information Questions					Answers
WH- WORD	**DO/DOES**	**SUBJECT**	**BASE FORM OF VERB**		
Who	do	I	**call**	for help?	Call your teacher.
What		you	**read**?		Novels.
Where	does	he	**live**?		He **lives** in the dorm.
		she			In Chicago.
When	do	we	**eat**	dinner?	At 7:00 every day.
Why		you	**exercise**?		For my health.
How		they	**play**?		They **play** well.

WH- WORD (SUBJECT)	BASE FORM OF VERB + -S/-ES			Answers
Who	lives	in Texas?		My father **does**.
What	smells	good?		Dinner.

⚠ When *who* or *what* is the subject of a question, do not use *do* or *does* or a subject pronoun
Who cleans the kitchen?   * Who does she clean the kitchen? (INCORRECT)

🎧 Listen to the questions. Write the words you hear.

1. _Where do_ you live?

2. _____ lives with you?

3. _____ you get to work?

4. _____ you eat lunch?

5. _____ you do on Saturday morning?

6. _____ the shopping?

7. _____ he go shopping?

8. _____ happens on Saturday night?

D2 Working on Information Questions

A. Read the statements. Write information questions about the underlined words or phrases.

1. Linda's father works <u>in a bank on Main Street.</u>

   Where does Linda's father work?

2. Lee's brother studies <u>medicine</u>.

   _____

3. Lynn and Paulo begin work <u>at 8:00 A.M.</u>

   _____

4. Larry drives <u>carefully</u>.

   _____

5. <u>Greg</u> drives his car to work.

   _____

6. Koji takes a bus <u>because he doesn't have a car.</u>

   _____

B. Work with a partner. Take turns asking and answering information questions with the phrases below.

   go home   live   study   eat lunch

   A: How do you go home?
   B: I take a bus.

A. Look at the pictures. Read the job descriptions and match them to the pictures.

_e_ **1.** A magician performs magic tricks.

____ **2.** A surgeon performs surgery.

____ **3.** An auto mechanic repairs cars.

____ **4.** A pastry chef bakes cakes, cookies, and other sweets.

____ **5.** A dog walker takes other people's dogs for walks.

____ **6.** An optician makes and sells eyeglasses.

B. Write one *Who* and one *What* question for each job description.

Who performs magic tricks?
What does a magician do?

C. Work with a partner. Take turns asking and answering your *Who* and *What* questions in part B.

A: Who performs magic tricks?
B: A magician.

The Simple Present

Examining Meaning and Use

Read the sentences and answer the questions below. Then discuss your answers and read the Meaning and Use Notes to check them.

    a. Los Angeles has over 3 million people.
    b. My mother makes spaghetti every Sunday.
    c. The word *enormous* means "very big."

1. Which sentence talks about a habit or routine (something that happens again and again)?

2. Which sentence gives a definition?

3. Which sentence gives factual information (that you can find in a book)?

4. Which verb expresses an action?

Meaning and Use Notes

Habits and Routines

1 Use the simple present to talk about habits and routines (things that happen again and again).

A: How **does** your father **get** to work?   A: What **do** you **do** in your free time?
B: He **takes** the train.   B: I **read** and **paint.**

Factual Information

2 Use the simple present to talk about factual information, such as general truths, definitions, and scientific facts.

General Truths   *Scientific Facts*
Most cars **use** gasoline for fuel.   Water **freezes** at 32°F.

Definitions
A: What does *rehearse* **mean**?
B: It **means** "to practice."

3 Stative verbs do not express actions. They express states and conditions such as physical descriptions, senses, possessions, measurements, feelings, and knowledge. We often use stative verbs in the simple present to express these states and conditions.

Descriptions	*Possessions*	*Feelings*
She **looks** beautiful.	Joe **owns** a motorcycle.	I **dislike** loud music.
The house **is** empty.	The book **belongs** to Ann.	They **love** each other.

Senses	*Measurements*	*Knowledge*
The flowers **smell** sweet.	The book **costs** $9.95.	She **understands** Thai.
The soup **tastes** good.	He **weighs** 139 pounds.	We **know** the answer.

⚠ We do not usually use stative verbs in the present continuous.

He **understands** that now.   The weather **seems** cold.

*He is understanding that now.   *The weather is seeming cold.
    (INCORRECT)   (INCORRECT)

E1 **Listening for Meaning and Use** ▶ Notes 1–3

🎧 Listen to the questions and answers. What are they about? Check (✓) the correct column.

	HABITS AND ROUTINES	FACTUAL INFORMATION	FEELINGS AND SENSES
1.	✓		
2.			
3.			
4.			
5.			
6.			
7.			
8.			

A. Describe Naomi and Alex's weekend routine. Use the verbs below.

call	cook	dance	go	make	take
clean	correct	give	eat	shop	watch

On Saturday mornings, Alex

cooks breakfast and Naomi
1

_____ a list of all their weekend
2

activities. Then they _____ the
3

house. On Saturday afternoons, Alex

_____ for the week's groceries
4

at the supermarket and Naomi

_____ her students' homework. On Saturday evenings, they _____ to
5   6

their favorite club and _____ until after midnight.
7

On Sunday mornings, Alex and Naomi _____ a late breakfast. Then they
8

_____ their parents. On Sunday afternoons, they _____ a long walk
9   10

in the park with their dog. In the evening, Naomi _____ the dog a bath
11

and Alex _____ a football game on TV.
12

B. Write six information questions about Naomi and Alex's routine in your notebook.

Who cooks breakfast on Saturday morning?

C. Work with a partner. Take turns asking and answering your questions in part B.

A: Who cooks breakfast on Saturday mornings?
B: Alex does. Who makes a list of all their weekend activities?

Beyond the Sentence

Linking Ideas in the Simple Present

Use sequence words such as *first, then, next, after that,* and *finally* when you describe actions in a sequence. Compare the two paragraphs below.

<table>
<tr><td>Without Sequence Words</td><td>With Sequence Words</td></tr>
<tr>
<td>On Saturdays I get up at nine o'clock. I take a shower. I eat breakfast and read the newspaper. I wash the dishes. I go shopping.</td>
<td>On Saturdays I get up at nine o'clock. First I take a shower. Then I eat breakfast and read the newspaper. Next I wash the dishes. After that, I go shopping.</td>
</tr>
</table>

E3) Linking Ideas with Sequence Words

A. Complete the chart. Write some things you do on a Monday morning and some things you do on a Monday afternoon.

MONDAY MORNING	MONDAY AFTERNOON
I get up early.	

B. Use the chart from part A to write two paragraphs about your typical Monday. In the first paragraph, describe your morning activities. In the second paragraph, describe your afternoon activities. Use a sequence word to introduce each new activity.

On a typical Monday morning, I get up at 6:00 A.M. First I take a shower and brush my teeth. Then I get dressed. . . .

A. Read the paragraph. In your notebook, write a question for each underlined word or phrase.

Archeologists study societies of the past. They examine the remains of ancient
<u>1</u>   <u>2</u>

buildings and graves. They dig very slowly and carefully. Their job is difficult
                           <u>3</u>

because they work in all weather conditions. Nautical archeologists work
                 <u>4</u>

under water. They use special diving equipment and digging tools in their work.
<u>5</u>   <u>6</u>

Who studies past societies?

B. Write three to five sentences about one of the jobs below. Look in a dictionary or encyclopedia for help. Use the description in part A as a model.

paleontologist   meteorologist   entomologist

A paleontologist studies fossils. . .

A. Complete this description. Use the correct form of the stative verbs below.

feel   hate   have   have   live   look   love   weigh

Susan Acosta _____lives_____ in Seattle with her family. She is married and
              1

_____ three children. During the week, she is a wife and mother. On the
  2

weekends, she is a long distance runner. Susan is 40 years old, but she

_____ young for her age. She _____ light brown hair and green
  3   4

eyes. She is 5 feet 2 inches tall, and she _____ only 100 pounds. Susan is
                                5

very fit. She exercises every day, and she runs in three marathons every year.

Susan _____ her sport, but she _____ competition. "Before a race,
          6   7

I _____ very nervous. I don't like it, but it helps me run fast!"
   8

B. Write a description of a friend or a family member. Use the description in part A as a model. Write five or six sentences. Use a variety of stative verbs.

My brother Chang looks very young for his age. He is six feet tall and thin. He is a law student . . .

F Combining Form, Meaning, and Use

F1 Thinking About Meaning and Use

Complete each conversation. Then discuss your answers in small groups.

1. **A:** _____

   B: In Florida.
   - **a.** Where do you live?
   - **b.** Who do you live with?
   - **c.** What do you do?

2. **A:** _____ after work?

   B: To the gym.
   - **a.** Where does she
   - **b.** Where she goes
   - **c.** Where does she go

3. **A:** Does Steve clean the house?

   B: _____
   - **a.** Yes, he is.
   - **b.** No. I do.
   - **c.** Yes, we do.

4. **A:** Who teaches your class?

   B: _____
   - **a.** A class of fifth graders.
   - **b.** A woman from Spain.
   - **c.** Spanish.

5. **A:** _____

   B: It cools the air.
   - **a.** What does an air conditioner do?
   - **b.** Who makes an air conditioner?
   - **c.** What is an air conditioner?

6. **A:** What does your brother look like?

   B: _____
   - **a.** He likes soccer.
   - **b.** He has dark hair.
   - **c.** He looks for his shoes.

7. **A:** Who owns that bicycle?

   B: _____
   - **a.** Ted is.
   - **b.** Ted does.
   - **c.** Ted has.

8. **A:** Does water freeze at 212° F?

   B: No. It _____ at 32° F.
   - **a.** is freezing
   - **b.** freezes
   - **c.** freeze

Find the errors in this paragraph and correct them.

Sun-hee ~~go~~ *goes* to a college in Southern California. This is her freshman year, and everything seem new and exciting to her. After three months at the college, she have many friends and don't feel lonely. She works hard and get good grades, but she also enjoy life with her friends. On Saturday mornings, they studies together at the library, but in the afternoons they take long walks or doing other outdoor activities. Sunday morning is her favorite part of the week. Her friends sleep late on Sundays, but Sun-hee get up at 7:00 and goes horseback riding in a forest near the college.

Beyond the Classroom

Searching for Authentic Examples

Look for an interview in an English-language newspaper or magazine, or on the Internet. Find six questions in the simple present. Write them in your notebook and share them with your class. Why does the writer use the simple present?

Writing

Follow the steps below to write an interview with a friend or classmate.

1. Interview a friend or a classmate. Write three *Yes/No* questions and three information questions about his or her daily routine. For example:

   What time do you get up?   How do you get to school?

2. Use the questions to interview your friend. Write his or her answers.

3. Write a first draft. Use the simple present.

4. Read your work carefully and circle grammar, spelling, and punctuation errors. Work with a partner to decide how to fix the errors and fix the content.

5. Rewrite your draft.

   Interviewer: What time do you get up in the morning?
   Paulo: I get up at 7:00 A.M.
   Interviewer: How do you get to school?
   Paulo: I take the bus to the park. Then I walk.

Adverbs of Frequency

A What Kind of Learner Are You?

A1 Before You Read

Discuss these questions.

Do you like to listen to lectures? Do you prefer to look at pictures and diagrams? Do you like to do experiments? Do you think everyone learns in the same way?

A2 Read

Read the article from a science magazine on the following page. What kind of learner are you?

A3 After You Read

Write *T* for true or *F* for false for each statement.

___T___ **1.** Teachers like good listeners.

_____ **2.** Good listeners don't always follow instructions.

_____ **3.** Julie Hong does well in school.

_____ **4.** Larry Dawson is good with details.

_____ **5.** Hands-on learners don't usually learn from books.

_____ **6.** Pete Donaldson spends a lot of time on the computer.

What Kind of Learner Are You?

Researchers say that there are at least three different types of learners.

Some learners are good listeners. Teachers like them because they always 5 follow instructions. Julie Hong is a student like this. She gets A's in all her classes at Deerfield High School in 10 Connecticut. She loves school, and her teachers love her because she always pays attention in class. "I pay attention because I don't want to miss important information," she says.

15 Some people learn from pictures and diagrams. They are very creative but don't like details. 20 Larry Dawson is a good example of this kind of learner. He is studying graphic design at Warfield Community College in Ohio.

25 He is usually very good with ideas and concepts but sometimes has problems with details. "New ideas are exciting, but I often get bored at the end of a big project," Larry admits.

30 Some learners rarely learn from books or pictures. They are "hands-on" learners. They learn from 35 experience. Pete Donaldson is a good example of a hands-on learner. Pete is studying computer science at the University of Florida. 40 Pete never reads computer manuals and seldom looks at diagrams. He just spends hours on the computer. "That's the best way for me to learn," he says.

So, what kind of learner are you?

45 Do you always learn the same way? Or do you learn one way in some classes and another way in others?

---

concepts: ideas or principles
creative: using skill or imagination to make new things
details: small facts or pieces of information

hands-on: learned by doing, not watching
manuals: books that explain how to do something
pay attention: listen to something or someone carefully

B Adverbs of Frequency

Examining Form

Read the sentences and complete the tasks below. Then discuss your answers and read the Form charts to check them.

    a. Good listeners are usually good learners.
    b. They always follow instructions.
    c. Some learners are often bad with details.
    d. Some learners rarely read books.

1. We use adverbs of frequency to say how often something happens. Underline the adverb of frequency in each sentence.

2. Look at the sentences with the verb *be*. Is the adverb of frequency before or after *be*?

3. Look at the sentences with other verbs. Is the adverb of frequency before or after the verb?

Affirmative Statements with *Be*

SUBJECT	BE	ADVERB	
I	am	**always** **seldom**	late.
She	is		
We	are		

Affirmative Statements with Other Verbs

SUBJECT	ADVERB	VERB	
I	**always** **seldom**	walk	home.
She		walks	
We		walk	

Negative Statements with *Be*

SUBJECT	ADVERB	BE + NOT	
I	**generally** **usually**	am not	late.
She		isn't	
We		aren't	

Negative Statements with Other Verbs

SUBJECT	ADVERB	DO/DOES + NOT	VERB	
I	**generally** **usually**	don't	walk	home.
She		doesn't		
We		don't		

Yes/No Question with *Be*			
BE	SUBJECT	ADVERB	
Is	he	**always**	happy?

Answers
Yes. Yes, he is. Yes, he **generally** is.

Yes/No Question with Other Verbs			
DO/DOES	SUBJECT	ADVERB	BASE FORM OF VERB
Do	you	**usually**	exercise?

Answers
No. No, I don't. No, I **never** do.

Adverbs of Frequency

- Use adverbs of frequency to say how often something happens.
- Adverbs of frequency can be positive or negative.

Positive Adverbs	*Negative Adverbs*
always, almost always,	rarely, seldom,
frequently, usually,	hardly ever,
generally, often,	almost never,
sometimes, occasionally	never

 Do not use negative adverbs of frequency in negative statements.

We **rarely** eat lunch.   * We don't rarely eat lunch. (INCORRECT)

Placement of Adverbs of Frequency

- In affirmative statements, adverbs of frequency come after the verb *be*. They come before other verbs.
- In negative statements, most adverbs of frequency come before *be + not* or *do + not*.
- However, *always* comes after *be + not* or *do + not*.

  She isn't **always** late.   She doesn't **always** eat lunch.

- In *Yes/No* questions and short answers, adverbs of frequency come after the subject.

Other Positions of Adverbs of Frequency

- *Frequently, usually, generally, sometimes,* and *occasionally* can also come at the beginning or end of a sentence.

  Sometimes I'm late.   I don't eat lunch **usually**.

🎧 Listen to the description. Write the adverbs of frequency you hear.

Some adults ___occasionally___

get very angry when they drive.

Experts call this "road rage." Road rage

is dangerous because angry drivers

_____ drive carelessly
2

and _____ cause
3

accidents. These drivers

_____ care about other drivers. They are _____
4   5

rude and hostile. Angry drivers _____ drive very fast, and they
6

_____ shout at other drivers.
7

Form sentences with adverbs of frequency in your notebook. Use the words and
phrases. There may be more than one correct order. Punctuate your sentences
correctly. Compare your sentences with a partner.

1. Lisa/gets angry/often

   Lisa often gets angry.

2. don't/watch TV/usually/I

3. is/always/on time/she/

4. rarely/eats lunch/Rick

5. work late/don't/we/generally

6. drinks coffee/she/never

B3 **Positioning Adverbs of Frequency**

Read the sentences. Write new sentences using the adverbs of frequency in parentheses. There may be more than one position for the adverb.

1. Jack is very slow in the morning. (frequently)

   Jack is frequently very slow in the morning. OR *Frequently, Jack is very slow in the morning.*

2. He needs a lot of time to get ready. (always)

   _____

3. He spends 30 minutes in the shower. (almost always)

   _____

4. He is on time for work. (never)

   _____

5. He stays out late with his friends. (usually)

   _____

6. He goes to bed before 2:00 A.M. (rarely)

   _____

B4 **Forming *Yes/No* Questions with Adverbs of Frequency**

A. Form *Yes/No* questions with adverbs of frequency in your notebook. Use the words and phrases. Punctuate your sentences correctly.

   1. you/usually/on time/are

      Are you usually on time?

   2. always/do/your friends/remember your birthday

   3. you/almost always/do/do your homework

   4. generally/you/are/in a good mood

   5. usually/the bus/take/you/do/to school

   6. sometimes/you and your friends/go to the movies/do

B. Work with a small group. Take turns asking and answering the questions in part A.

Adverbs of Frequency

Examining Meaning and Use

Read the sentences and complete the tasks below. Then discuss your answers and read the Meaning and Use Notes to check them.

a. Bob usually does his homework. He's an average student.
b. Ana rarely does her homework. She gets in trouble with her teacher.
c. Mike never does his homework. He's failing the class.
d. Teresa always does her homework. She's an excellent student.

Underline the adverbs of frequency in the sentences above. How often do these people do their homework? Write the letter of each sentence on the correct line of the chart below.

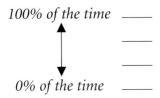

100% of the time _____
_____
_____
0% of the time _____

Meaning and Use Notes

Common Adverbs of Frequency

1A We use adverbs of frequency to express how often something happens.

100%
- always
- almost always
- frequently, often
- usually, generally
- sometimes, occasionally
- rarely, seldom
- almost never, hardly ever
0%
- never

1B We can use other frequency expressions such as *all the time, some of the time,* and *once in a while* instead of certain adverbs of frequency. These frequency expressions usually go at the end of the sentence.

I am **always** busy. = I am busy <u>all the time</u>.
She **sometimes** walks to work. = She walks to work <u>some of the time</u>.
They **occasionally** visit me. = They visit me <u>once in a while</u>.

2 These adverbs of frequency have opposite meanings.

Always / Never
He **always** tells the truth. He **never** lies.

Almost Always / Almost Never
We **almost always** bring our lunches. We **almost never** eat in a restaurant.

Frequently, Often / Seldom, Rarely
I **frequently/often** go out on weekends. I **seldom/rarely** stay home on weekends.

Using *Ever*

3A *Ever* means "at any time." We use *ever* in negative statements and in *Yes/No* questions. We also use *ever* in certain affirmative statements, for example, with *hardly*.

I **don't ever** work on weekends.
Do you **ever** go fishing?
We **hardly ever** walk to work.

3B We can use an adverb of frequency to answer a question with *Do you ever . . . ?*, but it is not necessary.

A: Do you **ever** study until midnight?
B: Yes, I do. OR I **sometimes** do.

C1 **Listening for Meaning and Use** ► Notes 1A–3A

🎧 Listen to Mark and Erica's conversation. Check (✓) the correct column.

	Mark	Erica
1. looks at diagrams	____	✓
2. follows instructions well	____	____
3. doesn't usually make things	____	____
4. frequently cooks	____	____
5. rarely collects recipes	____	____
6. usually fixes things.	____	____

A. Take this magazine quiz. Check (✓) the adverb of frequency that best describes your health habits.

How Healthy Are You?

DO YOU EVER...	ALWAYS	USUALLY	SOMETIMES	RARELY	NEVER
1. take vitamins?					
2. sleep eight hours a night?					
3. eat junk food or sweets?					
4. run or swim for twenty minutes?					
5. eat green vegetables?					
6. play sports?					
7. drink eight glasses of water a day?					
8. eat fast food?					

B. Work with a partner. Take turns asking and answering the questions in part A.

A: Do you ever take vitamins?
B: Yes. Sometimes I do. OR *No. I never do.*

C3 Expressing Opposites ► Note 2

These sentences are false. Make each sentence true by using the opposite adverb of frequency. More than one answer may be possible.

1. Cats hardly ever have more than one kitten.

   Cats frequently have more than one kitten.

2. It seldom rains in tropical areas of the world.

   _____

3. People often live for more than 100 years.

   _____

4. It is almost always hot in Canada in October.

   _____

Vocabulary Notes

How Often . . . ? and Frequency Expressions

Use *How often . . . ?* to ask about frequency. We often use frequency expressions to answer questions with *How often . . . ?*

every day/night/afternoon/Saturday	twice a year/week
once a day/week/month/year	three times a day/month

A: **How often** do you exercise?

B: (I exercise) **every day**.

A: **How often** do you clean your apartment?

B: (I clean my apartment) **once a week**.

C4) Asking Questions About Frequency

A. Work with a partner. Take turns asking and answering questions about the things on the list. Ask questions with *How often . . . ?* Answer with frequency expressions. Take notes on your partner's responses.

1. have lunch with your friends

   A: How often do you have lunch
   with your friends?
   B: Every Saturday.

2. go to a nightclub

3. talk on your cell phone

4. go to a bookstore

5. study in the library

6. visit your family

7. take a bus

8. do your laundry

B. Now tell the class about your partner.

Luisa has lunch with her friends every Saturday.

A. Rewrite each sentence with a different adverb of frequency. Do not change the meaning of the sentence. More than one answer may be possible.

1. Alan isn't usually friendly.

   Alan is rarely friendly. OR _Alan isn't often friendly._

2. His co-workers don't ever ask him to go to lunch.

   _____

3. He rarely talks to people in the office.

   _____

4. Alan doesn't usually help people.

   _____

5. Alan seldom remembers his co-workers' birthdays.

   _____

6. Alan's boss likes his work all the time.

   _____

7. Alan frequently cancels his vacation.

   _____

8. Alan gets a big raise every year.

   _____

B. Write five pairs of sentences about yourself. In the first sentence, use an adverb of frequency to say how often you do something. In the second sentence, use a more specific frequency expression to explain the first sentence.

I exercise frequently.
I go to the gym three times a week.

Combining Form, Meaning, and Use

D1 Thinking About Meaning and Use

Complete each conversation. Then discuss your answers in small groups.

1. **A:** Jack always does his homework on time.

   B: Yes. _____
   - (a.) He's a good student.
   - **b.** He rarely studies.
   - **c.** He seldom works hard.

2. **A:** Does it ever rain in Oman?

   B: _____
   - **a.** No, they don't.
   - **b.** Hardly ever.
   - **c.** Yes, it is.

3. **A:** Jenny is rarely home on Saturday night.

   B: _____
   - **a.** Where does she go?
   - **b.** She never goes out.
   - **c.** Is she always at home?

4. **A:** I'm frequently late for work.

   B: _____
   - **a.** Do you need a new alarm clock?
   - **b.** Does this happen often?
   - **c.** Are you ever late?

5. **A:** Do you often take vacations?

   B: No. _____
   - **a.** We sometimes do.
   - **b.** We rarely do.
   - **c.** We always do.

6. **A:** This bus never comes on time.

   B: I know. _____
   - **a.** It's never late.
   - **b.** It's usually on time.
   - **c.** It's always late.

D2 Editing

Some of these sentences have errors. Find the errors and correct them.

1. ~~Always~~ Lisa is *always* late.

2. He gets up rarely on time.

3. She seldom hears her alarm clock.

4. How often you call home?

5. I don't never study at night.

6. You always aren't on time.

7. Do you walk usually to work?

8. They almost always at home.

▶ Beyond the Classroom

Searching for Authentic Examples

Look for a survey in an English-language newspaper or magazine, or on the Internet. Share the survey with your class. Use adverbs of frequency to report the results of the survey to the class.

Writing

Follow the steps below to write a paragraph about your own learning style.

1. Use these questions to make notes.

   - What type of learner are you?
   - What things do you find easy or difficult?
   - What types of learning do you enjoy?
   - What do you do to remember things?

2. Write a first draft. Use adverbs of frequency.

3. Read your work carefully and circle grammar, spelling, and punctuation errors. Work with a partner to decide how to fix the errors and improve the content.

4. Rewrite your draft.

   I learn from pictures and diagrams. I often draw diagrams in my notebook. The diagrams usually help me remember the lesson.

The Past

The Simple Past of *Be*

A The Temples of Egypt

A1 Before You Read

Discuss these questions.

What do you know about the history and culture of ancient Egypt? Who were the pharaohs? What were the pyramids?

A2 Read

Read this excerpt from a history textbook. What was the difference between a temple and a pyramid?

THE TEMPLES OF EGYPT

The ancient Egyptians <u>were</u> great builders. Their temples and pyramids still stand today, and thousands of people visit them every year. However, 5 in ancient Egypt, the temples and pyramids (were not) for ordinary people. The pyramids were tombs for the pharaohs, the kings of ancient Egypt. The Egyptian temples were 10 very special places, too. But an Egyptian temple (was not) a tomb. For the ancient Egyptians, a temple <u>was</u> the home of a god.

The six parts of a temple were the 15 gate, the courtyard, the first hall, the second hall, the sanctuary, and the sacred lake.

The **gate** was the entrance at the front of the temple.

20 The **courtyard** was a large open room with no roof. Many pictures of

The Luxor Temple

the pharaoh and the gods were on the walls of the courtyard. The temple courtyard was open to ordinary 25 people only on special days.

The **first hall** was a large, dark room. It was light only in the center aisle. This hall was full of columns in the shape of water plants.

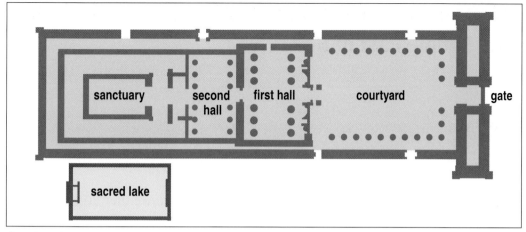

Floorplan of an Egyptian temple

30 The **second hall** was full of columns, too. It was very dark. It was open only to priests and the pharaoh.

The **sanctuary** was the most special and important part of the temple. It 35 was a dark and mysterious place. Like the second hall, this room was open only to priests and the pharaoh. A statue of the god was in the middle of the sanctuary.

40 The **sacred lake** was a pool of water next to the temple. The water from the sacred lake was important for special rituals.

---

god: a being that people worship
priest: a religious leader
ritual: a ceremony

sacred: holy
temple: a religious place
tomb: a place for a dead body

A3 **After You Read**

Match each part of the temple with its description.

_d_ **1.** gate

a. a special room with a statue of a god

_____ **2.** courtyard

b. a pool of holy water outside the temple

_____ **3.** first hall

c. an open room with pictures of the pharaoh

_____ **4.** second hall

d. an entrance at the front of the temple

_____ **5.** sanctuary

e. a dark room with light in the center aisle

_____ **6.** sacred lake

f. a very dark room open only to priests and the pharaoh

B   The Simple Past of *Be*

Examining Form

Look back at the excerpt on pages 170–171 and complete the tasks below. Then discuss your answers and read the Form charts to check them.

1. Look at the underlined examples of *be* in the simple past. Are they affirmative forms or negative forms? What are their subjects?

2. Look at the circled examples of *be* in the simple past. Are they affirmative forms or negative forms? Does the word *not* come before or after the verb?

3. Find four more affirmative examples of the simple past of *be*.

Affirmative Statements		
SUBJECT	WAS/WERE	
I	was	
You	were	
He She It	was	helpful.
We		
You	were	
They		

Negative Statements		
SUBJECT	WAS/WERE + NOT	
I	was not wasn't	
You	were not weren't	
He She It	was not wasn't	helpful.
We		
You	were not weren't	
They		

Yes/No Questions

WAS/WERE	SUBJECT	
Was	I	
Were	you	
Was	he she it	helpful?
Were	we you they	

Short Answers

YES	SUBJECT	WAS/WERE	NO	SUBJECT	WAS/WERE + NOT
Yes,	you	**were.**	**No,**	you	**weren't.**
	I	**was.**		I	**wasn't.**
	he she it	**was.**		he she it	**wasn't.**
	you	**were.**		you	**weren't.**
	we			we	
	they			they	

Information Questions

WH- WORD	WAS/WERE	SUBJECT	
Where	**was**	he	last week?
Why	**were**	you	in Hawaii?
What	**was**	that noise?	
When		we	in Boston?
Who	**were**	you	with?
How		the desserts?	

Answers

He **was** in London.
For Tom's wedding.
It was a barking dog.
In 1995.
My brother.
They **were** delicious!

WH- WORD (SUBJECT)	WAS		
Who	**was**		in Rome?
What			in the car?

We **were.**
My purse.

- The verb *be* has two past forms: *was* and *were*.
- In negative statements and negative short answers, combine *was* and *were* with *not* to make the contractions *wasn't* and *weren't*.

Listening for Form

🎧 Listen to each sentence. What verb form do you hear? Check (✓) the correct column.

	WAS	WASN'T	WERE	WEREN'T
1.	✓			
2.				
3.				
4.				
5.				
6.				
7.				
8.				

B2 **Working on Affirmative Statements**

Complete the paragraph with *was* or *were*.

Alexander the Great (356–323 B.C.)

_____was_____ a great Greek military leader.
1

His birthplace _____ Pella, the ancient
2

capital of Macedonia. Alexander's parents

_____ Philip II, king of Macedonia,
3

and Olympias, a princess of Epirus. His

teacher _____ the philosopher
4

Aristotle. As a king and general, Alexander

_____ very popular with his soldiers.
5

They _____ very loyal to him. By
6

Alexander the Great

323 B.C., countries from Turkey to Afghanistan _____ under his control. At
7

the time of his death, Alexander _____ only 33 years old.
8

The facts below are false. Correct each one by rewriting it as a negative statement. Then use the word or phrase in parentheses to write a true affirmative statement.

1. The pharaohs were generals. (kings)

   The pharaohs weren't generals. They were kings.

2. Cleopatra was a Persian general. (Egyptian queen)

   _____

3. Columbus was a lawyer. (explorer)

   _____

4. Picasso and Rembrandt were astronomers. (artists)

   _____

5. William Shakespeare was a French writer. (English)

   _____

6. Cervantes was an American inventor. (Spanish writer)

   _____

7. Marie Curie and Albert Einstein were doctors. (scientists)

   _____

8. Beethoven was a German king. (composer)

   _____

B4 Forming *Yes/No* Questions

A. Form *Yes/No* questions. Use the words and phrases. Punctuate your sentences correctly.

1. an only child _Were you an only child?_

2. a good student _____

3. your mother/a housewife _____

4. your hometown/large _____

5. your teachers/friendly _____

6. your home/near a beach _____

B. Work with a partner. Take turns asking and answering the questions in part A.

A: Were you an only child?
B: No, I wasn't.

B5 Forming Information Questions

A. Form information questions. Use the words and phrases. Punctuate your sentences correctly.

1. What/Persia _What was Persia?_

2. Who/Alexander the Great _____

3. When/the American Revolution _____

4. Where/the Mongols from _____

5. Who/Marie Curie and Albert Einstein _____

6. What/the pyramids _____

B. Answer the questions in part A in your notebook. Use the words and phrases.

1. the old name of Iran

   Persia was the old name of Iran.

2. a Greek military leader

3. in the eighteenth century

4. Mongolia

5. famous scientists

6. the tombs of pharaohs

C The Simple Past of *Be*

Examining Meaning and Use

Read the sentences and answer the questions below. Then discuss your answers and read the Meaning and Use Notes to check them.

a. My uncle was a doctor.
b. The weather is rainy.
c. Yesterday the children were happy.

d. Twenty years ago he was a great athlete.
e. They weren't in Brazil last year.
f. Shakespeare was from England.

1. Which sentences show situations that existed in the past? Which show situations that exist in the present?

2. Which sentences use a word or phrase that tells you exactly when a situation existed in the past? Underline the word or phrase in each sentence.

Meaning and Use Notes

> **Common Uses of *Be* in the Simple Past**
>
> **1** Use the simple past of *be* to talk about people, things, or situations that existed in the past.
>
> *Conditions*
> John and Sandra **were** sick yesterday.
> Keisha **was** hungry.
>
> *Physical Characteristics*
> Last year Soon-jin's hair **was** long.
> The school **was** small.
>
> *Occupations*
> Her brother **was** a taxi driver for four years.
>
> *Location and Origin*
> Those two new students **were** here yesterday.
> Alexander the Great **was** from Macedonia.

(Continued on page 178)

> **Past Time Expressions**
>
> **2** When we use the simple past of *be*, we often use a past time expression like *yesterday, last night/week/month*. We also use a period of time + *ago*. These past time expressions can occur at the beginning or end of a sentence.
>
> I wasn't in school **yesterday**.   **The day before yesterday** was Monday.
>
> **Last night** they were at a party.   **Last month** we were in Argentina.
>
> Irina's birthday was **ten days ago**.   **Five minutes ago** Mike was in the kitchen.

C1 Listening for Meaning and Use ▶ Note 1

🎧 Listen to each sentence. Is it about the past or the present? Check (✓) the correct column.

	PAST	PRESENT
1.	✓	
2.		
3.		
4.		
5.		
6.		

C2 Using Past Time Expressions with *Was/Were* ▶ Note 2

Complete each sentence. Use *was/wasn't* or *were/weren't* to make true statements.

1. I __wasn't__ at home last night.

2. My friends _____ in school yesterday.

3. My best friend _____ in New Orleans three days ago.

4. I _____ happy about the grades on my last test.

5. Our teacher _____ in class the day before yesterday.

6. The movie *Casablanca* _____ on TV last night.

Vocabulary Notes

Was Born and Were Born

When we talk about the birth of a person, we use *was born* and *were born*.

Alexander the Great **was born** in Macedonia.

The twins **were born** in 1978.

Use these questions to ask about a birthplace or birthday.

When **was** he **born**?   **Was** Alexander **born** in Macedonia?

Where **were** they **born**?   **Were** Ana and Rosa **born** in Uruguay?

C3 Guessing Where and When People Were Born

A. Guess where and when these famous people were born. Use the places and dates below to fill in the chart.

Places: China Egypt England Germany Holland Italy Poland Spain

Dates: 551 B.C. 69 B.C. 1451 1564 1606 1867 1879 1881

		PLACE OF BIRTH	YEAR OF BIRTH
1.	Cleopatra	Egypt	69 B.C.
2.	Columbus		
3.	Confucius		
4.	Marie Curie		
5.	Einstein		
6.	Picasso		
7.	Rembrandt		
8.	Shakespeare		

B. Work with a partner. Take turns asking and answering questions about the people in the chart.

A: Where was Cleopatra born?
B: That's easy. She was born in Egypt. When was she born?
A: Hmm . . . . In 69 B.C.?
B: I don't know. Let's see.

C. Now see Appendix 12 to check your answers. How many correct answers do you have?

C4 Guessing About the Past ▶ Note 1

Work with a partner. Think of a famous person from the past. Do not tell your partner the person's name. Take turns asking *Yes/No* questions about your partner's famous person. Try to guess the person's name.

A: *Was this person a man?*
B: *Yes, he was.*

A: *Was he a scientist?*
B: *Yes, he was.*

A: *Was he an astronaut?*
B: *No, he wasn't.*

A: *Is it Albert Einstein?*
B: *Yes, it is!*

C5 Talking About Your Past ▶ Notes 1, 2

A. Work with a partner. Take turns asking and answering the following questions about your lives. Make notes about your partner's answers.

1. Where were you ten years ago?

2. Were you a student? If not, what were you?

3. What were you like?

4. What were your hobbies?

5. Who were your best friends?

6. What were your best friends like?

B. Change partners. Tell your new partner about your first partner. Use your notes.

Ten years ago Yuji was in Japan. He was a student in the sixth grade of elementary school. He was a good athlete. . .

C6 Describing Places in the Past ▶ Note 1

A. What do you remember about your first school? Answer the questions.

1. Where was your first school?

2. How long were you a student there?

3. What was the school like?

4. Who was your favorite teacher?

5. What were your favorite lessons?

6. Were you a good student?

B. Write a paragraph describing your school. Use your answers in part A to guide you.

My first school was in Bogotá. I was a student there for six years. It was an old school with very big classrooms. My favorite teacher was Mr. Lopez. My favorite lessons were math, geography, and science. I was a good student.

D Combining Form, Meaning, and Use

D1 Thinking About Meaning and Use

Complete each conversation. Then discuss your answers in small groups.

1. **A:** _____

   B: No. It was very small.
      a. Where do you live?
      (b.) Was your house big?
      c. Who was in your house?

2. **A:** When were you born?

   B: _____
      a. Last night.
      b. Twenty years ago.
      c. In Tokyo.

3. **A:** What was the weather like in Miami?

   B: _____
      a. It was hot and rainy.
      b. It is cold.
      c. It rains.

4. **A:** Who was at the party?

   B: I don't know. _____
      a. I wasn't there.
      b. I am not there.
      c. I'm there.

5. **A:** _____

   B: In South America.
      a. When was your father born?
      b. Where was your grandmother born?
      c. What was your grandfather?

6. **A:** Marta's hair is very long.

   B: That's impossible! _____
      a. It was long yesterday.
      b. It was short last week.
      c. Marta's hair was dark.

7. **A:** _____

   B: The bus was late.
      a. When weren't you on time?
      b. Why weren't you on time?
      c. When were you on time?

8. **A:** Was Confucius a Chinese general?

   B: _____. He was a Chinese philosopher.
      a. No, he wasn't.
      b. Yes, he was.
      c. I think so.

Find the errors in this paragraph and correct them.

My best friend in elementary school ~~is~~ ^{was} Hanna. We was very close friends. Hanna born in Seoul in 1984. Her parents was teachers, and they very kind people. Their house was very beautiful. Her grandparents were also very kind, but they're very old. Hanna's little brother was very funny. His toys always on the living-room floor and his dog always with him. He not naughty like my little brother.

▶ Beyond the Classroom

Searching for Authentic Examples

Look in an English-language book or on the Internet for information about a person from the past. Find three examples of the past of *be*. Write them in your notebook and share them with your class.

Writing

Follow the steps below to write a paragraph about a famous person from the past.

1. Do research in the library or on the Internet. Use these questions to make notes.
    - What was this person's job or profession?
    - When was this person born?
    - What was this person like?
    - Why was this person famous or important?

2. Write a first draft. Use the simple past of *be*.

3. Read your work carefully and circle grammar, spelling, and punctuation errors. Work with a partner to decide how to fix the errors and improve the content.

4. Rewrite your draft.

    Confucius was a Chinese philosopher. He was born in the ancient province of Lu in about 551 B.C. . . .

The Simple Past

A Fashions in History

A1 Before You Read

Discuss these questions.

What are some of today's fashions? Do you like them? Why or why not? What do you know about fashions of the past?

A2 Read

Read the excerpt from a history textbook on the following page. What were some of the fashions in the eighteenth century and the nineteenth century?

A3 After You Read

Look at the chart. Is the fashion from the eighteenth century or the nineteenth century? Check (✓) the correct column.

	FASHION	EIGHTEENTH CENTURY (1700s)	NINETEENTH CENTURY (1800s)
1.	pale skin		✓
2.	gloves		
3.	elaborate hairstyles		
4.	high boots		
5.	heavy clothing		
6.	powdered wigs		

FASHIONS *in* HISTORY

Fashions are always changing. The fashions of past centuries often seem strange or funny to us. In the United States and Europe, for example, upper-class men and women of the
5 1700s wore white wigs. The wigs were white because people <u>covered</u> them with white powder. Wealthy women in France in the 1770s did something even stranger. They made a paste of flour and water. Then they
10 put it on their hair to make elaborate hairstyles. They often added feathers, lace, and ribbons. Some women even <u>placed</u> vases of real flowers and small birdcages with live birds in their hair.

French hairstyle from the 1770s

People often ask this question: Why did Napoleon Bonaparte keep one hand inside
15 his coat? Certainly, it was not because he did not have gloves. He actually owned 300 pairs! In the nineteenth century, many wealthy people wore gloves indoors and outdoors. Gloves became popular because they protected the hands and helped keep them soft. Soft hands showed that
20 a person was rich and did not need to work.

European nineteenth-century dress

In the nineteenth century, life was not easy for fashionable European women. They wore about 30 pounds of clothing. This often included a long dress of heavy material, several undergarments,
25 a big hat with flowers or feathers, a veil, and high boots. Each piece of clothing had a purpose. For example, they wore high boots because women needed to cover their legs down to the ankle. They never went out without a hat because
30 they wanted to have pale skin—another sign of wealth. For this reason, women also put white powder on their faces.

---

ankle: area where the foot connects to the leg
elaborate: complicated, detailed
lace: loosely knit material with beautiful patterns

ribbons: long, thin pieces of material
undergarments: clothing worn under another piece of clothing
veil: a net used to cover the face

B Simple Past Statements

Examining Form

Look back at the excerpt on page 185 and complete the tasks below. Then discuss your answers and read the Form charts to check them.

1. Look at the underlined examples of regular verbs in the simple past. What ending do we add to the base form of regular verbs ending in *-e*?

2. What ending do we add to the base form of all other regular verbs?

3. Look at the irregular verbs below and their irregular simple past forms. Do the simple past forms have a common ending?

   wear — wore   do — did   make — made   put — put

4. Look at the circled example of a negative form in the simple past. Find one more example of this form. How many parts does the negative form have? What are they?

REGULAR VERBS

Affirmative Statements		
SUBJECT	BASE FORM OF VERB + -D/-ED	
I		
You		
He She It	arrived worked	yesterday.
We		
You		
They		

Negative Statements			
SUBJECT	DID + NOT	BASE FORM OF VERB	
I			
You			
He She It	did not didn't	arrive work	yesterday.
We			
You			
They			

Affirmative Statements		
SUBJECT	SIMPLE PAST FORM	
I		
You		
He She It	**left went won**	yesterday.
We		
You		
They		

Negative Statements			
SUBJECT	*DID + NOT*	BASE FORM OF VERB	
I			
You			
He She It	**did not didn't**	**leave go win**	yesterday.
We			
You			
They			

Regular Verbs
- To form the simple past of most regular verbs, add -ed to the base form.

  work — work**ed**   cover — cover**ed**

- If the base form of a regular verb ends in -e, add -d.

  arrive — arrive**d**   place — place**d**

- See Appendix 6 for spelling rules for verbs ending in -ed.

Irregular Verbs
- Some verbs are irregular in the simple past tense. These are some common examples.

  BASE FORM — SIMPLE PAST

become — became	go — went	say — said
buy — bought	have — had	see — saw
come — came	hear — heard	spend — spent
do — did	keep — kept	speak — spoke
drive — drove	know — knew	take — took
eat — ate	leave — left	wake — woke
find — found	make — made	wear — wore
forget — forgot	meet — met	win — won
give — gave	put — put	write — wrote

- See Appendix 8 for irregular verbs and their simple past forms.

Negative Forms
- To form a negative statement in the simple past with a regular or irregular verb, use the base form of the verb after *did + not*.

🎧 Listen for the verb in each sentence. Is the verb in the simple past or the simple present? Choose the form you hear.

1. **a.** lives
   (b.) lived

2. **a.** call
   b. called

3. **a.** wear
   b. wore

4. **a.** think
   b. thought

5. **a.** play
   b. played

6. **a.** cover
   b. covered

7. **a.** seems
   b. seemed

8. **a.** is
   b. was

B2 **Working on Regular Simple Past Verbs**

Complete the paragraph. Use the simple past form of each verb in parentheses.

A strange thing <u>happened</u>
                        1
(happen) at our salon today. At about 10:00,

the door _____ (open) and a young
               2

man _____ (walk) in. He said he
          3

_____ (not want) a normal haircut.
       4

He _____ (want) a new hairstyle.
         5

He _____ (ask) me to cut only one
         6

side! I _____ (lift) my scissors and
            7

_____ (start) cutting. I _____
       8   9

(finish) one side, and I _____ (stop). He _____ (look) in the mirror and
                                10   11

_____ (smile). "It's perfect!" he _____ (exclaim). Then he _____
       12   13   14

(hand) me $10 and said happily, "A normal haircut is $20, so $10 should be fine!"

Complete the letter. Use the simple past form of each verb in parentheses.

Dear Marta,

I _had_ (have) a great time in Washington, D.C. The plane tickets
1

were very inexpensive, so I _____ (buy) two and _____ (take)
2   3

my friend Val with me. We _____ (go) to a lot of museums. In fact,
4

we _____ (spend) one day at the National Museum of American
5

History. We _____ (see) a really interesting exhibit on clothes of the
6

past. People _____ (wear) some very strange clothes in the old
7

days! We _____ (eat) very well, too! We _____ (find) a different
8   9

restaurant every night. We also _____ (meet) a lot of interesting
10

people. Write soon and tell me about San Francisco.

B4 Contrasting Negative and Affirmative Simple Past Statements

The statements below are false. Make each one true by changing it to a negative
statement. Then write a true affirmative statement. Use the words in parentheses
in place of the underlined words. Write in your notebook.

1. Nineteenth-century women wore <u>short dresses</u>. (long dresses)

   Nineteenth-century women didn't wear short dresses. They wore long dresses.

2. In the 1700s upper-class men and women covered their wigs with <u>black</u> powder. (white)

3. In the 1700s aristocratic French women had <u>simple hairstyles</u>. (elaborate hairstyles)

4. French women used <u>hairspray</u> on their hair. (paste)

5. Napoleon owned hundreds of <u>hats</u>. (gloves)

Pronunciation Notes

Pronunciation of Verbs Ending in *-ed*

The final *-ed* of regular simple past verbs has three pronunciations: /t/, /d/, and /ɪd/. The pronunciation depends on the final sound of the base form of the verb.

1. If the base form of the verb ends with the sounds /p/, /k/, /tʃ/, /f/, /s/, /ʃ/, or /ks/, then we pronounce the final *-ed* as /t/.

    laugh – laughed /læft/   slice – sliced /slaɪst/
    look – looked /lʊkt/   fix – fixed /fɪkst/

2. If the base form ends with a vowel sound or the sounds /b/, /g/, /dʒ/, /v/, /ð/, /z/, /ʒ/, /m/, /n/, /ŋ/, /l/, or /r/, then we pronounce the final *-ed* as /d/.

    try – tried /traɪd/   shave – shaved /ʃeɪvd/
    bang – banged /bæŋd/   rain – rained /reɪnd/

3. If the base form of the verb ends with the sound /d/ or /t/, then we pronounce the final *-ed* as /ɪd/. This adds an extra syllable to the word.

    need – needed /ˈnidɪd/   start – started /ˈstartɪd/
    decide – decided /dɪˈsaɪdɪd/ wait – waited /ˈweɪtɪd/

B5 Pronouncing Final *-ed*

A. 🎧 Look at the chart. Listen for each verb alone and in a sentence. What final sound do you hear? Check (✓) the correct column.

		/t/	/d/	/ɪd/
1.	needed			✓
2.	stopped			
3.	waited			
4.	knocked			
5.	gained			
6.	borrowed			
7.	helped			
8.	hated			

B. Work with a partner. Take turns saying each of the word pairs. Choose the correct pronunciation for each *-ed* ending.

1. try – tried   /t/   (/d/)   /ɪd/   **5.** fail – failed   /t/   /d/   /ɪd/

2. laugh – laughed   /t/   /d/   /ɪd/   **6.** hike – hiked   /t/   /d/   /ɪd/

3. rain – rained   /t/   /d/   /ɪd/   **7.** wash – washed   /t/   /d/   /ɪd/

4. invite – invited   /t/   /d/   /ɪd/   **8.** want – wanted   /t/   /d/   /ɪd/

B6) Changing the Simple Present to the Simple Past

A. Change the verbs in the paragraph from the simple present to the simple past. Rewrite the paragraph in your notebook.

Teresa wakes up at 7:00 and takes a shower. Then she dries her hair and brushes her teeth. She cooks a light breakfast and drinks a cup of coffee. She waits for her friend Eva on the corner, and they walk to the office together. On the way, they discuss their jobs and plan their day. At 8:45 they arrive at the office and start their day. Teresa works hard all day, and after work, she exercises and lifts weights at the gym. She gets home at 7:00 and prepares a simple meal. After dinner, she relaxes and listens to music. Then she watches the evening news and goes to bed.

Teresa woke up at 7:00 and took a shower. Then she . . .

B. Work with a partner. Find the past tense verbs in your paragraph in part A. Write them in the correct column.

REGULAR PAST TENSE FORMS			IRREGULAR PAST TENSE FORMS
/t/	/d/	/ɪd/	
			woke up

C. With your partner, take turns reading the paragraph you wrote in part A.

C Simple Past Questions

Examining Form

Read the sentences and answer the questions below. Then discuss your answers and read the Form charts to check them.

    1a. Do you eat breakfast?   **2a.** When does the class start?
    1b. Did you eat breakfast?   **2b.** When did the class start?

1. Which questions are in the simple past? How do you know?

2. Which is a *Yes/No* question in the simple past? What word comes before the subject? What form of the verb follows the subject?

3. Which is an information question in the simple past? What word comes between the *wh-* word and the subject? What form of the verb follows the subject?

Yes/No Questions			
DID	SUBJECT	BASE FORM OF VERB	
Did	I you he she it we you they	arrive leave	yesterday?

Short Answers						
YES	SUBJECT	*DID*	*NO*	SUBJECT	*DID + NOT*
Yes,	I you he she it you we they	did.	No,	I you he she it you we they	didn't.

Information Questions					Answers
WH- WORD	DID	SUBJECT	BASE FORM OF VERB		
Who		I	meet	at dinner?	Your friend Jane.
What		you	have	for breakfast?	I **had** cereal.
Where	did	he	go	last night?	To Steve's house.
When		we	call	them?	You **called** them last week.
Why		you	study	so late?	Because we **had** a big test.
How		they	enjoy	the film?	They **loved** it.

WH- WORD (SUBJECT)			SIMPLE PAST FORM		
Who			left	yesterday?	Pete.
What			arrived	in the mail?	A letter.

- Use *did* to form most questions in the simple past.
- Use the base form of the verb after the subject in most simple past questions. Do not use a simple past form.

    Who did Gloria **call**?   Did Alex **see** you?

⚠️ Do not use *did* in information questions when *who* or *what* is the subject.

    What **happened** last night?   Who **left** early?

C1 Listening for Form

🎧 Listen to each sentence. Check (✓) the form of *do* that you hear. For sentences with no form of *do*, check (✓) the last column (∅).

	DO	DOES	DID	∅
1.			✓	
2.				
3.				
4.				
5.				
6.				

A. Form simple past questions in your notebook. Use the words and phrases. Then look at the pictures and answer your questions with short answers. If an answer is *no*, write a true statement. Punctuate your sentences correctly.

1. Carl and Rosa/go to the bank

Did Carl and Rosa go to the bank?
No. They went to the mall.

2. Carl/buy/a shirt

3. Rosa/go to the hairdresser's

4. they/eat/hamburgers for lunch

5. they/look/at dolls

6. they/meet/their friends

B. Work with a partner. Take turns asking and answering the questions in part A.

C. Now write six *Yes/No* questions to find out about your partner's activities yesterday. Take turns asking and answering each other's questions.

A: Did you wake up early yesterday?
B: No, I didn't. I woke up at 11:00.

C3 Working on Information Questions

Write information questions about the underlined words or phrases in each statement.

1. Carol studied art <u>in Paris.</u>

   Where did Carol study art?

2. Carol made <u>her own clothes.</u>

   _____

3. Carol graduated from college <u>in 1999.</u>

   _____

4. <u>Carol</u> worked for a fashion designer.

   _____

5. <u>Her boss</u> taught her the latest fashions.

   _____

6. <u>The fashion designer</u> loved Carol's work.

   _____

7. Carol photographed <u>her designs.</u>

   _____

8. Carol won a prize <u>in 2001.</u>

   _____

Informally Speaking

Spoken Forms of *Did* + Pronoun

🔊 Look at the cartoon and listen to the sentence. How is the underlined form in the cartoon different from what you hear?

Josh! What <u>did you</u> do to my new floor?

We often use the spoken form of *did you* /ˈdɪdʒə/ and *did he* /ˈdɪdi/ in conversation.

STANDARD FORM	WHAT YOU MIGHT HEAR
Did you go yesterday?	"/ˈdɪdʒə/ go yesterday?"
Did he leave early?	"/ˈdɪdi/ leave early?"
Where **did you** study?	"Where /ˈdɪdʒə/ study?"

C4 Understanding Informal Speech

🎧 Listen to the conversation. Write the standard form of the words you hear.

1. **A:** _Did he_____ come home late last night?

   B: Yes. He got in at 9:00.

2. **A:** What time _____ call him?

   B: About 10:00.

3. **A:** How _____ get home from the airport?

   B: He took a taxi.

4. **A:** _____ have a good time in Hawaii?

   B: Yes. He loved it!

5. **A:** _____ invite him for dinner on Friday?

   B: Yes I did.

D | The Simple Past

Examining Meaning and Use

Read the sentences and answer the questions below. Then discuss your answers
and read the Meaning and Use Notes to check them.

   a. David works in Seattle.
   b. David worked in Seattle for a long time.

1. Which sentence shows that David has a job in Seattle now?

2. Which sentence shows that David does not have a job in Seattle now?

Meaning and Use Notes

Past Actions and States

1A   Use the simple past for actions that started and finished in the past. The actions
can be from the recent past (a short time ago) or from the distant past (a long
time ago).

Recent Past	*Distant Past*
She **washed** her hair <u>this morning</u>.	The war **started** <u>in 1776</u>.

1B   Use the simple past for states that were true in the past.

Recent Past	*Distant Past*
She **was** sick <u>this morning</u>.	Gloves **were** popular <u>in the nineteenth century</u>.

Past Time Expressions

2   As with the simple past of *be*, we often use past time expressions with verbs in the
simple past to say when an action happened. Past time expressions can come at
the beginning or at the end of the sentence.

They went to Japan **last week**.	**Last night** we saw a great movie.
He left **ten minutes ago**.	**Two years ago** I went to Mexico.
We stayed **for three hours**.	I was ill **yesterday**.

Listening for Meaning and Use ▶ Note 1A, 1B, 2

🎧 Listen to each sentence. Is the action or state in the past or present? Check (✓) the correct column.

	PAST	PRESENT
1.	✓	
2.		
3.		
4.		
5.		
6.		
7.		
8.		

D2 **Referring to Past Time Expressions** ▶ Notes 1A, 2

A. In your notebook, write questions with *when* in the simple past. Use the words and phrases. Then write a true answer to the questions. Use past time expressions. Punctuate your sentences correctly.

1. take/vacation

When did you take a vacation?
I took a vacation last month.

2. see/your friends

3. go/the movies

4. eat/pizza

5. take/a test

6. finish/high school

B. Write five more simple past questions with *when.*

When did you have your first English class?

C. Work with a partner. Take turns asking and answering each other's questions in part B. Use a time expression in each answer.

A: When did you have your first English class?
B: I had my first English class two years ago.

Beyond the Sentence

Connecting Ideas in the Simple Past

We can use sequence words such as *first, next, then,* and *later* with time expressions to help connect ideas in a story. Time expressions help us place events at **specific** times in the past. They also help us show the passage of time.

> **Five years ago** Derek met a beautiful woman at a party. **The next day** he saw her again at the library. **Later that evening** he called her and asked her out. They had their first date **two days later**. **The next week** they spent every day together. **A year later** they announced their engagement.

D3 Connecting Events in the Past

► Notes 1A, 2

Look at the pictures. Write a paragraph in your notebook to describe Amy's bad day. Use the time expressions and sequence words. Begin with:

Last week Amy had a really bad day. First, she got up late. Then, . . .

1. get up late

3. drop the coffee pot

5. arrive at work / see a sign on the door

2. burn her shirt

4. miss the bus

6. tell the story at work / they laugh

Meaning and Use • The Simple Past   199

D4) Writing About Events in the Past

▶ Notes 1A, 1B, 2

A. Think about a bad day you had. In your notebook, write a list of at least five events that happened.

I didn't hear my alarm clock.

B. Now write a paragraph. Connect the events with sequence words and past time expressions. Start with a sentence that tells when the events happened.

Last Monday I had a really bad day. First, I didn't hear my alarm clock, and I got to English class 20 minutes late. . . .

D5) Talking About the Past

▶ Notes 1A, 1B, 2

A. Work with a small group. Write questions about life one hundred years ago. Write a question for each topic.

	TOPIC	QUESTION
1.	transportation	How did people travel?
2.	jobs	
3.	school	
4.	food	
5.	clothes	
6.	families	
7.	communication	
8.	entertainment	

B. Take turns asking and answering the questions in part A. Offer as many different answers to each question as possible.

A: How did people travel?
B: People traveled by horse and cart.
C: They also traveled on foot.

Combining Form, Meaning, and Use

E1 Thinking About Meaning and Use

Complete each conversation. Then discuss your answers in small groups.

1. A: _____

    B: My ten-year-old brother.

        a. Who drove you to school?

        b. Who did you drive to school?

        c. When did you go?

2. A: What did you do yesterday?

    B: _____

        a. My homework.

        b. Last night.

        c. Yes, I did it.

3. A: I missed class on Monday.

    B: _____

        a. Why did you miss him?

        b. Are you in class now?

        c. Did you wake up late?

4. A: What started the fire?

    B: _____

        a. A cigarette.

        b. Two weeks ago.

        c. In a restaurant.

5. A: _____

    B: They used horses and wagons.

        a. Where did people go?

        b. When did people travel?

        c. How did people travel?

6. A: _____

    B: I have no idea.

        a. Why did Victorian women wear all those clothes?

        b. Why do Victorian women wear long dresses?

        c. Do Victorian women have long hair?

7. A: When did you arrive?

    B: _____

        a. By train.

        b. Yesterday evening.

        c. Yes, I did

8. A: Who _____

    B: Tom did.

        a. did he break the window?

        b. break the window?

        c. broke the window?

Find the errors in this paragraph and correct them.

graduated
I ~~graduate~~ from high school in 1995. My high school years are very difficult. For one thing, my school were very far from my house, so I didn't went out with my friends very often. In addition, my parents didn't like my friends. They worried about me, and they always ask me lots of questions. Where you went last night? Who you with? What time did you get home? I hated all of those questions. Sometimes I didn't told the truth. To be honest, I feeled bad about lying.

▶ Beyond the Classroom

Searching for Authentic Examples

Look for simple past sentences in English-language newspapers and magazines, or on the Internet. Find three regular and three irregular simple past verbs. Write the sentences in your notebook and share them with your class.

Writing

Follow the steps below to write a paragraph about life in your country one hundred years ago.

1. Use these questions to make notes.
   - Where did most people live?
   - What kind of work did most people do?
   - What kind of clothes did people wear?
   - What kind of transportation did people use?

2. Write a first draft. Use the simple past.

3. Read your work carefully and circle grammar, spelling, and punctuation errors. Work with a partner to decide how to fix the errors and improve the content.

4. Rewrite your draft.

   One hundred years ago, most Polish people lived in the countryside. They lived in small villages. . . .

The Past Continuous

A Unusual Disasters in History

A1 Before You Read

Discuss these questions.

What is a disaster? What kinds of things cause disasters? Can you think of any recent disasters?

A2 Read

Read this magazine article to find out about two unusual disasters. What were their causes?

Unusual DISASTERS in History

The Great Chicago Fire

According to legend, the worst disaster in the history of the city of Chicago began in a barn on the night of Sunday, 5 October 8, 1871. A woman named Mrs. O'Leary <u>was milking</u> her cow when the cow kicked over a lantern and started a fire. According to historians, a combination of bad planning and dry 10 weather allowed the fire to destroy the city. While firefighters <u>were fighting</u> the fire downtown, the wind blew it across the river. Suddenly, the city was burning on both sides of the river! The 15 firefighters didn't have enough men or equipment to fight the fire. Chicago was still burning when rain finally came on Tuesday and put out the fire. In the end, 2,000 acres of land and 18,000 20 buildings burned—all because of a cow. Amazingly, Mrs. O'Leary's house survived!

Boston's Sea of Molasses

January 15, 1919, was a beautiful Sunday in Boston. The sun was shining. Many
25 people were enjoying the unusually warm weather. Unfortunately, the beautiful weather caused a disaster. A huge tank with two million gallons of molasses was sitting in the hot sun at the
30 Purity Distilling Company in downtown Boston. The sun heated the molasses, the molasses expanded, and the huge tank exploded. Soon a giant wave of sticky molasses almost two stories high was
35 spreading through the streets. The river of molasses was not moving very fast, but it trapped many people in their houses. It killed 21 men, women, and children and destroyed many buildings. It took several weeks to clean up the city streets and
40 buildings. For many years after that the sweet smell of molasses filled the air on warm days.

---

barn: a building where farmers keep animals such as cows and horses

expand: become bigger

lantern: a light that you can carry, often with a flame

legend: a story that may or may not be true

molasses: a thick, dark, sticky syrup made from sugar

tank: a large container for gas or liquid

A3 **After You Read**

Write *T* for true or *F* for false for each statement. Then change the false statements to true ones.

_F_ **1.** Mrs. O'Leary started the Chicago fire.

Mrs. O'Leary's cow started the Chicago fire.

____ **2.** The Chicago fire burned for one day.

____ **3.** The fire destroyed 2,000 buildings.

____ **4.** Extremely cold weather caused the explosion at the Purity Distillery Company.

____ **5.** Twenty-one people died in the Purity Distilling Company explosion.

____ **6.** People smelled molasses in the air for years after the disaster.

B Past Continuous

Examining Form

Look back at the article on pages 204–205 and complete the tasks below. Then discuss your answers and read the Form charts to check them.

1. Look at the two underlined examples of the affirmative form of the the past continuous. Each has two words. What are they?

2. Find two more affirmative examples of the past continuous.

3. Look at the circled example of the negative form of the past continuous. How many words does it have? What are they?

SUBJECT	WAS/WERE	BASE FORM OF VERB + -ING	
I	was		
You	were		
He She It	was	working	at 5:00.
We			
You	were		
They			

Negative Statements

SUBJECT	WAS/WERE + NOT	BASE FORM OF VERB + -ING	
I	was not wasn't		
You	were not weren't		
He She It	was not wasn't	working	at 5:00.
We			
You	were not weren't		
They			

- In speaking and informal writing, we often use the contractions *wasn't* and *weren't* in negative past continuous statements.
- See Appendix 3 for spelling rules for verbs ending in *-ing*.

Yes/No Questions

WAS/WERE	SUBJECT	BASE FORM OF VERB + -ING	
Was	I		
Were	you		
Was	he she it	working	at 5:00?
Were	we you they		

Short Answers

YES	SUBJECT	WAS/WERE	NO	SUBJECT	WAS/WERE + NOT
	you	were.		you	weren't.
	I	was.		I	wasn't.
Yes,	he she it	was.	No,	he she it	wasn't.
	you			you	
	we	were.		we	weren't.
	they			they	

Information Questions

WH- WORD	WAS/WERE	SUBJECT	BASE FORM OF VERB + -ING
How	was	I	doing?
What	were	you	
Who	was	he	calling?
Why		we	
When	were	you	driving?
Where		they	

WH- WORD (SUBJECT)	WAS		BASE FORM OF VERB + -ING
Who	was		reading?
What			happening?

Answers

Great.
I **was cooking** dinner.
He **was calling** David.
Because the trains **weren't running**.
Yesterday morning.
On the highway.

Marta **was reading**.
The dogs **were barking**.

⚠ When *who or what* is the subject of the question, do not use a subject pronoun.

Listen to each sentence about a fire in a building. Choose the answer you hear.

1. a. is burning
   b. was burning
   c. burned

2. a. are walking
   b. were walking
   c. walked

3. a. are calling
   b. were calling
   c. called

4. a. are arriving
   b. were arriving
   c. arrived

5. a. is burning
   b. was burning
   c. burned

6. a. is working
   b. was working
   c. worked

B2 **Forming Affirmative and Negative Past Continuous Statements**

Form an affirmative and a negative statement about what Jack and his friends were and were not doing at 9:00 P.M. yesterday evening. Use the words and phrases. Punctuate your sentences correctly.

1. Jack/watch/TV/not do/his homework

   Jack was watching TV. He wasn't doing his homework.

2. Marta and Derek/play/chess/not watch/TV

3. Jenny/study/for a history test/not plan/Andre's party

4. Toshio and Ana/sit/at home/not dine/in a French restaurant

5. Robin/exercise/at home/not jog/in the park

6. Mark/walk/his dog/not make/dinner

Building Past Continuous *Yes/No* Questions

A. Build six *Yes/No* questions. Use one word or phrase from each column. Punctuate your sentences correctly.

Was she studying at 5:00 P.M.?

	Sara and Victor	raining	at 5:00 P.M.
was	she	studying	yesterday
were	it	barking	this morning
	the dogs	practicing	

B. Work with a partner. Write six *Yes/No* questions of your own. Then take turns asking and answering them.

A: Were you watching TV at 10:00 P.M. yesterday?
B: Yes, I was.

B4 **Working on Past Continuous Information Questions**

Complete the conversation about a frightening experience. Use the words in parentheses and the past continuous.

Yuji: Where __were you going__ (you/go)?
₁

Karen: I was going to Los Angeles.

Yuji: Who _____ (travel) with you?
₂

Karen: My brother was.

Yuji: Where _____ (you/sit)?
₃

Karen: In the middle section of the plane.

Yuji: What _____ (you/do)
₄
when you saw the smoke from the engine?

Karen: I was looking out the window.

Yuji: What about the other passengers? How _____ (they/act)?
₅

Karen: They were looking around and getting very nervous.

Yuji: And the flight attendants? What _____ (they/do)?
₆

Karen: They were helping everyone with their life vests. In the end, we didn't need

them. The pilot landed the plane safely.

The Past Continuous

Examining Meaning and Use

Read the sentences and answer the questions below. Then discuss your answers and read the Meaning and Use Notes to check them.

a. At 6:00 yesterday morning it was raining.
b. At 7:00 I was making breakfast, and the children were getting ready.
c. Suddenly, I heard a loud crash.

1. Which sentences talk about activities that were in progress at a specific time in the past? What is the form of the verb?

2. Which sentence talks about an event that happened at a specific time but did not continue? What is the form of the verb?

Meaning and Use Notes

Activities in Progress at a Specific Past Time

1A Use the past continuous to talk about activities that were in progress at a specific time in the past. The activities began before the specific time and might also have continued after that time.

A: What **were** you **doing** at 8:00 P.M.?
B: I **was watching** TV.

A: Why was the teacher angry yesterday?
B: Because the students **were talking**.

1B The simple past and the past continuous are different. Use the past continuous for activities in progress at a specific time. Use the simple past for actions that happened at a specific time but did not continue

Activity in Progress
At 5:00 P.M. Marta **was reading**.

Actions That Happened but Did Not Continue
Suddenly, the phone **rang**. She **answered** it.

Simultaneous Activities

2A Use the past continuous to talk about two or more activities that were in progress at the same time.

We **were telling** jokes and **laughing**.
I **was sleeping**, and Linda **was taking** a shower.

2B We often use *while* instead of *and* to connect two activities that were happening at the same time.

I was washing the dishes **while** Eva was baking a cake.
While Eva was baking a cake, I was washing the dishes.

Stative Verbs

3 We do not usually use stative verbs in the past continuous. We use the simple past instead.

I **knew** all their names.
*I was knowing all their names (INCORRECT)

C1 Listening for Meaning and Use ▶ Notes 1A, 1B

Listen to each sentence. Is it about an activity that was in progress or about an action that was not in progress? Check (✓) the correct column.

	ACTIVITY IN PROGRESS	ACTION NOT IN PROGRESS
1.	✓	
2.		
3.		
4.		
5.		
6.		
7.		
8.		

Complete this description of a historic disaster that occurred in Lakehurst, New Jersey, in 1937. Use the verbs in parentheses. Think about each verb. Use the past continuous for activities in progress, or the simple past for actions that happened but did not continue.

The *Hindenburg* was a large balloon airship. It _____made_____ (make)
1

its last trip on May 6, 1937. On that day it _____ (rain), and the
2

wind _____ (blow) hard. At exactly 7:00 P.M. the *Hindenburg*
3

_____ (begin) to descend. A few seconds later, a fire
4

_____ (start) aboard the airship. At that moment, many photographers
5

_____ (take) pictures, and a reporter _____ (describe) the
6   7

event. However, at first no one _____ (notice) anything strange. Then
8

suddenly, everyone on the ground _____ (see) smoke. The *Hindenburg*
9

_____ (burn)! Just 37 seconds later, the balloon _____ (fall)
10   11

from the sky, and _____ (hit) the ground. Miraculously, 62 of the 97
12

people on board _____ (survive) the disaster.
13

The *Hindenburg*

C3 **Describing Activities in Progress**   ▶ Notes 1A–2A, 3

A. Read these opening paragraphs of two stories. Circle the verbs that show activities in progress at a specific time.

On that June day I (was walking) in the park. It was a beautiful day. It was warm and bright. The sun was shining, and the birds were singing. I was walking near the lake. Suddenly, I heard a woman's voice. She was singing softly in a strange language. I followed the sound of her voice.

One night I was at home with my brother Danny. The weather was terrible. It (was snowing,) and the wind was blowing. We were watching a scary movie on TV. In the movie, a monster was chasing two young boys. The boys were running away from the monster, and they were screaming. Suddenly, we heard a loud crash in the kitchen. We ran to the window and looked out.

B. Continue this story. Write three or four more sentences after the first sentence to describe activities in progress. Use the past continuous.

Last week I had a very strange experience. _I was walking to work . . ._

_____

_____

_____

Suddenly, I saw a bright light in the sky.

In a fire drill, people practice what to do in case of a real fire. This university had a fire drill yesterday. Look at the pictures and complete the sentences about what these people were doing when the fire alarm rang.

1. Pete and Rick _were eating lunch._

4. Yuki _____

2. Tyrone and Jorge _____

5. Steve and Celia _____

3. Mr. Simms _____

MATH TEST TODAY.

6. The students _____

D Combining Form, Meaning, and Use

D1 Thinking About Meaning and Use

Complete each conversation. Then discuss your answers in small groups.

1. **A:** You got home at 11:00 last night.

   B: Yes. I _____
   - **a.** visited a friend.
   - **b.** was visiting a friend.
   - **c.** visiting a friend.

2. **A:** Was the weather bad this morning?

   B: _____
   - **a.** No. The sun was shining.
   - **b.** Yes. The sun shone.
   - **c.** Yes. It's raining.

3. **A:** Hi Mike. Did I wake you up?

   B: _____
   - **a.** No, I slept.
   - **b.** No, I am sleeping.
   - **c.** No, I wasn't sleeping.

4. **A:** Did Gloria come home late?

   B: I don't think so. She _____ in her room at 9:00 last night.
   - **a.** studied
   - **b.** was studying
   - **c.** studying

5. **A:** Why was John angry last night?

   B: _____
   - **a.** He was trying to study while Dan was playing loud music.
   - **b.** Dan is playing loud music.
   - **c.** No. Dan wasn't playing loud music.

6. **A:** Did you own a bike ten years ago?

   B: Yes. I _____ a red mountain bike.
   - **a.** owning
   - **b.** owned
   - **c.** own

7. **A:** Your phone line was busy a moment ago.

   B: Yes. I _____ to Nedra.
   - **a.** am talking
   - **b.** was talking
   - **c.** talk

8. **A:** Did you sleep well?

   B: No. The children _____ a lot of noise.
   - **a.** were making
   - **b.** make
   - **c.** making

Some of these sentences have errors. Find the errors and correct them.

1. We were ~~work~~ *working* at 10:00 A.M.

2. Where was she going?

3. He wasn't wanting any food.

4. We looked up and they are coming.

5. We were working hard while the children watching TV.

6. I didn't go because I was having a bad cold.

▶ Beyond the Classroom

Searching for Authentic Examples

Look for examples of the past continuous in news stories in English-language newspapers and magazines, or on the Internet. Find three examples. Write them in your notebook. Share your examples with the class.

Speaking

Follow the steps below to prepare a one-minute presentation for your classmates.

1. Think of a disaster or news event during your lifetime. Use these questions to make notes.

   • When did it happen?
   • What were you doing at the time?
   • How did you hear about it?
   • How did you feel?

2. Use your answers to prepare your presentation for your classmates. Remember to use the past continuous to describe past events in progress. Use the simple past to describe events that were not in progress.

Last year my best friend was coming to my house for her winter vacation. She was traveling by train from Washington, D.C., to New York. I was cleaning the house and listening to the radio. Suddenly, I heard a news announcement about a train crash outside of Washington. Was it my friend's train? I called her cell phone. My hands were shaking. Luckily, she was safe. It wasn't her train. . . .

Articles; Quantity Expressions; There Is and There Are

Articles

A How to Enjoy a New City

A1 Before You Read

Discuss these questions.

Do you like visiting new cities? Why or why not? What is your favorite city? What is interesting about it?

A2 Read

Read the magazine article on the following page about moving to a new city. What suggestions does it make?

A3 After You Read

Write *T* for true or *F* for false for each statement.

__T__ 1. It's sometimes hard to meet people in a big city.

_____ 2. It's a good idea to carry a map of the city.

_____ 3. It's a good idea to talk to local people.

_____ 4. It's not a good idea to use public transportation.

_____ 5. It's not a good idea to talk to taxi drivers.

_____ 6. It's a good idea to eat in ethnic neighborhoods.

Taxi drivers know a lot about their city.

Museums are good places to visit.

How to ENJOY a New CITY

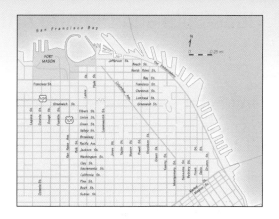

For some people, a new city is exciting. For other people, however, a move to a new city can be difficult. Cities are big places and sometimes it's hard to meet
5 people. Here are a few ways to get to know a new city and its people.

Buy a guidebook before you get to the city. Read the guidebook in your free time. Look for interesting places to go.
10 When you get there, buy a city map. Keep the map in your pocket or purse. Look at the map and find a park. Buy a newspaper and read it in the park, or just watch the people. Look back at the
15 guidebook. Find the interesting places on your map. Make plans to visit them.

Buy a bus map. On sunny days, ride buses and look out a window. With the bus map and your guidebook, it is easy
20 to travel around the city. Talk to people. A bus stop is a very good place for a conversation with a stranger.

Taxi drivers know a lot about their city. Take taxis and talk to the drivers.
25 Ask them about ethnic neighborhoods in the city. Visit the neighborhoods. Walk around for an hour or two. Shop in the stores. Find a good ethnic restaurant and eat delicious new food.
30 Think about your special interests. Are you a sports fan? Find a sports stadium or arena. Buy a ticket to a game. Go to the game and start a conversation with other fans. Are you
35 interested in museums? Choose a museum. Spend a few hours in the museum on a rainy day.

---

arena: an enclosed area for sporting events
ethnic: connected with a particular culture

guidebook: a book for tourists with information about interesting places
stadium: a large building used for sports events

B Indefinite and Definite Articles

Examining Form

Read the sentences and complete the tasks below. Then discuss your answers and read the Form charts to check them.

a. Buy a map. Take the map with you.

b. Do you like art? Visit a museum.

c. Take taxis and talk to the drivers.

d. Ethnic food is delicious. Try the food in ethnic restaurants.

1. Underline the count nouns in the sentences. Circle the noncount nouns.

2. When do we use the article *a* or *an*? When do we use the article *the*? When do we use no article (Ø)? Check (✓) the correct columns in the chart below.

	A/AN	THE	Ø
before singular count nouns			
before plural count nouns			
before noncount nouns			

Indefinite Article

A/AN	SINGULAR COUNT NOUN
a	city
an	hour evening

Ø	PLURAL COUNT NOUN
	cities hours evenings

Ø	NONCOUNT NOUN
	information milk work

Definite Article

THE	SINGULAR COUNT NOUN
the	city hour evening

THE	PLURAL COUNT NOUN
the	cities hours evenings

THE	NONCOUNT NOUN
the	information milk work

B1 Listening for Form

Paul was in Paris last year. Listen to Paul talk about his experiences. Write the article you hear. Use Ø for no article. Use a capital letter when needed.

Paris is __an__ exciting city. It is ____ great city to visit. I spent ____ time there last
      1   **2**   **3**
year. I liked ____ museums best. My favorite museum was the Musée d'Orsay. This
             4
museum is in ____ old train station. ____ station closed in 1939. ____ museum
           5   **6**   **7**
opened in 1986. It has ____ famous paintings and sculptures. It was ____ wonderful
                    8   **9**
place to spend ____ afternoon.
            10

The interior of the Musée d'Orsay

Form sentences with the words and phrases. Use *a*, *an*, or no article with the underlined words. Punctuate your sentences correctly.

1. I/left/<u>sweater</u>/at your house

   <u>I left a sweater at your house.</u>

2. I/love/<u>Thai food</u>

   _____

3. he/is working/on/<u>university degree</u>

   _____

4. Celia/bought/<u>new furniture</u>

   _____

5. my friends/rented/<u>house</u>/in San Antonio

   _____

6. Rosa/met/<u>wonderful man</u>

   _____

7. <u>guidebook</u>/is/<u>book</u>/for tourists

   _____

8. Keiko/doesn't like/<u>museums</u>

   _____

9. Paris/is/<u>beautiful city</u>

   _____

10. <u>new cars</u>/are/expensive

   _____

B3 Working with Indefinite and Definite Articles

Rewrite each phrase with *a* or *an* if possible. Write ✗ where no change is possible.

1. the old man   _an old man_

2. the boy   _____

3. the information   _____

4. the interesting book   _____

5. the equipment   _____

6. the answer   _____

7. the new store   _____

8. the woman   _____

9. the university   _____

10. the expensive car   _____

B4 Choosing the Correct Article

Choose the correct article or articles. More than one answer may be possible.

1. Please buy _____ apples.
   a. a   **b.** an   **(c.)** Ø

2. Juan loves _____ classical music.
   a. a   **b.** an   **c.** Ø

3. It was late, but _____ stores were still open.
   a. a   **b.** the   **c.** Ø

4. Sara loves _____ modern art.
   a. a   **b.** an   **c.** Ø

5. _____ Italian restaurants in New York are fantastic.
   a. An   **b.** The   **c.** Ø

6. Take _____ taxi to the airport.
   a. a   **b.** the   **c.** Ø

7. They serve _____ delicious food there.
   a. a   **b.** an   **c.** Ø

8. _____ teacher asked my name.
   a. A   **b.** The   **c.** Ø

Indefinite and Definite Articles

Examining Meaning and Use

Read the sentences and answer the questions below. Then discuss your answers and read the Meaning and Use Notes to check them.

a. I saw a great movie last night.
b. The movie was interesting.
c. It was about an English soldier.
d. The soldier lost his memory.

1. Underline the article and noun in each sentence.

2. Which sentences introduce a noun for the first time?

3. Which sentences mention the noun for the second time?

Meaning and Use Notes

Introducing a Noun

1A Use *a*, *an*, or no article to introduce a noun for the first time. The speaker has a specific noun in mind. The listener does not.

A: I have **a new apartment**.
B: Where is it?

A: I have **new jeans**.
B: And I have **new shoes**!

A: Do you want to hear **a joke**?
B: Sure. Go right ahead.

1B Sometimes the speaker does not have a specific noun in mind either.

A: I'm looking for **a new car**, but I don't know what kind.
B: Are you looking for **a big car** or **a small car**?

2 Use *the* to talk about a noun for the second time (after you introduce the noun).

In a Newspaper
Local investors built <u>a new factory</u> in Jamestown. **The factory** opened last week.

Customer to a Computer Repair Person
A: I bought <u>new software</u>, but it doesn't work.
B: Who installed **the software**?

At the Office
A: I had <u>a sandwich</u> and <u>soup</u> for lunch.
B: How was **the soup**?

Shared Information

3 Use *the* when the speaker and the listener have a specific noun in mind because they share common information.

Father to Son
Please wash **the car**.

Boss to Employee
Have you finished **the report**?

C1 **Listening for Meaning and Use** ► Notes 1A–2

Look at the chart. Listen to the conversation. Is each noun mentioned for the first time or the second time? Check (✓) the correct column.

		FIRST MENTION	SECOND MENTION
1.	vacation	✓	
2.	trip		
3.	tour		
4.	tour		
5.	guide		
6.	trip		
7.	accident		
8.	park		

C2 Using Indefinite and Definite Articles   ▶ Notes 1A–3

Complete the conversations. Use *a, an, the,* or no article (∅). Use a capital letter when needed.

1. **A:** Do you like __∅__ pets?
      ₁

   B: Yes, I do. I have ____ dog and ____ cat. ____ dog isn't very intelligent, but ____
      ₂   ₃   ₄   ₅
   cat is very smart.

2. **A:** Where are ____ car keys, Michael? I'm late for work.
      ₁

   B: Oh, I saw them on ____ kitchen table about ____ hour ago.
      ₂   ₃

3. **A:** Do you need ____ help?
      ₁

   B: Yes. I'm looking for ____ suit.
      ₂

   A: Do you want ____ business suit or ____ casual suit?
      ₃   ₄

C3 Contrasting Indefinite and Definite Articles   ▶ Note 3

A. Complete the conversations. Use *a, an,* or *the.*

__NS__ **1. A:** Would you like __a__ salad with your sandwich?

   B: No, thanks. I'm not very hungry.

____ **2. A:** Don't forget to lock ____ door.

   B: Don't worry, Mom.

____ **3. A:** The car is making a funny noise!

   B: We need ____ new car!

____ **4. A:** Sara, did you take ____ contract to Mr. Ruiz's office?

   B: No, I'm working on it right now.

____ **5. A:** ____ TV is too loud. Please close your door.

   B: Sure. No problem.

B. Look at the underlined noun in each conversation in part A. Does the speaker have a specific noun or a nonspecific noun in mind? Write *S* for specific or *NS* for nonspecific.

D Combining Form, Meaning, and Use

D1 Thinking About Meaning and Use

Complete each conversation. Then discuss your answers in small groups.

1. **A:** What is _____ good present for Ana?

   B: Buy her a CD.
   - **a.** a
   - **b.** an
   - **c.** the

2. **A:** Do you like _____ classical music?

   B: Well, I prefer rock 'n' roll.
   - **a.** ∅
   - **b.** the
   - **c.** a

3. **A:** These eggs are delicious.

   B: _____ recipe is really easy.
   - **a.** ∅
   - **b.** A
   - **c.** The

4. **A:** Dad, I'm going to _____ mall.

   B: OK. I'll see you later.
   - **a.** ∅
   - **b.** the
   - **c.** an

5. **A:** Hurry up! _____ train leaves at 5:00.

   B: All right, all right!
   - **a.** The
   - **b.** An
   - **c.** A

6. **A:** I'm really hungry. Let's buy lunch.

   B: Do you want _____ sandwich?
   - **a.** ∅
   - **b.** the
   - **c.** a

D2 Editing

Some of these sentences have errors. Find the errors and correct them.

1. Buy a̶n̶ map. *(a)*

2. Prague is the wonderful city.

3. Is a telephone call for me?

4. Please put a stamp on this letter.

5. Museums are fun on the rainy days.

6. My uncle is a policeman.

▶ Beyond the Classroom

Searching for Authentic Examples

Look in an English-language travel guidebook or on the Internet for a short description of a place you want to visit. Find six examples of definite and indefinite articles used before count nouns. Write them in your notebook and share them with your class. Discuss which examples introduce a noun for the first time and which refer to a noun for a second time.

Writing

Imagine a friend is visiting your hometown. Follow the steps below to write a paragraph with instructions for your friend.

1. Use these questions to make notes.
   - What does your friend need to know before he or she visits?
   - What does your friend need to take with him or her?
   - What kind of tourist sights do you have in your hometown: museums, parks, sports stadiums? Which is your favorite?
   - What kind of public transportation do people use?
   - Do you have different types of restaurants? Which ones do you recommend?

2. Write a first draft. Pay attention to how you use *a/an, the,* or no article.

3. Read your work carefully and circle grammar, spelling, and punctuation errors. Work with a partner to decide how to fix the errors and improve the content.

4. Rewrite your draft.

   Rome is the capital of Italy. It's on a river. It has many churches and famous art museums. You'll love Rome. But don't forget to take comfortable shoes because Rome is a large city. Also, remember to take a camera because Rome is a beautiful place. . . .

Quantity Expressions

Ghost Towns

A1 Before You Read

Discuss these questions.

What is a ghost town? Do you know of any ghost towns? Where are they?

A2 Read

Read the magazine article on the following page. What is a ghost town?

A3 After You Read

Check (✓) the things that some ghost towns have today.

✓ **1.** old empty buildings   ___ **5.** empty mines

___ **2.** many residents   ___ **6.** job opportunities

___ **3.** gold   ___ **7.** interesting names

___ **4.** a lot of history   ___ **8.** movie sets

A ghost town in Arizona

GHOST TOWNS

What Are Ghost Towns?

Ghost towns were once busy towns like many others in the western United States. Then, for one reason or another, the
5 residents moved away, and the towns resembled empty movie sets—places with a lot of buildings but no people. Today, each ghost town is different. Some ghost towns have a few residents. Others don't
10 have any residents at all. Some ghost towns have just a little history. Others have a lot of history and are popular tourist attractions.

Where Did Ghost Towns Come From?

15 Many ghost towns began as mining camps. When the mine had no more gold, silver, or other minerals, people didn't have much work. No work meant no money. As a result, everyone—or
20 almost everyone— moved away. They went to new places where they could make some money.

Where Are These Ghost Towns?

You can visit thousands of ghost towns in
25 the western United States. The state of Arizona alone has over 275. The names of the towns tell us something about their history. Some towns have Spanish names, such as Agua Caliente and Dos
30 Cabezas. Others, like Adaman and Aravaipa, have Native American names. Others, Coalville and Copper Hill, tell us about the type of mining in the town. Places with names like Paradise or Fort
35 Misery tell us about the miners' dreams and difficulties.

---

mine: a hole that people dig under the ground to obtain metals and minerals

mining: the business of taking metals and minerals from the earth

movie set: a place with false buildings where people make movies

resident: a person who lives in a place

B Quantity Expressions

Examining Form

Look back at the article on page 233 and complete the tasks below. Then discuss your answers and read the Form charts to check them.

1. Look at the underlined phrases. Each phrase contains a quantity expression and a noun. Circle the noun in each phrase.

2. Which quantity expressions go with plural count nouns? Which quantity expressions go with noncount nouns? Look at the quantity expressions below. Check (✓) the correct columns in the chart below.

QUANTITY EXPRESSIONS	PLURAL COUNT NOUNS	NONCOUNT NOUNS
a lot of		
some		
a few		
a little		
many		
much		

Affirmative Statements

	QUANTITY EXPRESSION	PLURAL COUNT NOUN
The town has	a lot of many some a few no	tourists.

	QUANTITY EXPRESSION	NONCOUNT NOUN
The town has	a lot of some a little no	history.

Negative Statements

	QUANTITY EXPRESSION	PLURAL COUNT NOUN
It doesn't have	a lot of many any	residents.

	QUANTITY EXPRESSION	NONCOUNT NOUN
It doesn't have	a lot of much any	traffic.

- Quantity expressions can come before plural count nouns and noncount nouns.
- Some quantity expressions are used with both plural count nouns and noncount nouns. Some are used only with plural count nouns or only with noncount nouns.

WITH PLURAL COUNT NOUNS OR NONCOUNT NOUNS	WITH PLURAL COUNT NOUNS	WITH NONCOUNT NOUNS
a lot of	many	much
some	a few	a little
any		
no		

- Use *no* with the affirmative form of a verb. Use *any* with the negative form of a verb.

Yes/No Questions

	QUANTITY EXPRESSION	PLURAL COUNT NOUN
Does the town have	**a lot of** **many** **any**	residents?

	QUANTITY EXPRESSION	NONCOUNT NOUN
Does the town have	**a lot of** **much** **any**	traffic?

Information Questions with *How Many* and *How Much*

HOW MANY	PLURAL COUNT NOUN	
How many	residents	does the town have?

HOW MUCH	NONCOUNT NOUN	
How much	traffic	does the town have?

- *Much, many, a lot of,* and *any* are common in *Yes/No* questions. We sometimes use *a few, a little,* and *some,* but they are less common.
- It is not necessary to repeat the noun in the answer to questions with quantity phrases.
  - A: Do you want **some** coffee?
  - B: Yes, I want **some**.
  - A: **How much** traffic does the town have?
  - B: **A little**.
- *A lot of* shortens to *a lot* when we use it without a noun.
  - A: Does Texas have any oil?
  - B: Yes, **a lot**.

🎧 Listen to each sentence. Write the quantity expression you hear.

1. __Some_____ people don't like this neighborhood, but I love it.

2. It's very quiet. We have almost _____ traffic.

3. _____ families with small children live here.

4. We don't have _____ bars or art galleries.

5. However, we have _____ ethnic restaurants.

6. The city park is _____ blocks away.

B2) **Replacing *A Lot Of* with *Much* and *Many***

Rewrite the paragraph. Replace *a lot of* with *much* or *many*.

People from a lot of different countries live in my neighborhood. On the street you hear a lot of languages. People here don't have a lot of money, but they are very friendly. For example, Mr. Lee, the Chinese grocer, doesn't speak a lot of Spanish, but he always says *buenos días* to his Spanish-speaking customers. The residents also celebrate a lot of holidays. In February a lot of residents go to the Chinese New Year celebration. And no one does a lot of work on Cinco de Mayo, a Mexican holiday. Come to my neighborhood and you can experience a lot of different cultures in one afternoon.

People from many different countries live in my neighborhood. . . .

_____

_____

_____

_____

_____

_____

B3) Working on Quantity Expressions

Complete each sentence. Choose the correct quantity expression in parentheses.

(A little / (Many)) ghost towns don't have (some / any) people. Of course,
  1

ghost towns have (no / any) real ghosts, but (some / any) ghost towns have
       3   4

(much / a lot of) visitors.
 5

  Ghost towns don't usually have (no / any) schools or other public buildings.
              6

They don't have (some / many) problems either. For example, they don't have
      7

(much / a little) traffic and generally they have (a few / no) crime. This is an
 8   9

advantage because they don't need (a lot of / some) police officers either.
          10

B4) Working on *A Few* and *A Little*

Complete the conversations. Use *a few* or *a little*.

Conversation 1

Elena: Excuse me, Mr. Reed. I need __a little__ help with my homework.
          1

Do you have _____ time for _____ questions?
     2   3

Mr. Reed: Of course. I have _____ minutes before my next class. What's the
         4

problem?

Elena: Well, I missed _____ classes, and I'm having _____ trouble
        5   6

with these verbs.

Conversation 2

Rosa: Hi, Jack. How was Japan?

Jack: Good, but we only had _____ days there so we didn't see everything.
          1

We had _____ time in Tokyo, so we visited _____ museums.
    2   3

We did _____ shopping, too. It was great fun!
    4

B5 **Forming *Yes/No* Questions with Quantity Expressions**

A. Form *Yes/No* questions with quantity expressions. Use the words and phrases. Punctuate your sentences correctly.

1. a lot of/Arizona/have/ghost towns/does

   Does Arizona have a lot of ghost towns?

2. ghost towns/much/have/do/crime

3. a ghost town/many/does/have/businesses

4. do/a lot of/Coalville/visit/tourists

5. ghost towns /live/many people/do/in/

6. ghost towns/much/do/have/traffic

7. do/some/a lot of history/have/ghost towns

8. residents/Coalville/have/does/a lot of

B. Look back at the questions in part A. Choose the correct answer for each question. Both answers may be possible.

1. **a.** Yes, it does. *(circled)*
   b. Yes, many. *(circled)*

2. **a.** No, not many.
   b. No, not much.

3. **a.** No, not many.
   b. No, not much.

4. **a.** Yes, they do.
   b. Yes, a lot.

5. **a.** No, not many.
   b. No they don't.

6. **a.** No, not a lot.
   b. No, not many.

7. **a.** Yes, they do.
   b. Yes, many.

8. **a.** No, they don't.
   b. No, it doesn't.

A. Luisa wants to buy a house. Complete her questions to the real estate agent. Use *how much* or *how many*.

1. _____How many_____ rooms does the house have?

2. _____ years did the last owners live here?

3. _____ work does the house need?

4. _____ noise does the area get from the airport?

5. _____ schools are in the neighborhood?

6. _____ crime does the neighborhood have?

7. _____ people live next door?

8. _____ space does the backyard have?

B. Imagine you are the home buyer in the picture. Think of four more questions for the real estate agent. Use the words below and *how much* or *how many*.

bedrooms   public transportation   shops   traffic

How many bedrooms does the house have?

Quantity Expressions

Examining Meaning and Use

Read the sentences and answer the questions below. Then discuss your answers
and read the Meaning and Use Notes to check them.

    a. Phoenix has many residents. It has a lot of traffic.
    b. Mineral Springs has a few residents. It has a little traffic.
    c. Coalville has no residents. It has no traffic.
    d. Tempe has a lot of residents. It doesn't have much traffic.

1. Underline the quantity expressions in the sentences.

2. Which expressions refer to large numbers or amounts? Which expressions refer to
small numbers or amounts?

3. Which expression means *none*?

Meaning and Use Notes

Expressing General Quantities

1   Some quantity expressions refer to a general amount of something. They do not
refer to exact amounts.

Large Quantities	• many, much, a lot of	A city has **many** residents.
	• some	He has **some** money.
	• a few, a little	The town has **a few** residents.
Small Quantities	• no	The town has **no** water.

Large Quantities

2A   Use *much, many,* and *a lot of* for large amounts. *A lot of* is more common.
(Remember, we usually don't use *much* in affirmative statements.)

Plural Count Nouns
Many tourists visit the town.
The town has **a lot of** residents.

Noncount Nouns
He has **a lot of** time.
She doesn't have **much** money.
Does she have **a lot of** money?

2B In informal speech, we often use *lots of* instead of *a lot of.*

He has **lots of** time.

Lots of tourists visit the town.

Small Quantities

3 Use *a few* and *a little* for small amounts. *Some* can express a slightly greater amount.

Plural Count Nouns

A few people live in Mineral Springs.

Some people live in Mineral Springs.

Noncount Nouns

He has **a little** money.

He has **some** money.

None

4 Use *no* + noun with an affirmative verb or *any* + noun with a negative verb to express none at all.

The town has **no** water. = The town does**n't have any** water.

The town has **no** residents. = The town does**n't have any** residents.

C1 Listening for Meaning and Use ▶ Notes 1–4

Look at the chart. Listen to the information. How much of each thing does the speaker mention? Check (✓) the correct column.

		LARGE QUANTITIES	SMALL QUANTITIES	NONE
1.	food stores	✓		
2.	Italian food			
3.	years			
4.	money			
5.	money			
6.	people			
7.	kinds			
8.	celebrities			

C2 Expressing Opinions with Quantity Expressions ▶ Notes 1–4

Complete each statement. Use a quantity expression + noun. Use a variety of different quantity expressions. Then compare your answers with your class.

1. Young children need _a lot of love_ .

2. The students in our class have _____ .

3. Good teachers have _____ .

4. Students often buy _____ .

5. Our school needs _____ .

6. Writers need _____ .

7. Most people don't want _____ .

8. My neighborhood doesn't have _____ .

C3 Asking and Answering Questions about Quantity ▶ Notes 1–4

A. Complete each question. Use *any, a lot of, much,* or *many.* Use each quantity expression twice. More than one answer is possible.

1. Do you have _____many_____ relatives in other countries?

2. Do you have _____ free time?

3. Do you get _____ exercise?

4. Do you eat _____ fruits and vegetables?

5. Do you need _____ sleep?

6. Do you drink _____ coffee?

7. Do your teachers give you _____ homework?

8. Do you listen to _____ music?

B. Work with a partner. Take turns asking and answering the questions in part A. Use quantity expressions in your answers.

A: Do you have many relatives in other countries?
B: No, I don't have any relatives in other countries. My relatives live in this country.

Work with a partner. Look at the pictures and think about life in big cities and small towns. List three advantages and three disadvantages of each. Use quantity expressions. Write affirmative and negative statements. Punctuate your sentences correctly.

BIG CITIES

Advantages

Big cities have a lot of cinemas.

_____

_____

Disadvantages

Big cities have a lot of traffic.

_____

_____

SMALL TOWNS

Advantages

_____

_____

_____

Disadvantages

_____

_____

_____

Life in a big city

Life in a small town

Complete this magazine survey. Then discuss your answers with a partner.

How Much Effort Are You Making to Improve Your English?

1 How often do you study outside of class?

_____ **a.** Every day. _____ **b.** A few days a week. _____ **c.** Never.

2 Do you speak any English outside of class?

_____ **a.** Yes, a lot. _____ **b.** Yes, some. _____ **c.** No, none.

3 Do you have many English-speaking friends?

_____ **a.** Yes, a lot. _____ **b.** No, only a few. _____ **c.** No, none.

4 Do you listen to many English-language radio programs?

_____ **a.** Yes, a lot. _____ **b.** Yes, some. _____ **c.** No, none.

5 How many songs do you know in English?

_____ **a.** A lot. _____ **b.** A few. _____ **c.** None.

6 Did you read any English-language novels last month?

_____ **a.** Yes, two or three. _____ **b.** Yes, one. _____ **c.** No, none.

7 How many English-language newspaper articles did you read last week?

_____ **a.** A lot. _____ **b.** A few. _____ **c.** None.

8 How often do you use an English-language dictionary?

_____ **a.** Every day. _____ **b.** A few times a week. _____ **c.** Never.

Scoring: Give yourself 2 points for every *a*, 1 point for every *b*, and 0 points for every *c*.

13–16 You are making a lot of effort. Keep up the great work!

9–12 You are making good effort. Well done!

5–8 You are making some effort.

0–4 You are not making much effort. Look at the survey for some ideas.

D Combining Form, Meaning, and Use

D1 Thinking About Meaning and Use

Complete each conversation. Then discuss your answers in small groups.

1. **A:** Does your neighborhood have much traffic?

   B: Yes, _____
   - **a.** it has a lot.
   - **b.** it has little.
   - **c.** it has many.

2. **A:** Do you want more coffee?

   B: _____
   - **a.** Yes. Just a little, please.
   - **b.** No. Only a few, please.
   - **c.** Yes. Just a few, please.

3. **A:** How much work did you do?

   B: _____
   - **a.** Many.
   - **b.** Much.
   - **c.** A lot.

4. **A:** _____

   B: I only need a little.
   - **a.** We don't have many carrots.
   - **b.** We don't have much sugar.
   - **c.** We have no eggs.

5. **A:** Do you have any homework?

   B: _____
   - **a.** Yes, many.
   - **b.** Yes, some.
   - **c.** A few.

6. **A:** Did many people come?

   B: _____
   - **a.** A little.
   - **b.** A few.
   - **c.** Much.

D2 Editing

Find the errors in this paragraph and correct them.

As a first-year university student, I had ~~much~~ *many* problems. I didn't have no friends and I was very lonely. I also didn't speak a lot English then, so I had a few trouble communicating. At the beginning lot of things were strange, like the food and the subways. Luckily, I met a little students from my country, and they helped me. Today I know much people. I also speak more English, so now I don't have any problems.

▶ Beyond the Classroom

Searching for Authentic Examples

Look in an English-language college catalog or on the Internet for general information about a college or university in the United States. Find three examples of quantity expressions. Write them in your notebook and share them with your class.

Writing

A friend of yours is thinking about attending your school next year. Follow the steps below to write him or her a short letter about your school.

1. Use these questions to make notes.

   - Does it have a lot of different programs? What courses are popular? Who takes them?
   - How many students does the school have? Does it have many foreign students?
   - Does it have any cultural or sporting events?

2. Write a first draft. Use a variety of quantity expressions.

3. Read your work carefully and circle grammar, spelling, and punctuation errors. Work with a partner to decide how to fix the errors and improve the content.

4. Rewrite your draft.

   Dear Sally,

   Here's some information about my university. The school has many different programs. A lot of students take liberal arts courses, but some people study business, and a few people are in the nursing program. The school has a lot of students—over 10,000! Many students are from San Antonio, but the school also has a lot of foreign students. . . .

There Is and *There Are*

A Wonderful Gift

A1 Before You Read

Discuss these questions.

Is there an art museum in your area? Do you like art? What kind of art is your favorite? Why?

A2 Read

Read this newspaper article about a piece of art. Then read the two letters to the editor on the following page. What are the writers' opinions about the piece of art?

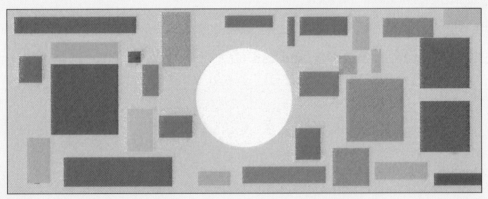

Lowell Public Library Gets Valuable Painting

A View from Lowell, by Mitch Jacoby

FEBRUARY 2—There is a new painting by artist Mitch Jacoby at the Lowell Public Library. Mr. David Grady, president of Grady Industries, recently donated the 5 work to the library. Experts say that the painting, *A View from Lowell*, is worth half a million dollars. Local art critic Melissa Sawyer said, "We are very lucky. There's 10 no other painting like this in the whole state." Mayor Frank Kurty said that the town will pay for a new security system for the painting. "There isn't enough security in the library for such a valuable 15 piece of art."

Dear Editor:

I went to the library yesterday to see *A View from Lowell*. It's ridiculous! <u>There are</u> houses and gardens in
20 Lowell. There are no houses and gardens in this painting. <u>There are</u> stores in Lowell. There aren't any stores in this painting either. What is there in this painting? Well, it's all
25 gray! There are dark gray squares and light gray rectangles. <u>There's</u> a gray circle in the middle. Is this Lowell? No way! Is this art? Absolutely not. It's a geometry lesson!
30 Experts say that this painting is worth half a million dollars. Let's sell it and buy a real piece of art.

DR. ARTHUR MONTGOMERY
Lowell

35 Dear Editor:

A recent letter to the editor was very critical of Mitch Jacoby's painting, *A View from Lowell*. Local doctor Arthur Montgomery does not believe that this
40 painting is art. Of course, there are always many different opinions about art. Dr. Montgomery has a right to his opinion, but no one is telling him to hang this painting in his home.
45 Frankly, when I have a health problem, I'll ask Dr. Montgomery's opinion. About art, I'll trust the experts.

SARAH CALDWELL
Lowell

---

art critic: a person who gives professional opinions about art
critical: saying what is wrong with somebody or something

expert: a person who knows a lot about a subject
valuable: worth a lot of money

A3) After You Read

Write *T* for true or *F* for false for each statement.

__F__ **1.** The library doesn't need a security system.

____ **2.** The painting, *A View from Lowell*, is now worth a million dollars.

____ **3.** There is no local art critic in Lowell.

____ **4.** There are many paintings like it in the state.

____ **5.** Dr. Montgomery is an art expert.

____ **6.** The painting is very colorful.

B There Is and There Are

Examining Form

Look back at the article and the two letters on pages 248–249 and complete the tasks below. Then discuss your observations and read the Form charts to check them.

1. Look at the underlined examples of *there is* and *there are*. Circle the noun or noun phrase that follows each example.

2. Which form of *there is/there are* comes before a singular noun? Which form comes before a plural noun?

3. Look back at the article and the two letters on pages 248–249. Find more examples of *there is* and *there are*.

Singular Affirmative Statements		
THERE + IS	**NOUN PHRASE**	
There is **There's**	a library a lot of traffic	in town.

Plural Affirmative Statements		
THERE	**ARE**	**NOUN PHRASE**
There	**are**	two libraries a lot of cars	in town.

Singular Negative Statements		
THERE	**IS + NOT**	**NOUN PHRASE**	
There	**is not** **isn't**	a museum much traffic	in town.

Plural Negative Statements		
THERE	**ARE + NOT**	**NOUN PHRASE**	
There	**are not** **aren't**	any museums many cars	in town.

Yes/No Questions			
IS/ARE	**THERE**	**NOUN PHRASE**	
Is	**there**	a museum any traffic	in town?
Are		any banks	

Short Answers					
YES	**THERE**	**IS/ARE**	**NO**	**THERE**	**IS/ARE + NOT**
Yes,	**there**	**is.**	No,	**there**	**isn't.**
		are.			**aren't.**

Questions About Quantity with *How Much* and *How Many*

HOW MUCH/HOW MANY	NOUN	IS/ARE	THERE	
How much	traffic	**is**	**there**	in town?
How many	schools	**are**		

- In a statement, a noun follows *there is* and *there are*. Use *there is* with a singular count noun or a noncount noun. Use *there are* with a plural noun.

- We use an indefinite article *(a, an)* before a singular count noun in sentences with *there is*.
  There is **a** red car in the driveway.

- We often use *some* or another quantity expression before plural nouns in sentences with *there are*.
  There are **some** new shops in town.
  There are **a lot of** new shops in town.

- In spoken English, we usually use *there isn't* or *there aren't* in negative statements. *There is not* and *there are not* are uncommon.

- Use *no* in affirmative statements to express the same idea as *not any* or *not a/an* + noun.
  There is **no** traffic. = There is **not any** traffic.
  There are **no** museums in town. = There are **not any** museums in town.
  There is **no** bookstore in town. = There **isn't** a bookstore in town.

- ⚠ Do not use *no* and *not* in the same sentence.
  *There are not no gardens in the painting. (INCORRECT)

- Use *any* in questions with plural count nouns and noncount nouns.
  Are there **any** libraries in town?
  Is there **any** traffic in your area?

- With *how much* and *how many*, the noun comes before *is/are* + *there*.

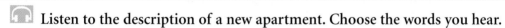

B1 Listening for Form

Listen to the description of a new apartment. Choose the words you hear.

1. **a.** there's
   b. there are

2. **a.** there are
   b. there aren't

3. **a.** there's
   b. there are

4. **a.** there's no
   b. there isn't

5. **a.** there's
   b. there isn't

6. **a.** there isn't
   b. there aren't

Change each affirmative sentence to a negative sentence. Write each negative sentence in two ways. Punctuate your sentences correctly.

1. There's traffic in my neighborhood.

   There isn't any traffic in my neighborhood.

   There's no traffic in my neighborhood.

2. There are some stores on this street.

3. There is a hospital in our town.

4. There is some crime in that neighborhood.

5. There are some children in the park.

6. There is a jewelry store at the mall.

7. There is a bus stop on my street.

8. There are some noisy people in this neighborhood.

Work with a partner. Look at the pictures. How are they different? Discuss each item below.

1. stoplight

   There is a stoplight in picture B.
   There are no stoplights in picture A.

2. supermarket

3. stop sign

4. movie theater

5. drugstore

6. children

7. bakery

8. dogs

Read each answer. Write a *Yes/No* or an information question for each answer.

1. **A:** Is there a gas station on Maple Street?

   B: No, there isn't. There isn't a gas station on Maple Street.

2. **A:** _____

   B: Yes, there are. There are some public telephones in the library.

3. **A:** _____

   B: There are 200 students at this school.

4. **A:** _____

   B: No, there isn't. There isn't a bank on Green Street.

5. **A:** _____

   B: Yes, there are. There are some expensive hotels downtown.

6. **A:** _____

   B: There are two hours of homework every night.

A. Write affirmative or negative statements with *there is* or *there are* in your notebook.

1. a good bookstore in this area

   There is a good bookstore in this area.

2. a lot of children in my neighborhood

3. interesting shows on TV tonight

4. a good article in the newspaper today

B. Work with a partner. Ask and answer questions with *there is/there are* about the information in part A.

A: Is there a good bookstore in this area?
B: Yes, there is. There is a good bookstore on the corner of Clara Avenue and Duck Street.

There Is and There Are

Examining Meaning and Use

Read the sentences and answer the questions below. Then discuss your answers and read the Meaning and Use Notes to check them.

   a. "Dr. Jones, there's a patient on the telephone. He's very upset."
   b. "Dr. Jones, the patient is on the telephone again. He's very upset."

1. Which sentence talks about the patient for the first time? How do you know?

2. In which sentence does the doctor already know about the patient? How do you know?

Meaning and Use Notes

Introducing a Noun

1 We use *there is/there are* with *a/an*, no article, or a quantity expression to talk about someone or something for the first time. After we introduce someone or something, we use *the* + noun, or a pronoun to mention that person or thing again.

Introducing a Noun	*Mentioning the Noun Again*
There's <u>a</u> drugstore on my street.	<u>The</u> drugstore is next to the bakery.
There are <u>a lot of</u> students in the class.	<u>They</u> are from different countries.

Expressing Existence, Location, and Facts

2 Sentences with *there is/there are* describe the location or the existence of someone or something, and usually state factual information.

Location
There's a man at the door.

Existence
Guess what! **There's** a new John Grisham novel.

Fact
There are 365 days in a year.

(Continued on page 256)

⚠ Do not confuse *there is/there are* with the adverb *there*. We use the adverb *there* when we are pointing to someone or something to tell its location.

There Is/There Are	*There (Adverb)*
There's a sweater on the bed.	**There** is my red sweater! I left it on the bed.
There are two blankets in the closet.	**There** are the blankets! I put them in the closet.

⚠ Do not confuse *there is/there are* with the possessive adjective *their*. We use *their* to express ownership or possession of something.

There Is/There Are	*Their (Possessive Adjective)*
There's a car in the driveway.	**Their** car is in the driveway.

C1 Listening for Meaning and Use
▶ Notes 1, 2

 Listen to each sentence. Does it introduce a noun, express possession, or point to a noun? Check (✓) the correct column.

	INTRODUCES A NOUN (*THERE IS/THERE ARE*)	EXPRESSES POSSESSION (*THEIR*)	POINTS TO A NOUN (ADVERB *THERE*)
1.		✓	
2.			
3.			
4.			
5.			
6.			

C2 Writing Facts
▶ Note 2

Write factual statements with *there is/there are* about each phrase in your notebook. Punctuate your sentences correctly.

1. days in a year

   There are 365 days in a year.

2. months with 28 days

3. hours in a day

4. planets in the solar system

5. sunrises every day

6. full moons every month

7. pennies in a dollar

8. states in the United States

Work with a partner. Describe one of the pictures in each pair. Ask your partner to guess which picture you are describing.

There is a path in this picture. There are . . .

A. Look at the map of a neighborhood. Choose five of the places below and draw them on the map.

bank	gas station	hospital	hotel	library
museum	park	police station	post office	supermarket

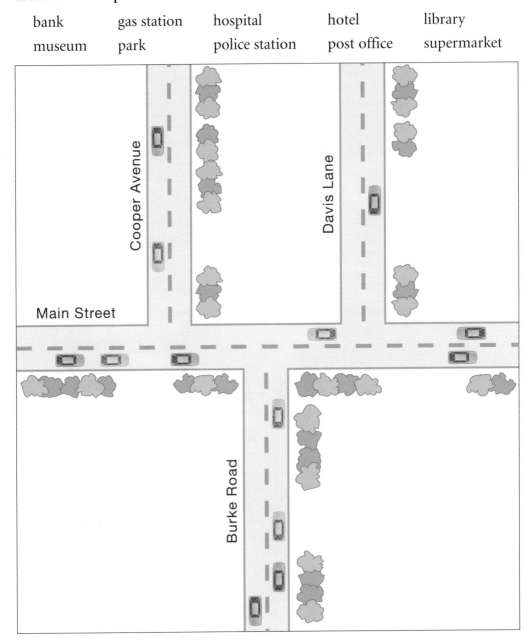

B. Now work with a partner. Ask questions to find out which places in part A are in your partner's neighborhood and where they are.

A: *Is there a bank in your neighborhood?*
B: *Yes, there is.*
A: *Is it on Burke Road?*
B: *No, it isn't. It's on Cooper Avenue.*

Beyond the Sentence

Combining Sentences with *But*

But can be used to combine sentences with contrasting information. Often the information is surprising. Use a comma when combining two complete sentences with *but*.

> There's a plate on the table. There's no food on the plate.
>
> There's a plate on the table, **but** there's no food on it.

When we write, we combine sentences because it makes our writing sound more natural. Compare these two paragraphs.

A.	**B.**
There isn't much to do in our town. There are a lot of supermarkets. There aren't any movie theaters. We have three gas stations. We don't have any good restaurants. The young people have plenty of time. They don't have any after-school activities. They have money. There are no shops.	There isn't much to do in our town. There are a lot of supermarkets, **but** there are no movie theaters. We have three gas stations, **but** we don't have any good restaurants. The young people have plenty of time, **but** they don't have any after-school activities. They have money, **but** there are no shops.

C5 Combining Sentences with *But*

Rewrite the paragraph below. Use *but* to combine the underlined sentences. Punctuate your sentences correctly.

There's a new student in our class. Her first name is Ana. I don't know her last name. Her English seems pretty good. She never says much in class. She's from South America. There are four students in my class from Venezuela. Ana is the only one from Argentina.

_____

_____

_____

_____

_____

D Combining Form, Meaning, and Use

D1 Thinking About Meaning and Use

Complete each conversation. Then discuss your answers in small groups.

1. **A:** Is there a drugstore in your neighborhood?

   B: _____

   a. No, it isn't.

   b. No, there isn't.

   c. Yes, they are.

2. **A:** Put the books on the table, please.

   B: _____

   a. There isn't any room.

   b. There's the table.

   c. No, there isn't.

3. **A:** _____

   B: No, there isn't.

   a. How many hotels are there in your hometown?

   b. Is there a hotel in your hometown?

   c. Are there many hotels in your hometown?

4. **A:** Are there any children in your house?

   B: _____

   a. Yes, they are.

   b. No, there isn't.

   c. Yes, there are two.

5. A: Is the book on the desk?

   B: _____

       a. No, it isn't.

       b. Yes, there is.

       c. Yes, there are.

6. A: _____

   B: Yes, there is.

       a. Is their car in the driveway?

       b. Are there cars in the driveway?

       c. Is there a car in the driveway?

D2) Editing

Some of these sentences have errors. Find the errors and correct them.

  1. There *are* ~~is~~ three boys here.

  2. Is their car at the mechanic's?

  3. Is there any oranges in the kitchen?

  4. Are there any English class in the morning?

  5. Is there a telephone message for me?

  6. There are no children at school today.

  7. There are some book here.

  8. There aren't no chairs.

  9. There are any students in the hall?

10. Look in the refrigerator. Are there any sandwich?

▶ Beyond the Classroom

Searching for Authentic Examples

Look in an English-language encyclopedia or on the Internet for a description of a city in the United States. Look for examples of *there is* and *there are.* Write two examples of each structure in your notebook and share them with your class.

Writing

Follow the steps below to write a paragraph about your neighborhood.

1. Use these questions to make notes.
   - What are three good things about your neighborhood?
   - What are three bad things about your neighborhood?

2. Write a first draft. Use *there is* and *there are.*

3. Read your work carefully and circle grammar, spelling, and punctuation errors. Work with a partner to decide how to fix the errors and improve the content.

4. Rewrite your draft.

> My neighborhood is good in many ways. There are many supermarkets, and there are a lot of nice people. They are helpful and friendly. There is a big park, too. There are also bad things about my neighborhood. For example, there aren't many restaurants, and there isn't a movie theater. . . .

The Future

PART
7

The Future with *Be Going To*

A Sports News Now

A1 Before You Read

Discuss these questions.

Do you read magazines? What kind of magazines do you like? Why?

A2 Read

Read this page from the table of contents of a magazine. What sports teams does the magazine talk about?

SPORTS NEWS NOW

BASEBALL.. page **22**

The New Jersey Diamonds are going to play for their second championship this season. Are they going to win? What do the fans think? Alex Cortes has the predictions.

5 *"The Diamonds aren't going to win it again this year. They were lucky last year, and they were lucky this year. That luck is going to end soon." Larry Markle, mechanic, Patterson*

"The Diamonds are probably going to do it. The team is healthy, and they have a good manager. The Sharks are
10 *probably going to give them some trouble, but the Diamonds have a good chance." Amy Reed, nurse, Perth Amboy*

SOCCER.. page **31**

It's official—Victor Mundsen isn't going to play for the Lancaster Lions next season. What is he going to do? Is he going to retire?
15 Carol Gray has the answers.

"I'm not going to lie. It was a hard decision, but it's the right decision. I'm going to miss Lancaster, and of course, all the fans." Victor Mundsen

BASKETBALL.................................... page **35**

20 Women's basketball is the hot sport this year, and the Miami Twisters are the hot team. But just last week, the Twisters' star player, Marta Sanchez, announced her retirement. Who is going to emerge as the new star of the Twisters? As Sally Gordon reports, many people think Holly Jones <u>is going to be</u>
25 the one.

"Holly is the one to watch. She's a fantastic athlete. She's going to be a top scorer." Twisters coach, Gloria Harris

"Holly is great for the team. She's young, but everyone respects her. She's going to be a terrific leader."
30 *Twisters center, Sara Witt*

---

championship: a series of competitions to find the best player or team

coach: a person who trains people to compete in sports

emerge: to come forward

fan: a person who is very enthusiastic about a sport, movie star, etc.

top scorer: the player who scores the most points

A3 After You Read

Write *T* for true or *F* for false for each statement.

__T__ **1.** The New Jersey Diamonds won the championship last year.

_____ **2.** Amy Reed thinks The Diamonds are going to win the championship.

_____ **3.** Victor Mundsen is going to play for the Lancaster Lions next season.

_____ **4.** The Lancaster Lions are a baseball team.

_____ **5.** Marta Sanchez retired from the Twisters.

_____ **6.** Holly Jones is probably going to score a lot of points.

B The Future with *Be Going To*

Examining Form

Look back at the table of contents on pages 266–267 and complete the tasks below. Then discuss your answers and read the Form charts to check them.

1. Look at the underlined examples of the future with *be going to*. Which one is singular? Which one is plural? What verb form follows *to*?

2. Find two examples of negative forms of *be going to*. How do we form the negative of *be going to*?

Affirmative Statements			
SUBJECT	BE	GOING TO	BASE FORM OF VERB
I	am		
You	are		
He She It	is	going to	help.
We			
You	are		
They			

CONTRACTIONS		
I'm		
You're		
He's She's It's	going to	help.
We're		
You're		
They're		

Negative Statements				
SUBJECT	BE	NOT	GOING TO	BASE FORM OF VERB
I	am			
You	are			
He She It	is	not	going to	help.
We				
You	are			
They				

CONTRACTIONS		
I'm not		
You're not You aren't		
He's not He isn't	going to	help.
They're not They aren't		

Yes/No Questions

BE	SUBJECT	GOING TO	BASE FORM OF VERB
Am	I		
Are	you		
Is	he	going to	help?
	we		
Are	you		
	they		

Short Answers

YES	SUBJECT	BE	NO	SUBJECT + BE + NOT
Yes,	you	are.	No,	you **aren't.** you**'re not.**
	I	am.		I**'m not.**
	he	is.		he **isn't.** he**'s not.**
	you			you **aren't.** you**'re not.**
	we	are.		we **aren't.** we**'re not.**
	they			they **aren't.** they**'re not.**

Information Questions

WH- WORD	BE	SUBJECT	GOING TO	BASE FORM OF VERB	
How	am	I		**help**	Mary?
What	are	you		**cook?**	
When	is	he	going to	**call**	us?
Where		we		**put**	the sofa?
Who	are	you		**invite?**	
Why		they		**drive**	to school?

Answers

You**'re going to** pick her up.
Chicken.
Tomorrow.
In the living room.
Our friends.
Because they're late.

WH- WORD (SUBJECT)	BE		GOING TO	BASE FORM OF VERB	
Who	is		going to	**call?**	
What				**happen?**	

Karen.
Nothing.

⚠ Do not use contractions with affirmative short answers.

⚠ When *who* or *what* is the subject of an information question, do not use a subject pronoun.

🎧 Listen to the interview with Victor Mundsen, a soccer player. What form of *be going to* do you hear? Choose the correct answer.

1. **(a.)** are you going to
   b. you're going to

2. **a.** I'm not going to
   b. I'm going to

3. **a.** the fans are going to
   b. are the fans going to

4. **a.** you're going to
   b. are you going to

5. **a.** I'm going to
   b. am I going to

6. **a.** we're going to
   b. we're not going to

B2 **Working on Affirmative and Negative Statements with *Be Going To***

A. Complete the conversations. Use the correct affirmative form of *be going to* and the verb in parentheses. Use contractions when possible.

Conversation 1

Rob: The Yankees ___are going to be___ (be) good again this year.
                              1

Derek: And how about the Boston Red Sox? They're always good. They

   _____ (have) a great year, too.
                    2

Conversation 2

Tom: Our new pitcher _____ (help) us a lot.
                                                    1

   He _____ (give) the other teams a hard time.
                    2

Yuji: The fans _____ (enjoy) this season.
                              3

Tom: I know. It _____ (be) very exciting!
                              4

B. Rewrite the sentences below in your notebook. Change the affirmative statements to negative statements. Use contractions when possible.

1. The next Summer Olympic Games are going to be in Antarctica.

   The next Summer Olympic Games aren't going to be in Antarctica.

2. People are going to live on the moon in the next ten years.

3. I am going to meet the president.

4. The population of the world is going to decrease by 2010.

5. Scientists are going to discover life on Mars.

Informally Speaking

Reduced Forms of *Going To*

Look at the cartoon and listen to the conversation. How is the underlined form in the cartoon different from what you hear?

> What are your plans for the weekend?

> We're <u>going to</u> go to a party.

We often pronounce *going to* as /gənə/ in informal speech.

STANDARD FORM	WHAT YOU MIGHT HEAR
I'm **going to** call at 8:00.	"I'm /gənə/ call at 8:00."
John is **going to** go now.	"John is /gənə/ go now."
We're **going to** eat lunch soon.	"We're /gənə/ eat lunch soon."

B3 Understanding Informal Speech

Listen to the sentences. Write the standard form of the verb you hear.

1. My sister _____is going to get_____ tickets for the game this weekend.

2. All my friends _____ here.

3. They _____ me play.

4. Our team _____ tonight.

5. The Astros _____ tonight.

6. The weather _____ nice for our game this weekend.

7. Our game _____ exciting.

8. My friends and I _____ to dinner after the game.

Write *Yes/No* questions with *be going to.* Use the phrases in parentheses. Punctuate your sentences correctly.

1. **A:** _Are you going to join a soccer league?_ (join a soccer league)

   B: No, I'm not. I don't play soccer.

2. **A:** _____ (attend the games)

   B: Yes, we are. We go to all the games.

3. **A:** _____ (rain tomorrow)

   B: No, it isn't. The newspaper said no rain until Friday.

4. **A:** _____ (the Tigers lose)

   B: No, they aren't. They always win at home.

5. **A:** _____ (have practice tonight)

   B: Yes, we are. The coach thinks we need it.

6. **A:** _____ (win the championship)

   B: Of course we are.

Imagine you are going to interview a famous athlete. In your notebook, form information questions to ask in the interview. Use the words and phrases below. Punctuate your sentences correctly.

1. retire/when/you/going/are/to?

   When are you going to retire?

2. you/are/where/going to/play/next year

3. are/why/going to/you/change teams

4. what/you/do/going to/after you retire/are

5. a championship/your team/going to/win/is/when

6. is/your new coach/who/be/going to/next season

The Future with *Be Going To*

Examining Meaning and Use

Read the sentences and answer the questions below. Then discuss your answers and read the Meaning and Use Notes to check them.

a. I'm going to study in Ireland this summer. I already have my plane ticket.
b. Be careful! Your shoe is untied. You're going to trip.

1. Which sentence talks about a future plan?

2. Which sentence talks about a belief about the near future?

Meaning and Use Notes

Expressing Future Plans

1 Use *be going to* to talk about future plans.

I**'m going to study** in Greece this summer. I got my tickets yesterday.
We**'re going to study** hard for the test next week. We need good grades.

Making Predictions

2 Use *be going to* for predictions (beliefs about the future), especially when you have evidence that something is about to happen.

Be careful! That glass **is going to fall**!
It's cloudy. I think it**'s going to rain** soon.

Expressing Less Certain Plans and Predictions

3 Use *probably* with *be going to* when a plan or prediction is not certain.

A Plan
We**'re probably going to get** tickets for the concert, but they're very expensive.

A Prediction
I**'m probably going to get** a B, but I'm not sure.

🎧 Listen to the sentences. Are they plans or predictions? Check (✓) the correct column.

	PLANS	PREDICTIONS
1.		✓
2.		
3.		
4.		
5.		
6.		
7.		
8.		

C2 **Talking About Future Plans** ▶ Notes 1, 3

A. Write three things that you plan to do after class today. Use *be going to* + verb. Punctuate your sentences correctly.

1. <u>Tonight I'm going to make dinner for my friends.</u>

2. _____

3. _____

Write three things that you plan to do this weekend. Use *be going to* + verb.

4. _____

5. _____

6. _____

Write two things that you plan to do after you complete this course. Use *be going to* + verb.

7. _____

8. _____

B. Ask several classmates about their plans.

A: *What are you going to do after class today?*
B: *I'm going to wash my car.*

Vocabulary Notes

Future Time Expressions

We use certain expressions to refer to future time. Some refer to a specific time, but others refer to general time.

Specific Time The following phrases refer to a specific time.

tomorrow	next (week/month/year/Monday)
the day after tomorrow	this (afternoon/evening/week/year)

It's going to rain **tomorrow**.

Irina is going to arrive **the day after tomorrow**.

I'm going to graduate **next year**.

She's going to cook **this afternoon**.

General Time The following phrases refer to general time.

later   soon   someday

They're going to help us **later**.

We're going to leave **soon**.

I'm going to write a book **someday**.

C3 Using Future Time Expressions

A. Write plans for the future. Use *be going to* and the future time expression in parentheses. Punctuate your sentences correctly.

1. <u>We're going to have a math test tomorrow morning.</u> (tomorrow morning)

2. _____ (next semester)

3. _____ (later)

4. _____ (next Friday)

5. _____ (the day after tomorrow)

6. _____ (someday)

B. Work with a partner. Take turns asking and answering information questions about the plans in part A. Use complete sentences as answers.

A: When are we going to have a math test?
B: We're going to have a math test tomorrow morning.

Look at the pictures. Make predictions about what is going to happen.

1. <u>The plane is going to land.</u> 4. _____

2. _____ 5. _____

3. _____ 6. _____

D Combining Form, Meaning, and Use

D1 Thinking About Meaning and Use

Complete each conversation. Then discuss your answers in small groups.

1. **A:** We're going to leave for the show at 7:00. Do you need a ride?

   B: _____

   a. Sorry. I'm busy right now.

   b. That's great. Thanks!

   c. What time did you go?

2. **A:** I'm going to take biology.

   B: _____

   a. Was it hard?

   b. Are you enjoying it?

   c. Who is going to teach the class?

3. **A:** Oh no! Look at those black clouds!

   B: _____

   a. It's probably going to rain.

   b. It rains.

   c. It rained.

4. **A:** Are you going to leave early?

   B: Yes, _____

   a. I left at 5:00.

   b. I have an appointment at 5:00.

   c. It was 5:00.

5. **A:** It's going to be hot today.

   B: _____

   a. Let's go swimming.

   b. Wear a sweater.

   c. Is it snowing?

6. **A:** Dan and Lisa are going to get married.

   B: Really? _____

   a. Was her dress pretty?

   b. Where did they get married?

   c. Did you get an invitation?

7. **A:** The test was awful. I'm not going to pass the course.

   B: _____

   a. Don't worry. I'm sure you are.

   b. That's a good plan.

   c. Was it easy?

8. **A:** I'm going to get up early tomorrow.

   B: _____

   a. Did you?

   b. Why?

   c. I did.

Some of these sentences have errors. Find the errors and correct them.

1. We *are* ~~be~~ going to eat at 8:00.

2. Where are you going be tomorrow?

3. Are they going to happy?

4. They're not going to win.

5. Who is going to being your coach?

6. Carl is going to not be a great player.

▶ Beyond the Classroom

Searching for Authentic Examples

Look in an English-language sports magazine or on the Internet. Find five examples of sentences with *be going to* and write them in your notebook. Explain why they are plans or predictions. Share your examples with your class.

Speaking

Use one of the outlines below to prepare a short presentation about a current famous person or sports team. Use *be going to.*

A Famous Person

- Tell the name of the person and say why he or she is famous.
- Discuss what the person is doing currently. Discuss some of his or her projects or plans. Is the person going to be successful?
- Make three predictions about what he or she is going to do in the future.

A Sports Team

- Tell the name of the team and where they are from.
- Discuss how they are doing this season. How well is the team playing? Are they going to win a championship? Are some good players going to leave the team?
- Make three predictions about the team.

  The New York Yankees are my favorite baseball team. The players are very talented. A few years ago they won the World Series. Next season, they are going to win a lot of games.

The Future with *Will*

A | Couch Potatoes Beware

A1 Before You Read

Discuss these questions.

Do you exercise regularly? What kind of exercise do you do?

A2 Read

Read the advertisement on the following page. What product is it for? Do you think anyone will buy the product? Why or why not?

A3 After You Read

Write *T* for true or *F* for false for each statement.

__F__ **1.** A couch potato is an exercise machine.

_____ **2.** The ad says that being in shape is easy.

_____ **3.** The machine will make you slim in three days.

_____ **4.** The company will bill you in six payments.

_____ **5.** The exercise equipment costs almost $180.

_____ **6.** If you are unhappy with the machine, you'll get your money back.

Couch Potatoes BEWARE . . .

Winter Doesn't Last Forever!

It's wintertime. It's cold and dark. You spend a lot of time in front of the TV. You eat a lot and don't move much. In short, you're a
5 couch potato.

Well, be careful! You'll be sorry in the summer! You won't be in shape. Your clothes won't fit, and you'll probably be embarrassed at the beach.

10 What can you do?
The answer is easy! Buy our **Stomach-System Exercise Equipment,** and you'll be ready for summer!

Are you afraid that exercise
15 **will be boring?**
Don't worry! Just ten minutes a day with our magic machine and you'll be slim and fit in just a few weeks!

Call us today, and we'll send your
20 **Stomach-System Exercise Equipment** immediately! We'll bill you in six small payments of only **$29.99.** And don't worry. If you're unhappy for any reason, send the equipment back, and we'll
25 return your money.

---

beware: be careful

couch potato: informal expression for a person who watches TV and doesn't exercise

in shape: physically fit and healthy

in short: in a few words

slim: thin

B The Future with *Will*

Examining Form

Read the sentences and complete the task below. Then discuss your answers and read the Form charts to check them.

a. You will be fit in just a few weeks.
b. We will bill you in six payments.

Look at the sentences. Underline the subject of each sentence. Does the form of *will* change or stay the same with different subjects?

Affirmative Statements			
SUBJECT	*WILL*	BASE FORM OF VERB	
I			
You			
He She It	will	be	late.
We			
You			
They			

Negative Statements				
SUBJECT	*WILL*	*NOT*	BASE FORM OF VERB	
I				
You				
He She It	will	not	be	late.
We				
You				
They				

CONTRACTIONS		
I'll		
You'll		
He'll She'll It'll	be	late.
We'll		
You'll		
They'll		

CONTRACTIONS			
I			
You			
He She It	won't	be	late.
We			
You			
They			

Yes/No Questions

WILL	SUBJECT	BASE FORM OF VERB	
Will	I you he she it we you they	**finish**	tomorrow?

Short Answers

YES	SUBJECT	WILL	NO	SUBJECT	WILL + NOT
Yes,	you I he she it you we they	**will.**	No,	you I he she it you we they	**won't.**

Information Questions

WH-WORD	WILL	SUBJECT	BASE FORM OF VERB	
How		I	**do**	on the exam?
What		you	**do**	now?
When	**will**	she	**get**	here?
Where		we	**park**	the car?
Who		you	**ask**	to the opera?
Why		they	**leave**	early?

WH- WORD (SUBJECT)	WILL		BASE FORM OF VERB	
Who	**will**		**win**	the game?
What			**happen?**	

Answers

You**'ll** do fine.
I**'ll** get a new job.
Soon, I hope.
We**'ll** park the car in the garage.
Our neighbors.
They need to study.

I don't know.
Nothing.

- Use the same form of *will* with every subject.
- We usually use the contracted subject pronoun + *'ll* in conversations.
- When *who* or *what* is the subject of an information question, do not use a subject pronoun.

Listening for Form

Listen to the conversation. Do you hear the simple present, the future with will, or the future with *be going to*. Check (✓) the correct column.

	SIMPLE PRESENT	FUTURE WITH *WILL*	FUTURE WITH *BE GOING TO*
1.			✓
2.			
3.			
4.			
5.			
6.			

B2 **Working on Affirmative and Negative Statements with *Will***

Complete the sentences from ads. Use *will* or *won't* and the verbs in parentheses. Use contractions when possible.

1. Use Aura and your hair _____will shine_____ (shine).

2. You _____ (be) a loser in Rabino running shoes.

3. You _____ (look) like a millionaire in your new Lexia.

4. Buy a ticket on Northeastern Airlines and your friend _____ (fly) for free.

5. Take your children to Water Fun, and they _____ (forget) it.

B3 **Forming Questions with *Will***

Form information questions with *will* and write them in your notebook. Use the words and phrases. Punctuate your sentences correctly.

1. get/your family/when/a new car/will

   When will your family get a new car?

2. will/when/dinner/be ready

3. where/in five years/will/be/your best friend

4. you/who/will/marry

5. tomorrow/what/you/will/wear

6. how/she/home/get/will

Informally Speaking

Reduced Forms of *Will*

 Look at the cartoon and listen to the sentence. How is the underlined form in the cartoon different from what you hear?

> Don't worry. <u>Jenny will</u> be great with the kids.

In informal speech, we sometimes use the reduced form of *will* (*'ll*) with *wh-* words and nouns.

STANDARD FORM	WHAT YOU MIGHT HEAR
Kim **will** help you.	"/ˈkɪməl/ help you."
The weather **will** be good.	"The /ˈwɛðərəl/ be good."
When **will** he leave?	"/ˈwɛnəl/ he leave?"

B4 Understanding Informal Speech

Listen to each sentence. Write the full form of the contraction with *will* that you hear.

1. Use our lotion today and your _____skin will_____ feel softer.

2. Some of my _____ believe anything.

3. Oh no! _____ your parents say?

4. The cold _____ end tomorrow.

5. _____ be the winner? You decide! Send your vote by e-mail.

6. Use this product and your _____ be incredibly white!

C The Future with *Will*

Examining Meaning and Use

Read the conversations and answer the questions below. Then discuss your answers and read the Meaning and Use Notes to check them.

a.   **Carl:** Do you want milk or soda?
     Paul: I'll have milk.

b.   **Father:** You need to improve your grades.
     Son: I know. I'll work very hard this term.

c.   **Mike:** Do you think Greg will finish first?
     Steve: No, Greg won't win. Tom will.

1. Which conversation makes a prediction about the future?

2. Which conversation makes a promise?

3. Which conversation expresses a quick decision at the moment of speaking?

Meaning and Use Notes

Predictions

1A   Use *will* to make predictions about the future.

I think the president **will solve** the problem. He always does.

1B   Add *probably* to make the prediction less certain.

She **will probably attend** college in the fall.
I **will probably move** next year.

Promises

2   Use *will* to express a promise, especially with *I* or *we*.

Please let me borrow your laptop. I **won't break** it.
Please let me watch this TV show. I**'ll do** my homework later.

3 Use *will* for decisions that you make at the moment of speaking.

In a Restaurant	*At Home*
A: Would you like coffee or tea?	A: Oh no! We're out of milk.
B: **I'll have** coffee.	B: That's OK. **I'll go** to the store and get some.

C1 Listening for Meaning and Use ▶ Notes 1A–3

🎧 Listen to each sentence. Is it a prediction, a promise, or a quick decision? Check (✓) the correct column.

	PREDICTION	PROMISE	QUICK DECISION
1.		✓	
2.			
3.			
4.			
5.			
6.			
7.			
8.			

C2 Making Promises ▶ Note 2

Read each situation. Write a promise for each one in your notebook. Use the first-person subject pronoun *I*.

1. Holly came home very late. Her father is worried. What does she say?

I won't be late again.

2. Rob's apartment is a mess. His roommate is angry. What does Rob say?

3. Ana borrowed her friend's white dress. She spilled black coffee on it. What does Ana say to her friend?

4. Carl fell asleep in a meeting. His boss is very angry. What does Carl say to his boss?

5. Keiko washed the dishes. She is very tired. What does her husband say?

6. Rosa was driving over the speed limit. A policeman stopped her. What does Rosa say?

A. Read the statements about life in the twenty-first century. Then make predictions about life in the next century. Write them in your notebook.

Robots will do the housework.

TWENTY-FIRST CENTURY	
1.	Women do most of the housework.
2.	Children go to school five days a week.
3.	Most people work from nine to five.
4.	Computers are very expensive.
5.	People travel by car.
6.	Cars use gas.
7.	Dogs are popular pets.
8.	People watch TV for relaxation.

B. Work with a partner. Compare your predictions. Do you agree?

C4 **Expressing Quick Decisions** ▶ Note 3

Work with a partner. Make a decision using *will* in each situation.

1. **Waiter:** I'm sorry. We don't have strawberry ice cream, only chocolate or vanilla.

   A: I'll have vanilla.
   B: I'll have chocolate.

2. **Ticket agent:** The 9:20 train is full. Tickets for the 9:50 and the 10:20 trains are available.

3. **Sales clerk:** That sweater comes in brown, blue, or red.

4. **Registrar:** There are two sections of History 101. Section A meets on Monday, and Section B meets on Wednesday.

5. **Hotel clerk:** The room on the fifth floor has a view of the mountains, and the room on the sixth floor has a view of the ocean.

6. **Receptionist:** The doctor is in tomorrow and on Thursday.

D Combining Form, Meaning, and Use

D1 Thinking About Meaning and Use

Complete each conversation. Then discuss your answers in small groups.

1. **A:** I'll write to you every day.

   B: _____
   - **a.** Do you promise?
   - **b.** Did you?
   - **c.** You're writing.

2. **A:** Don't worry. You'll pass the test.

   B: _____
   - **a.** It's a test.
   - **b.** I hope so.
   - **c.** Are you?

3. **A:** Do you need any help?

   B: _____
   - **a.** We'll be fine.
   - **b.** We didn't.
   - **c.** I am.

4. **A:** Do you want the blue one or the red one?

   B: _____
   - **a.** I took the blue one.
   - **b.** I take the blue one.
   - **c.** I'll take the blue one.

5. **A:** _____

   B: It'll be dry by tonight.
   - **a.** Do you paint well?
   - **b.** When will the paint be dry?
   - **c.** Do you have paint?

6. **A:** The chocolate cake looks delicious. Do you want some?

   B: _____
   - **a.** I'll have a small piece.
   - **b.** Yes, you do.
   - **c.** It's a chocolate cake.

D2 Editing

Some of these sentences have errors. Find the errors and correct them.

1. She will works late tonight.
2. Larry will be here tomorrow.
3. I'll to wait for you right here.
4. We willn't be home tonight.
5. Dinner will be ready at 6:00.
6. Who will goes to the library with her?
7. Will he at work next week?
8. They won't come not.

▶ Beyond the Classroom

Searching for Authentic Examples

Look for ads in English-language magazines and newspapers, or on the Internet.
Find two promises and two predictions with *will*. Write them in your notebook
and share them with your class.

Speaking

Imagine that you are running for president of your class or university. Write at
least six promises about what you will do as president. Then put your promises in
a speech. Your speech will have three parts.

1. Introduce yourself.

2. List your promises.
   - What will you do as president?
   - Why will you do these things?

3. Ask people to vote for you.
   - How will things be better for them?

*My name is Juan Montoya. I'm running for class president. As a president, I will
be a strong leader. . . .*

Modals

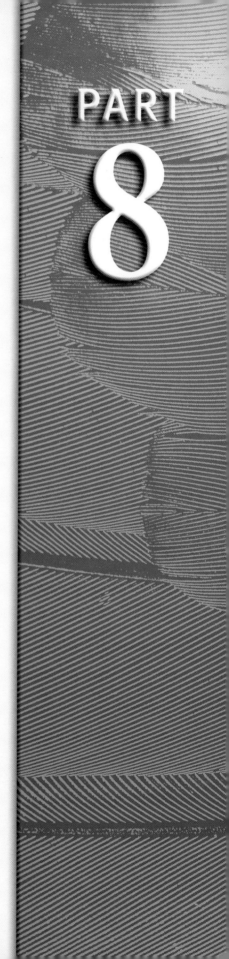

May and *Might* for Present and Future Possibility

Optimist or Pessimist?

Discuss these questions.

Do you usually believe good things will happen in the future? Why or why not?
Do you ever worry about the future? Why or why not?

A2 Read

Read and complete this quiz from a psychology magazine. What kind of person are you?

Optimist **or** Pessimist?

Is the glass half empty or half full? If you are an optimist, you probably think the glass is half full. If you are a pessimist, you probably think the glass is half empty. Are you an optimist or a pessimist? Take this quiz and find out.

5 **Read each pair of sentences. Choose the sentence that sounds more like you.**

1
  a. "I'm really excited about the party. We <u>may meet</u> some interesting people."
  b. "I don't want to go to the party. People might not talk to me."

2
  a. "That class is difficult, but it's interesting. You might enjoy it."
  b. "Don't take that class. It's difficult, and you might not pass."

10 **3**
  a. "Open the envelope. It <u>may be</u> good news."
  b. "Oh no! A letter. Don't open it. It <u>might be</u> a bill."

4
  a. "Explain the problem to your parents. They <u>may understand</u>."
  b. "Don't tell your parents. They may not listen."

5
  a. "I'm not really qualified, but I'm going to apply anyway. I <u>might be</u> lucky."
15 **b.** "I'm not going to apply for that job. I'll never get it."

How many *a*'s did you choose? How many *b*'s?

If you chose more *a*'s than *b*'s, you are an optimist. You always take chances because you believe that the
20 future will be OK.

If you chose more *b*'s than *a*'s, you are a pessimist. You worry that bad things might happen. You ignore opportunities, and you don't like to
25 take risks.

---

optimist: a person who believes good things are going to happen

pessimist: a person who believes bad things are going to happen

qualified: having the skills or knowledge that you need in order to do something

risks: possibilities that bad things might happen

A3   After You Read

Read the questions. Check (✓) the correct column.

	WHICH PERSON PROBABLY...	OPTIMIST	PESSIMIST
1.	worries a lot?		✓
2.	thinks things will go wrong?		
3.	takes more risks?		
4.	is afraid about the future?		
5.	sees opportunities in life?		
6.	smiles more?		

B *May* and *Might*

Examining Form

Look back at the quiz on pages 294–295 and complete the tasks below. Then discuss your answers and read the Form charts to check them.

1. Look at the underlined examples of *may* + verb and *might* + verb. Circle the subjects. Do *may* and *might* have different forms with different subjects? What form of the verb follows *may* and *might*?

2. Find one negative form with *may* and one with *might*. How do we form the negative of *may* and *might*?

Affirmative Statements			
SUBJECT	*MAY/MIGHT*	BASE FORM OF VERB	
I			
You			
He She It	may might	finish	today.
We			
You			
They			

Negative Statements				
SUBJECT	*MAY/MIGHT*	*NOT*	BASE FORM OF VERB	
I				
You				
He She It	may might	not	finish	today.
We				
You				
They				

- *May* and *might* are modal verbs. Modal verbs are auxiliary verbs. We use modals to add meaning to a main verb.
- Like all modals, *may* and *might* come before the base form of the verb. They also have the same form with all subjects.
- *May* and *might* often have the same meaning. We use both for present and future possibility.
- Do not use contractions with *may* or *might*.
  - *We mayn't go. (INCORRECT)

Yes/No Questions

WILL	SUBJECT		BASE FORM OF VERB
Will	you		**call**?

BE	SUBJECT	GOING TO	BASE FORM OF VERB
Are	they	**going to**	**call**?

Short Answers

SUBJECT	MAY/MIGHT		SUBJECT	MAY/MIGHT	NOT
I	**may. might.**		I	**may might**	**not.**

SUBJECT	MAY/MIGHT		SUBJECT	MAY/MIGHT	NOT
They	**may. might.**		They	**may might**	**not.**

Information Questions

WH- WORD (SUBJECT)	MIGHT	BASE FORM OF VERB
What	**might**	happen
Who	**might**	come?

Answers

He **might** not graduate.

Lynn's aunt.

- We do not usually use *may* or *might* in *Yes/No* questions about the future. We use *will* or *be going to* instead.
- We usually use *might* in information questions with *wh-* word subjects.

B1 Listening for Form

Listen to the conversation. Does the speaker use *may, might,* or no modal? Check (✓) the correct column.

	MAY	MIGHT	NO MODAL
1.		✓	
2.			
3.			
4.			
5.			
6.			
7.			
8.			

B2 Forming Affirmative and Negative Statements

Form affirmative and negative statements with *may* or *might*. Use the words and phrases. Punctuate your sentences correctly.

1. give/may/the teacher/us/next week/an exam

   The teacher may give us an exam next week.

2. to Taiwan/go/we/may/next month

   _____

3. in a meeting/be/might/Claudia

   _____

4. not/he/might/the job/take

   _____

5. the governor/win/not/may/the election

   _____

6. not/they/might/any/money/have

   _____

B3 Asking and Answering Questions

Work with a partner. Take turns asking and answering the questions. Use short answers with *may (not)* or *might (not).*

1. Is it going to rain tonight?

   It might.

2. Are you going to watch a movie tonight?

3. Will we have homework this week?

4. Are you going to eat at a restaurant tonight?

5. Are you going to relax this weekend?

6. Is your best friend going to call you tonight?

7. Who might visit you this year?

8. What might happen after class?

Present and Future Possibility

Examining Meaning and Use

Read the sentences and answer the questions below. Then discuss your answers
and read the Meaning and Use Notes to check them.

1a. He might fail the test tomorrow.   **2a.** The lights are on. They might be at home.
1b. He will fail the test.   **2b.** They're at home.

1. Which sentence refers to a possibility in the future? Which sentence refers to a possibility
at the present time?

2. Which sentences show that the speaker is certain?

Meaning and Use Notes

Present and Future Possibility

1A Use *may* and *might* to talk about present or future possibility.

Present Possibility

A: Where's Greg?

B: I don't know. He **may be** in the library.

A: Who's that man?

B: He **might be** Dana's father.

Future Possibility

It feels cold. It **may snow** tonight.

Tom didn't arrive on the ten o'clock bus.
  He **may come** on the next one.

1B Use *may* or *might* when something is possible but not certain. If you are certain
about the present, use the simple present or the present continuous. If you are
certain about the future, use *will* or *be going to.*

Possible but Not Certain

A: Where's Emily?

B: I don't know. She **might be** upstairs.

A: We need to be in class by 9:00.

B: The bus **might not be** on time.
  It's often late.

Certain

A: Where's Robin?

B: She's in the kitchen. I just saw her.

A: We need to be in the city by 8:00.

B: The train **will be** on time.
  It's never late.

🎧 Listen to the conversation. Is the speaker expressing possibility or certainty? Check (✓) the correct column.

	POSSIBILITY	CERTAINTY
1.		✓
2.		
3.		
4.		
5.		
6.		
7.		
8.		

Complete the telephone conversation. Use *might* or *will*.

Juan: What are your plans for the summer?

Paul: We don't know yet. We _____ *might* _____ visit Celia's parents in Brazil,
   1

or we _____ go to Europe. Our son Ben is in Madrid for a year,
   2

so we _____ visit him before he comes home. How about you?
   3

Juan: Well, one thing is certain. We _____ not take an expensive
   4

vacation this year! Our daughter Lisa _____ be a senior next
   5

year, so we're saving money for college.

Paul: Oh, I understand! But aren't you going to go anywhere?

Juan: Well, we _____ visit my wife's sister in Georgia for a week,
   6

or we _____ go on a camping trip to California.
   7

Paul: That's great! Do you plan to go to Yosemite again?

Juan: We don't know yet. We _____ try somewhere new.
   8

Write at least two statements about each situation. Use *may, might,* or *will* to make statements that express possibility or certainty.

1. Your sister is planning an outdoor wedding in March.

    It might not be a good idea. It will still be cold. She may be sorry.

2. Your nephew is skateboarding. He's not wearing a helmet.

    _____

3. Your roommate has an exam at 10:00. It's 9:30. He's still in bed.

    _____

4. Your friend drives too fast. You're worried about him.

    _____

5. Your brother bought a lottery ticket. You want to wish him good luck.

    _____

C4 **Talking About Possibility and Certainty**   ▶ Notes 1A, 1B

Work with a partner. Read each situation, then have a conversation. Student A is a pessimist and Student B is an optimist. Use *may, might,* or *will.* Change roles after each conversation.

1. **A:** A co-worker invited you to a party. You are new at your job and don't know anyone very well. Explain why you don't want to go.
    B: Give your partner three reasons for going to the party.

    A: I don't want to go. People might not speak to me.
    They might not like me.
    B: Of course they'll like you. You'll have a good time.
    You might make new friends.

2. **A:** You received flying lessons as a birthday present. Explain why you don't want to take the lessons.
    B: Give your partner three reasons for taking the flying lessons.

3. **A:** You want to ask your boss for a promotion. Explain why you feel nervous.
    B: Give your partner three reasons for asking for a promotion.

Look at the pictures. What is going to happen in each situation? Write at least one possibility and one certainty for each picture.

1. <u>He's going to fail the class.</u>

   <u>He might not tell his parents.</u>

   <u>He may take the class again.</u>

3. _____

   _____

   _____

2. _____

   _____

   _____

4. _____

   _____

   _____

D Combining Form, Meaning, and Use

D1 Thinking About Meaning and Use

Complete each conversation. Then discuss your answers in small groups.

1. **A:** I might go to the party.

   B: _____
      a. Where are you going?
      b. Why won't you go?
      (c.) I may go too.

2. **A:** Where is she going to stay?

   B: She's not sure. _____
      a. She'll stay with me.
      b. She might stay in a hotel.
      c. She may come.

3. **A:** _____

   B: Yes, it is. It may snow.
      a. It's really cold outside tonight.
      b. It's very warm today.
      c. What's the weather like?

4. **A:** I may not have time to go to the store.

   B: _____
      a. That's OK. I'll go.
      b. Please buy some milk at the store.
      c. Did you stop at the store?

5. **A:** _____

   B: I might go to the park on Saturday.
      a. What did you do last weekend?
      b. When will you go home?
      c. What are you going to do this weekend?

6. **A:** The car won't start.

   B: _____
      a. It might be out of gas.
      b. The window might be broken.
      c. Will it start?

D2 Editing

Some of these sentences have errors. Find the errors and correct them.

1. She ~~mayn't~~ *may not* arrive on time.

2. We might to leave at noon.

3. Dan may sees her today.

4. I may visit them in June.

5. She might not be here right now.

6. What might happens tomorrow?

7. They might probably take the train tomorrow.

8. There is someone at the door. It may Jenna.

▶ Beyond the Classroom

Searching for Authentic Examples

Look in the current events section of an English-language newspaper or on the Internet for two statements about the future and two statements about the present with *may* or *might*. Write them in your notebook and share them with your class.

Writing

Imagine you are moving to a new city. Follow the steps below to write a paragraph about what might or might not happen.

1. Use these questions to make notes.
   - What do you think will happen?
   - Will you be happy or sad?
   - Will you try to make new friends?
   - Will you stay at home?
   - Will you keep in touch with your old friends and co-workers?

2. Write a first draft. Write affirmative and negative statements with *may, might,* and *will.*

3. Read your work carefully and circle grammar, spelling, and punctuation errors. Work with a partner to decide how to fix the errors and improve the content.

4. Rewrite your draft.

   At first I'll probably be sad about moving because I'll miss my old friends. However, I won't stay home alone. I might join a sports club. . . .

Can and *Could* for Present and Past Ability

A The Youngest in His Class

A1 Before You Read

Discuss these questions.

Do you know any very smart children? What are they good at? Do they have any problems?

A2 Read

 Read the magazine article about Jacob, a child prodigy, on the following page. What problems did he have as a young child? What problems does he have now?

A3 After You Read

Write *T* for true or *F* for false for each statement.

__T__ **1.** Jacob goes to class with older students.

_____ **2.** Jacob was reading at six months old.

_____ **3.** Jacob tied his shoes at age two.

_____ **4.** Jacob made friends easily.

_____ **5.** Jacob plays on the college soccer team.

_____ **6.** Jacob has a lot of friends in college.

An unusual college student

The Youngest in His CLASS

Life Is Not Always Easy for a Child Prodigy

Jacob is an unusual college student. Why? Because he is only ten years old. Why is a young boy like Jacob in college? The answer is that Jacob is a child prodigy,
5 a young genius. At the age of ten, Jacob can take undergraduate courses at the local university.

Even as a baby, Jacob was remarkable. He could speak at ten months. He could
10 read soon after his first birthday, and he could do math problems at the age of fourteen months. "The differences with other children in his kindergarten class were enormous," explains Holly Franklin,
15 Jacob's mother. "For example, the other children could draw simple pictures, but they couldn't read or write. However, Jacob was already drawing molecules and reading adult literature."

20 Not surprisingly, Jacob didn't make friends with other children easily. Life can be difficult for child prodigies. Parents of other children are often jealous. And the older students in the school can be
25 unfriendly or even hostile.

Child prodigies can do amazing things, but physically and emotionally they are still children. For example, at age two, Jacob could talk intelligently about
30 dinosaurs, but he couldn't tie his shoes. When he was six, he could discuss philosophy but easily cried when he was upset.

So how does Jacob like life as a college
35 student? "Sometimes, it's lonely," he says. "I can't really be friends with my classmates. They're too old. And I like soccer, but I can't play on the team because I'm too small. However, I can't be in a
40 regular school because I'm too smart."

What are Jacob's plans for the future? He is going to be a doctor. "In the future, I hope I can find a cure for cancer," he says. "And I hope I can have a normal life with
45 friends and a family when people my own age grow up."

---

child prodigy: an extremely smart or talented child
enormous: very great or large
hostile: very unfriendly

jealous: upset because you want something that someone else has
kindergarten class: a class for five-year-old children

B *Can* and *Could*

Examining Form

Look back at the article on page 307 and complete the tasks below. Then discuss your answers and read the Form charts to check them.

1. Look at the underlined examples of *can* + verb and *could* + verb. Circle the subjects. Do *can* and *could* have different forms with different subjects? What form of the verb follows *can* and *could*?

2. Find one negative verb form with *can* and one with *could*. How do we form the negative of *can* and *could*?

CAN FOR PRESENT ABILITY

Affirmative Statements			
SUBJECT	CAN	BASE FORM OF VERB	
I			
You			
He She It	can	drive	a car.
We			
You			
They			

Negative Statements			
SUBJECT	CAN + NOT	BASE FORM OF VERB	
I			
You			
He She It	cannot can't	drive	a car.
We			
You			
They			

Yes/No Questions			
CAN	SUBJECT	BASE FORM OF VERB	
Can	you she they	dance?	

Short Answers					
YES	SUBJECT	CAN	NO	SUBJECT	CAN'T
Yes,	I she they	can.	No,	I she they	can't.

Information Questions					Answers
WH- WORD	*CAN*	SUBJECT	BASE FORM OF VERB		
Who	can	you	**trust?**		I **can** only trust Paulo.
What			**play?**		The piano and the violin.

COULD FOR PAST ABILITY

Affirmative Statements		
SUBJECT	*COULD*	BASE FORM OF VERB
I		
You		
He She It	**could**	**swim.**
We		
You		
They		

Negative Statements		
SUBJECT	*COULD + NOT*	BASE FORM OF VERB
I		
You		
He She It	**could not couldn't**	**swim.**
We		
You		
They		

Yes/No Questions		
COULD	SUBJECT	BASE FORM OF VERB
Could	you she they	**swim?**

Short Answers					
YES	SUBJECT	*COULD*	NO	SUBJECT	*COULDN'T*
Yes,	I she they	**could.**	No,	I she they	**couldn't.**

Information Questions					Answers
WH- WORD	*COULD*	SUBJECT	BASE FORM OF VERB		
When	could	he	**walk?**		At 11 months.
What			**do?**		He **could** read and write.

> ### *Can* and *Could*
> - *Can* and *could* are modal verbs.
> - Like all modals, *can* and *could* come before the base form of the verb. They also have the same form with all subjects.

(Continued on page 310)

- *Cannot* is the negative form of *can*. *Can't* is the contraction.
- *Could not* is the negative of *could*. *Couldn't* is the contraction.
- In affirmative sentences with *can* and *could*, we stress the main verb. We do not stress *can* or *could*. The vowel sound in both words is very short.

    I can go. — I /kən/ go.   I could go. — I /kəd/ go.

- In negative sentences with *can* and *could*, we stress *can't* and *couldn't*. We pronounce the *a* in *can't* like the *a* in *ant*. We pronounce the *ou* in *couldn't* like the *oo* in *good*.

    I can't go. — I /kænt/ go.   I couldn't go. — I /ˈkʊdnt/ go.

B1) Listening for Form

Listen to the conversation. Write the form of *can* or *could* you hear.

Dan: My brother is really smart. He's only six and he ____can____ read the newspaper.
1

Amy: Well, my cousin Sara is smart, too. She's sixteen years old, and she just graduated

from college. She _____ speak five languages. She _____ read at the
2   3

age of three, and she _____ do high school math in elementary school.
4

Dan: Wow! Some people _____ do elementary school math in high school!
5

Amy: Life isn't always easy for Sara. She _____ talk to professors, but she
6

_____ talk to other teenagers. She doesn't know what to say to them. She
7

_____ be in class with kids her own age, so she never had many friends.
8

Dan: Was she lonely?

Amy: Yes. She _____ read and talk to adults, but she _____ be just a kid.
9   10

B2) Forming Sentences with *Can* and *Can't*

Form sentences with *can* and *can't*, and write them in your notebook. Use the words and phrases. Punctuate your sentences correctly.

1. David/drive/can/his father's/car
David can drive his father's car.

2. can't/Teresa/speak/Spanish

3. cannot/swim/Irina/very well

4. Julie/the piano/play/and/the guitar/can

5. eat/can't/solid food/the baby

6. Tomek/fast/run/can't/very

Forming Questions with *Can*

Form *Yes/No* questions and information questions with *can*, and write them in your notebook. Use the words and phrases. Punctuate your sentences correctly.

1. you/swim/can

   Can you swim?

2. languages/you/speak/can/many

3. play/any instruments/can/Hanna

4. ride/a bicycle/can/you

5. what/cook/can/Alex

6. who/me/can/beat/at tennis

B4 **Working on *Could* and *Couldn't***

A. Eva was a child prodigy. Look at the information in the chart. Write sentences in your notebook about what Eva could and could not do as a four-year-old child. Punctuate your sentences correctly.

   Eva could speak Mandarin.

		YES	NO
1.	speak Mandarin	✓	
2.	roller-skate		✓
3.	tie her shoes		✓
4.	draw beautiful pictures	✓	
5.	ride a bicycle		✓
6.	play the piano	✓	
7.	play tennis		✓
8.	write simple poetry	✓	

B. With a partner look back at the information in the chart in part A. Take turns asking and answering *Yes/No* questions with *could*. Respond with short answers.

   A: Could Eva speak Mandarin?
   B: Yes, she could.

Present and Past Ability

Examining Meaning and Use

Read the sentences and answer the questions below. Then discuss your answers and read the Meaning and Use Notes to check them.

    a. I can't remember her address.
    b. Hiro could speak Japanese and Korean at the age of eight.
    c. Can you name five twentieth-century American writers?
    d. Could you write your name at the age of four?

1. Which sentences refer to present ability?

2. Which sentences refer to past ability?

Meaning and Use Notes

Present Ability with *Can*

1   Use *can* and *can't* to talk about ability in the present. An ability is something you know how to do.

    I **can run** 4 miles in an hour.   She **can do** math problems in her head.

    She **can't climb** trees! She's 85!   We **can't speak** French very well.

Past Ability with *Could*

2   Use *could* and *couldn't* to talk about ability in the past.

    I **could ride** a bike at age 5.   My uncle **could** still **roller-skate** at 75!

    They **couldn't read** in kindergarten.   He got lost because he **couldn't speak** French.

C1 Listening for Meaning and Use

► Notes 1, 2

🎧 Listen to each situation. Choose the statement that is true.

1. **a.** John can ski well.
   b. John can't ski.

2. **a.** He can't hear the teacher.
   b. He can hear the teacher.

3. **a.** John Wayne can act well.
   b. John Wayne could act well.

4. **a.** They can't read Japanese.
   b. They couldn't read Japanese.

5. **a.** She can't make a cake.
   b. She couldn't make a cake.

6. **a.** He couldn't wake up on time.
   b. He can't wake up on time.

7. **a.** They can both play instruments.
   b. They could both play instruments.

8. **a.** He can't see the board.
   b. He couldn't see the board.

C2 Talking About Present Abilities

► Note 1

A. Work in groups of four. Write the names of your three partners at the top of the chart. Then take turns asking and answering questions about the activities in the chart. Check (✓) the things you and your classmates can do. Record the results in the Totals column.

A: Can you ride a bike?
B: Yes, I can.

		ME	_____	_____	_____	TOTALS
1.	ride a bike	✓				
2.	drive a car					
3.	dance the tango					
4.	play the piano					
5.	speak three languages					
6.	do 100 sit-ups					
7.	bake cookies					
8.	type 50 words a minute					
9.	ski					
10.	fly an airplane					

B. Compare your totals with the other groups. What can a lot of people do? What can only a few people do?

Meaning and Use • *Can* and *Could* for Present and Past Ability   313

C3 Talking About Past Ability

► Note 2

A. Complete the sentences. Use *could* or *couldn't* to make true statements.

1. At five years old I _I couldn't swim_____ .

2. At the age of ten _____ .

3. Ten years ago _____ .

4. In my first English class _____ .

5. On my first day at school _____ .

6. At the end of first grade _____ .

B. Discuss your answers with a partner.

A: At five years old I couldn't swim.
B: I could!

C4 Contrasting Past and Present Ability

► Notes 1, 2

Complete the paragraph. Use *can, can't, could,* or *couldn't*.

Five years ago some of my friends ___could___ drive, but I
1
_____. This was a problem
2
because I lived on a farm in those
days, and I _____ go many
3
places on my own. Last year I got
my driver's license. Today I

_____ drive, but I still _____ go places by car because I don't own
4   5
one. I'm not complaining, though. I live in a big city now, and I _____ go
6
everywhere by bus or subway. Back on the farm, I _____ take buses or
7
trains because there was no public transportation in my area. I visited a few
neighbors on my bike, but I _____ cycle to town. It was just too far away.
8

D Combining Form, Meaning, and Use

D1 Thinking About Meaning and Use

Complete each conversation. Then discuss your answers in small groups.

1. **A:** Could you swim at the ago of six?

   B: _____
   - **a.** No, I couldn't.
   - **b.** No, I can't.
   - **c.** Yes, I can.

2. **A:** Are you going to go to the party?

   B: No. _____
   - **a.** I don't have any homework.
   - **b.** I went to bed early.
   - **c.** I didn't get an invitation.

3. **A:** _____

   B: No, not anymore.
   - **a.** When can you play the piano?
   - **b.** Can you play the piano?
   - **c.** Who can play for us?

4. **A:** Can you speak Russian?

   B: _____
   - **a.** No, I studied German.
   - **b.** No, I'm not.
   - **c.** Yes, I am.

5. **A:** Why were you afraid of the water?

   B: _____
   - **a.** I can swim.
   - **b.** I couldn't swim.
   - **c.** I am swimming.

6. **A:** Who can dance well?

   B: _____
   - **a.** Celia. She was a great dancer.
   - **b.** Victor doesn't sing well.
   - **c.** I can.

D2 Editing

Some of these sentences have errors. Find the errors and correct them.

1. We cann't leave right now.

2. They can to see in the dark.

3. She can runs very quickly.

4. She was very fit. She could do 100 sit-ups.

5. Could he spoke German?

6. What you can cook?

7. She cans sing and dance.

8. Greg is bilingual. He can't speak two languages.

▶ Beyond the Classroom

Searching for Authentic Examples

Choose a kind of animal, for example, a cheetah, turtle, bee, or dolphin. Look for information about your animal in an English-language book or on the Internet. Find four sentences that talk about your animal's abilities with *can* or *can't*. Write the sentences in your notebook and share them with your class.

Writing

Follow these steps to write two paragraphs about your abilities in the past and your abilities today.

1. Use these questions to make notes.
   - What things could you do as a five-year-old child? Did you have any special athletic or academic abilities? What things couldn't you do?
   - What things can you do now? What things can't you do? Do you have any special athletic or academic abilities? Do you have any job-related abilities?

2. Write a first draft. Use *can* and *could* in some of your sentences.

3. Read your work carefully and circle grammar, spelling, and punctuation errors. Work with a partner to decide how to fix the errors and improve the content.

4. Rewrite your draft.

   As a five-year-old child, I didn't have many special abilities. I could say the alphabet and I could write my name, but I couldn't really read or write. I was an athletic child. I could run fast and I could catch, but I couldn't hit a baseball or throw a ball very far.

   Now . . .

Modals of Request and Permission

A Standing Up for Yourself

A1 Before You Read

Discuss these questions.

Do you always express your true feelings, or do you hide your feelings?

A2 Read

Read this newspaper interview. Dr. Grey talks about three types of people. What are they? Which type of person are you?

Books

Standing Up for Yourself

Our reviewer, Paul Harris, spoke with Dr. Stanley Grey, the author of *Standing Up for Yourself*. Here is part of the conversation.

5 **HARRIS:** Dr. Grey, your new book is about assertiveness. <u>Can you explain the term?</u>

GREY: Of course. Assertiveness means expressing your feelings and needs
10 honestly. Americans generally value assertiveness. However, sometimes people confuse assertiveness with aggression.

HARRIS: <u>Could you tell us the difference between aggressive and assertive people?</u>

15 **GREY:** Sure. Aggressive people are often rude. They think about their own needs, and they don't care about the needs of others. This makes others feel hurt or
20 angry. Assertive people respect the needs of other people, but they also express their
25 own needs so others can respect them in return.

Dr. Stanley Grey

HARRIS: <u>Would you give us an example?</u>

30 **GREY:** Of course. Say it's your birthday and your family is having a special dinner for you at 6:00. At 4:30 your boss says: "I need your help. <u>Will you work until 8:00?</u>" An unassertive person will call home and
35 apologize, then stay and do the work. An aggressive person might say, "No, I won't. My hours are 9:00 to 5:00. I have plans after work." This is rude and will also make the boss angry. An assertive person
40 might say, "Could I come in early tomorrow and do the work then?"

HARRIS: How can we become more assertive?

GREY: Well, you can start with these
45 three tips:

1. **Be open about your needs.** Suppose your term paper is due tomorrow and your computer doesn't work. Ask a friend for help. Say, "My paper is due
50 tomorrow and my computer is broken. Can I use yours?" Your friend may need the computer too. Ask another person if necessary.

2. **Be honest about your feelings.** Your
55 roommate loves jazz, but you don't.

Don't pretend you do. Say, "Can you use your earphones, please? I don't want to listen to jazz right now."

3. **Say no to unreasonable requests.**
60 Your best friend asks, "May I wear your new sweater tonight?" Don't say yes just to be
65 polite. Say, "I'm sorry, I want to wear it first. Do you want to borrow
70 another one?"

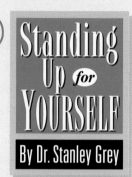

Standing Up **for** YOURSELF
By Dr. Stanley Grey

---

aggressive: ready to argue or fight or to use force

assertive: expressing your feelings and needs clearly and firmly

respect: to think highly of, care about

rude: not polite

standing up for yourself: protecting your feelings or needs

unassertive: not expressing your feelings and needs

value: to think something is good, to appreciate

A3 **After You Read**

Read each situation. Write *UN* for unassertive, *AG* for aggressive, or *AS* for assertive.

__UN__ **1.** John's roommate borrowed his new CD player and broke it. John is upset. He says, "Don't worry. I can buy another one."

_____ **2.** Jenny's friend wants to go to a horror movie. Jenny hates horror movies. She says, "Horror movies give me bad dreams. Can we see something else?"

_____ **3.** Tamika's brother wants her to help him with his homework. She says, "Do it yourself!"

_____ **4.** Jorge is very busy. His mother asks him to go to the store. He says, "I'd like to finish this first. Can I go later?"

_____ **5.** Fumiko's best friend asks to borrow some money. Fumiko is worried about money herself. She says, "Sure. No problem."

_____ **6.** A classmate asks to copy Rob's homework. Rob spent three hours doing it. He says, "I'm sorry, but I don't share my work."

B Modals of Request and Permission

Examining Form

Look back at the interview on pages 318–319 and complete the tasks below. Then discuss your answers and read the Form charts to check them.

1. Look at the underlined questions. Find the modal of request in each question. What subject do the questions have in common? Does the modal come before or after the subject?

2. Look at the circled questions. Find the modal of permission in each question. What subject do the questions have in common? Does the modal come before or after the subject?

MODALS OF REQUEST: *CAN, COULD, WILL, WOULD*

Yes/No Questions			
MODAL	**SUBJECT**	**BASE FORM OF VERB**	
Can			
Could	you	**explain**	that?
Will			
Would			

Short Answers					
YES	**SUBJECT**	*CAN/ WILL*	*NO*	**SUBJECT**	*CAN/WILL + NOT*
Yes,	I	can.	No,	I	can't.
		will.			won't.

- We generally use modals of request in questions with *you*.
- We usually use *can* and *will* in affirmative short answers. *Could* and *would* are less common.
- The short answer *I won't* can sound angry and impolite. Do not use it in polite answers.
- We often use *please* in *Yes/No* questions with modals of request. *Please* can come at the end of a sentence or after the subject. In written English, we use a comma before *please* if it comes at the end of a sentence.

  Could you explain that, **please**?   Would <u>you</u> **please** explain that?

Affirmative Statements

SUBJECT	CAN/ MAY	BASE FORM OF VERB	
You	can	sit	here.
	may		

Negative Statements

SUBJECT	CAN/MAY + NOT	BASE FORM OF VERB	
You	cannot can't	sit	here.
	may not		

Yes/No Questions

MODAL	SUBJECT	BASE FORM OF VERB	
Can			
Could	I we	borrow	your car?
May			

Short Answers

YES	SUBJECT	CAN/ MAY		NO	SUBJECT	CAN/MAY + NOT
Yes,	you	can.		No,	you	cannot. can't.
		may.				may not.

Wh- Questions

WH- WORD	MODAL	SUBJECT	BASE FORM OF VERB	
What	can		call	you?
Where	may	I we	park	the car?
When	could		visit	you?

Answers

You **can call** me Rob.
You **may park** in the driveway.
Next month.

- We generally use modals of permission in questions with *I* or *we*.
- Use *can* and *may* in statements. Do not use *could*.
- Use *can, could,* and *may* in *Yes/No* questions. Do not use *could* in short answers.
- There is no contracted form of *may not*.
- We often use *please* in *Yes/No* questions with modals of permission. *Please* can come at the end of a sentence or after the subject. In written English, we use a comma before *please* if it comes at the end of a sentence.

   Could I borrow your car, **please**?   May we **please** borrow your car?

Listen to each sentence. What modal do you hear? Check (✓) the correct column.

	CAN	COULD	MAY	WILL	WOULD
1.					✓
2.					
3.					
4.					
5.					
6.					
7.					
8.					

A. Form statements with modals of permission and write them in your notebook. Use the words. Punctuate your sentences correctly.

1. take/you/not/the/may/tomorrow/test

   You may not take the test tomorrow.

2. park/you/here/can't/car/your

3. early/you/leave/may/not

4. may/my/computer/borrow/they

5. can't/you/talk/him/to/now

B. Form questions with modals of request and permission and write them in your notebook. Use the words. Punctuate your sentences correctly.

1. you/me/could/please/help

   Could you help me, please? OR *Could you please help me?*

2. ride/us/can/give/a/you

3. close/the/you/would/please/door

4. have/could/time/I/more/please

5. can/when/call/I/him

Complete each conversation with a subject pronoun and *can, will,* or *can't.*

1. **A:** Can I take the test tomorrow?

   B: No, _____you can't_____. Today is the last day of the semester.

2. **A:** Will you teach me to play chess?

   B: Yes, _____. Where's the board?

3. **A:** Could you tell me the time?

   B: No, _____. I don't have my watch.

4. **A:** Can I borrow a pen?

   B: Yes, _____.

5. **A:** Can we play outside, Mom?

   B: Yes, _____, but don't cross the street.

6. **A:** Could I see the newspaper, please?

   B: Yes, _____.

7. **A:** Would you take care of my cat while I'm gone?

   B: Yes, _____. No problem.

8. **A:** Could you bring me a piece of apple pie, please?

   B: No, _____. There isn't any more. Could I get you
   something else instead?

   A: Yes, _____. Do you have any chocolate cake?

9. **A:** Professor Brown, could you please write a letter of recommendation for me?

   B: Yes, _____. It will be a pleasure.

10. **A:** Will you take out the trash?

    B: No, _____. I'm waiting for an important phone call.

Making Requests and Asking for Permission

Examining Meaning and Use

Read the sentences and answer the questions below. Then discuss your answers and read the Meaning and Use Notes to check them.

a. Can I borrow this book?

b. Would you carry these books for me?

c. May I use this glass?

d. Could I borrow your jacket tonight?

e. Will you tell the teacher I'm sick?

f. Could you lend me ten dollars?

1. Which sentences make a request for someone to do something?

2. Which sentences ask someone for permission?

Meaning and Use Notes

Making Requests

1 Use *can*, *could*, *will*, and *would* to ask someone to do something. We usually use *can* and *will* in less formal conversations, with friends and family. *Could* and *would* make a request sound more polite. We use them in more formal conversations, with strangers or people in authority.

Less Formal	*More Formal*
To a Friend: **Can** you hold this for me?	*To a Stranger:* **Could** you tell me the time?
To a Child: **Will** you clean your room?	*To Your Boss:* **Would** you sign this?

Agreeing to and Refusing Requests

2 We generally use *can* and *will* to agree to a request. *Could* and *would* are less common. We often use *can't* and *won't* to refuse a request. *Won't* is very strong and sounds impolite.

Agreeing to a Request	*Refusing a Request*
A: Could you take Amy to school?	A: Dan, **will** you answer the door?
B: Yes, I **can**.	B: Sorry, I **can't**. I'm on the phone. (polite)
A: Would you go to the post office?	A: Ava, will you answer the phone?
B: Yes, I **will**.	B: No, I **won't**! You answer it! (impolite)

3 Use *can, could,* and *may* to ask for permission. *Can* and *could* are less formal than *may. May* sounds more formal and polite. We often use *may* when we speak to strangers or people in authority.

Less Formal	*More Formal*
Son to Father: **Can/Could** I go out tonight?	*Stranger to Stranger:* **May** I sit here?

Giving and Refusing Permission

4 Use *can* or *may* to give permission. Do not use *could.* Use *may not, can't,* and *cannot* to refuse permission. *May* and *may not* are more formal.

Giving Permission	*Refusing Permission*
A: Can I use your computer?	A: Can I give you the report tomorrow?
B: Yes, you **can**. (less formal)	B: No, you **can't**. Sorry. (less formal)
A: May I take the test tomorrow?	A: May I borrow the car?
B: Yes, you **may**. (more formal)	B: No, you **may not**. I need it. (more formal)

Using *Please, Sorry,* and Other Expressions

5A Use *please* to make questions sound more polite.

Making a Request	*Asking for Permission*
Will you **please** open the door for me?	May I **please** have a glass of water?
Could you answer the phone, **please**?	Could I talk to you, **please**?

5B Use *I'm sorry* or *sorry* and an excuse to make refusals sound softer and more polite.

Refusing a Request	*Refusing Permission*
A: Could you drive me to the mall later?	A: Can I borrow your bike?
B: **Sorry**, I have a doctor's appointment.	B: I'm **sorry**, I lent it to Dan.

5C We often use expressions such as *sure, OK, certainly,* or *of course* to agree to requests and give permission.

Agreeing to a Request	*Giving Permission*
A: Would you take Amy to school?	A: Can I borrow your pen?
B: **Sure** I will.	B: **Certainly**.
A: Could you go to the store for me?	A: May I sit here?
B: **OK**.	B: **Of course**. Go right ahead.

C1 Listening for Meaning and Use

🎧 Listen to each question. Is the speaker making a request or asking for permission? Check the correct column.

	PERMISSION	REQUEST
1.	✓	
2.		
3.		
4.		
5.		
6.		

C2 Making and Responding to Requests

Complete the conversations. Use appropriate modals and appropriate responses. Make at least two refusals.

Conversation 1: Paulo is in a clothing store.

Paulo: _Could_ you help me, please?

Clerk: _Of course I can. What size do you wear?_

Conversation 2: Josh and his friends are in a restaurant.

Josh: _____ you give us a table near the window?

Waiter: _____

Conversation 3: Sally and Ruth are taking a test.

Ruth: Sally, _____ you tell me the answer to number 2?

Sally: _____

Conversation 4: Irina is on a public bus.

Irina: Driver, _____ you stop at the next corner, please?

Driver: _____

Conversation 5: Corey is at home.

Corey: Mom, _____ you make lasagna for dinner tonight?

Mom: _____

A. Write a question with *can, could,* or *may* to ask permission in each situation. Use explanations and polite expressions when appropriate. Use each modal at least once. Punctuate your sentences correctly.

1. You are at work. You have a doctor's appointment. Ask your boss for permission to take a long lunch break.

   I have a doctor's appointment. Could I take a long lunch

   break today?

2. You are in line at the bank. You don't have a pen. The man in front of you is writing a check. Ask to borrow his pen.

3. You are in a restaurant. You need another chair at your table. Ask the person at the next table for permission to take an empty chair.

4. You are at home. You have an important message for your friend Rosa Gomez. You call her home and her father answers. Ask to talk to Rosa.

5. Your computer isn't working. You have to write a paper. Ask to use your roommate's computer.

6. You have a date. Ask your friend Marcus for permission to use his car.

B. Work with a partner. Take turns asking and answering your questions in part A.

   A: Could I have a long lunch break today? I have a doctor's appointment.
   B: Certainly, go right ahead. OR *I'm sorry, you can't. Did you forget about the big meeting?*

Write a short dialogue for each situation. For A, make a request or ask for permission. For B, write a response. More than one answer is possible.

1. **A:** _Can I borrow the car?_

   B: _No, you can't._

4. **A:** _____

   B: _____

2. **A:** _____

   B: _____

5. **A:** _____

   B: _____

3. **A:** _____

   B: _____

6. **A:** _____

   B: _____

D Combining Form, Meaning, and Use

D1 Thinking About Meaning and Use

Complete each conversation. Then discuss your answers in small groups.

1. **A:** _____

   B: Sorry, I can't. This is my only one.
   - a. Can you lend me a pen, please?
   - b. Can you get a pen?
   - c. Will you buy a pen?

2. **A:** How can I help you?

   B: _____
   - a. Yes, you can.
   - b. I'm looking for a white blouse.
   - c. I'm a customer.

3. **A:** _____

   B: Certainly, sir. What size do you wear?
   - a. When can you help me?
   - b. May I help you?
   - c. Could you help me, please?

4. **A:** Would you tell me the time, please?

   B: _____
   - a. Maybe later.
   - b. Sorry, I'm not wearing a watch.
   - c. Yes, I could.

5. **A:** May I please use the phone?

   B: _____
   - a. Of course you may.
   - b. Sorry, you won't.
   - c. Sure you will.

6. **A:** _____

   B: No, you had pizza last night.
   - a. Could you have pizza for dinner?
   - b. Can we have pizza for dinner?
   - c. When may we have pizza?

7. **A:** May I sit here?

   B: _____
   - a. You certainly will.
   - b. You could.
   - c. Yes, you can.

8. **A:** Could you open the window for me?

   B: _____
   - a. Yes, you may.
   - b. Yes, I will.
   - c. No, I can.

Some of these sentences have errors. Find the errors and correct them.

Could

1. ~~Will~~ I borrow your car?

2. No, you mayn't smoke here.

3. Where can we sit?

4. Would I leave now, please?

5. May you help me?

6. Would please you help me?

7. Will you open the door, please?

8. Sure, I can't help you now. I'm busy.

▶ Beyond the Classroom

Searching for Authentic Examples

Watch an English-language TV program or movie. Listen for examples of people making requests and asking for permission. Write three examples of each in your notebook. Share them with your class.

Speaking

Before you come to class, choose one of the situations below. Think of different ways the conversations might develop. What reasons might each person give?

1. A 13-year-old wants to go to a rock concert. He asks one of his parents for permission. The parent is not happy about the idea, but is open-minded. They discuss the situation. Then the parent decides.

2. An employee wants to go to night school. He will need to adjust his work schedule to take the necessary courses. He asks his boss for permission. The boss doesn't like the idea, but she is an open-minded person. They discuss the situation. Then the boss decides.

In class, work with a partner. Discuss your ideas. Then act out two dialogues: one where the parent or boss gives permission and the other where the parent or boss refuses permission. Use modals of request and permission.

A: Dad, can I go to the Red Spider concert?
B: I'm not sure. Is it on a week night?

Modals of Advice, Necessity, and Prohibition

A | Rule Followers and Rule Breakers

A1 Before You Read

Discuss these questions.

What do you think about rules? Are they necessary? Do you usually follow rules? Why or why not?

A2 Read

Read and complete this quiz from a magazine. Are you a rule follower or a rule breaker?

Rule Followers and Rule Breakers

There are two kinds of people in the world: people who follow rules and people who break them. Rule followers think that every rule exists for a good reason, even if they

5 don't know what it is. They think that people <u>should</u> always <u>follow</u> the rules. One of my friends is a rule follower. He says, "Rules are important. We have to follow them. Rules make life orderly." Another friend of mine

10 hates rules. His philosophy? He thinks that he doesn't have to follow rules that are unreasonable. He says, "A person <u>should</u> only <u>obey</u> rules that make sense."

What do you think? Are you a rule follower, a rule breaker, or somewhere in
15 **between? Take the following quiz and find out.**

1

You're standing at a corner and waiting to cross the street. There aren't any cars on the road, but the sign says, "Don't Walk." What should 20 you do?

a. You should wait.
b. You should cross the street.
c. You should look both ways, then cross the street.

2

25 What does a stop sign mean to you?

a. Every car must stop.
b. The car behind your car has to stop.
c. You have to slow down and be careful.

3

You're at a swimming pool and you 30 see a sign that says, "No Running." What does this mean to you?

a. You must not run.
b. Other people shouldn't run.
c. You have to run carefully.

4

35 On the first day of class your teacher says, "Students must spend at least an hour a week in the language lab." You . . .

a. sign up for an hour of lab time each week.
40 **b.** don't think you need an hour, so you sign up for half an hour.
c. check the lab schedule and decide to go when you have time.

5

You take your dog for a walk in the park.
45 He hates leashes, but a sign in the park says, "Dogs Must Not Run Free." What should you do?

a. Keep him on a leash.
b. Let him walk near you without the leash.
50 **c.** Let him run free. He won't cause you any trouble.

KEY
Mostly _a_ answers: You're a rule follower.
Mostly _b_ answers: You're a rule breaker.
Mostly _c_ answers: You sometimes follow rules and sometimes break them.

---

leash: a long piece of rope or leather that is attached to a collar around a dog's neck
to make sense: to be logical

philosophy: a set of beliefs
unreasonable: not logical

A3 **After You Read**

Compare your answers to the quiz with four other students. Who is most like you?

B *Should, Must,* and *Have To*

Examining Form

Look back at the quiz on pages 332–333 and complete the tasks below. Then discuss your answers and read the Form charts to check them.

1. Look at the underlined examples of *should* + verb and *must* + verb. What is the subject of each example? Do *should* and *must* have different forms with different subjects? What form of the verb follows *should* and *must*?

2. Look at the circled examples of the phrasal modal *have to* + verb. What is the subject of each sentence? Does *have to* have different forms with different subjects? What form of the verb follows *have to*?

SHOULD/MUST

Affirmative Statements

SUBJECT	SHOULD/ MUST	BASE FORM OF VERB
I		
You		
He She It	should must	leave.
We		
You		
They		

Negative Statements

SUBJECT	SHOULD/MUST + NOT	BASE FORM OF VERB
I		
You		
He She It	should not shouldn't must not	leave.
We		
You		
They		

Yes/No Questions

SHOULD	SUBJECT	BASE FORM OF VERB
Should	I	
	she	leave?
	we	

Short Answers

YES	SUBJECT	SHOULD	NO	SUBJECT	SHOULD + NOT
Yes,	you		No,	you	
	she	should.		she	shouldn't.
	we			we	

Information Questions					Answers
WH- WORD	SHOULD	SUBJECT	BASE FORM OF VERB		
What	should	I	do?		Talk to your boss.
		she			She **should** work harder.

- *Should* and *must* are modals. Like all modals, they come before the base form of the verb. They also have the same form with all subjects.
- The form *mustn't* is not very common in American English.
- In questions, *have to* (see below) is more common than *must*.

HAVE TO

Affirmative Statements

SUBJECT	HAVE TO	BASE FORM OF VERB
I	**have to**	
You		
She	**has to**	**leave.**
We		
You	**have to**	
They		

Negative Statements

SUBJECT	DO/DOES + NOT	HAVE TO	BASE FORM OF VERB
I	**don't**		
You			
She	**doesn't**	**have to**	**leave.**
We			
You	**don't**		
They			

Yes/No Questions

DO/DOES	SUBJECT	HAVE TO	BASE FORM OF VERB
Do	I	**have to**	**leave?**
Does	he		

Short Answers

YES	SUBJECT	DO/DOES	NO	SUBJECT	DO/DOES + NOT
Yes,	you	**do.**	No,	you	**don't.**
	he	**does.**		he	**doesn't.**

Information Questions

WH- WORD	DO/DOES	SUBJECT	HAVE TO	BASE FORM OF VERB
When	**do**	we	**have to**	**study?**
What	**does**	she		

Answers

Tomorrow.
Chapter 24.

(Continued on page 356)

- *Have to* is different from *should* and *must*. It is not a true modal. It has a different form for the third-person singular.

    You **have to** call him.   She **has** to call him.

- *Have to* has no contracted form.

- We use *do* with *have to* in negative statements and questions.

    I **don't have to** call him.   **Do I have to** call him?

- *Have to* usually replaces *must* in questions.

    Do I **have to** be home by 10:00 P.M.?

B1) Listening for Form

🎧 Listen to each conversation. Which modal do you hear? Check (✓) the correct column.

	(DON'T) HAVE TO	MUST (NOT)	SHOULD (NOT)
1.	✓		
2.			
3.			
4.			
5.			
6.			

B2) Building Sentences with *Should, Must,* and *Have To*

Build four affirmative and four negative sentences. Use a word or phrase from each column. You may omit the second and fourth column in some of your sentences. Punctuate your sentences correctly.

I must take the test.

I		must		take the test
you	(don't)	should	(not)	make a speech
the other students	(doesn't)	have to		go by plane
Sara		has to		study tonight

B3) Forming *Yes/No* Questions with *Should* and *Have To*

Form *Yes/No* questions with *should* and *have to*. Use the words and phrases. Remember to add *do* or *does* if necessary. Punctuate your sentences correctly.

1. we/watch a movie tonight/should

Should we watch a movie tonight?

2. you/go to class tomorrow/have to

_____

3. your friend/study chemistry next year/have to

_____

4. we/have homework on the weekends/should

_____

5. the school library/be open all night/should

_____

B4) Writing Information Questions with *Should* and *Have To*

Write information questions with *should* and *have to*. Use the responses and question words to help you. Punctuate your questions correctly.

1. A: _What time should young children go to bed?_ (what time)

B: Young children should go to bed at eight o'clock.

2. A: _____ (what)

B: We have to read Chapter 6 for tomorrow.

3. A: _____ (who)

B: The accountants should check the deposits.

4. A: _____ (how long)

B: You have to wait about two weeks for the test results.

5. A: _____ (when)

B: Julie and Mark have to leave at noon.

C Modals of Advice, Necessity, and Prohibition

Examining Meaning and Use

Read the sentences and answer the questions below. Then discuss your answers and read the Meaning and Use Notes to check them.

a. You should watch movies in English. You will improve your listening skills.
b. Wait a minute. I have to answer the phone.
c. You must not park here. It's a no parking zone.
d. You must take two writing courses in order to graduate.

1. Which sentence gives advice?

2. Which sentence says that something is not allowed?

3. Which two sentences say that something is necessary? Which one is more formal?

Meaning and Use Notes

Giving Advice and Expressing Opinions

1A Use *should* to give advice.

You **should study** for the test tonight.   He **shouldn't go** to the party this weekend.

1B Use *should* to express opinions.

Everyone **should exercise** regularly.   People **shouldn't smoke** cigarettes.

Expressing Necessity

2A Use *have to* and *must* to talk about something that is necessary. Use *must* in formal or more serious situations.

We **have to leave** now. Class starts in five minutes!
You **must ask** permission to leave work early.

2B Use *must* to express rules, laws, and requirements, especially in writing.

Students **must pay** their tuition before the first day of class.

2C We often use *have to* instead of *must* to talk about rules and laws in conversation.

We **have to pay** our tuition today. The business office is open until 8:00 P.M.
You **have to wear** your seatbelt at all times.

Expressing Lack of Necessity and Prohibition

3 The negative forms of *must* and *have to* have very different meanings. *Don't/doesn't have to* means that something is not necessary for you to do (but you can). *Must not* means that something is prohibited (you cannot do it). There is no choice.

Not Necessary	*Prohibited*
I'm on vacation. I **don't have to get up** early.	Visitors **must not** block the entrance.

C1 Listening for Meaning and Use ▶ Notes 1A–3

🎧 Listen to each statement. Choose the correct use of the modal.

1. necessity   (opinion)
2. advice   necessity
3. advice   opinion
4. necessity   lack of necessity
5. advice   necessity
6. necessity   prohibition
7. necessity   lack of necessity
8. prohibition   lack of necessity

C2 Giving Advice ▶ Note 1A, 1B

Work with a partner. Read each situation. Take turns giving advice with *should* and *should not*.

1. Paulo is the coach of his soccer team. The team lost many games. Many members of the team feel discouraged. Some want to quit. What should Paulo do?

   He should have extra practice sessions. He shouldn't . . .

2. Linda wants to feel and look better. She works too hard. What should Linda do?

3. Brad is upset because his roommate plays loud music. It's difficult for Brad to study. Brad talked to his roommate, but it didn't make a difference. What should Brad do?

A. Work with a partner. Study the chart and think about your school's rules and requirements. Check (✓) the correct column.

		REQUIRED	NOT REQUIRED	PROHIBITED
1.	be late for class			✓
2.	wear a uniform			
3.	buy a dictionary			
4.	smoke in the classroom			
5.	eat in the computer lab			
6.	do homework			
7.	carry a student ID			
8.	pay school fees			

B. Write full sentences in your notebook to describe the rules and requirements at your school. Use the information in the chart. Use *must* and *must not* to describe rules and requirements. Use *don't have to* to describe what is not a rule or requirement.

Students must not be late for class.

D Combining Form, Meaning, and Use

D1 Thinking About Meaning and Use

Complete each conversation. Then discuss your answers in small groups.

1. **A:** This is a dangerous neighborhood.

   _____

   B: Don't worry. I'll be fine.

   a. You have to lock your door at night.

   b. You don't have to leave the windows open.

   c. You must not lock your apartment.

2. **A:** _____

   B: Maybe a book. She loves to read.

   a. Do I have to get Sara a present for her birthday?

   b. What should I buy Sara for her graduation?

   c. Who should get Sara a birthday present?

3. **A:** Oh no! My parents are going to be here soon, and this place is a mess.

   B. _____ I'll do it.

   a. You don't have to clean the living room.

   b. You must not clean the kitchen.

   c. You should clean the apartment.

4. **A:** We can't park here. Look at that sign.

   B: You're right! _____

   a. Visitors must not use this lot.

   b. Visitors must park here.

   c. Visitors don't have to park here.

5. **A:** I'm hungry. I'm going to make a sandwich.

   B: _____. We're meeting the Haddads at the restaurant in an hour.

   a. You have to eat.

   b. You must eat now.

   c. You shouldn't eat now.

6. **A:** Ms. Anderson, can I take your math class?

   B: No, I'm sorry. It's too late. _____

   a. Students must register before the first day of class.

   b. Students shouldn't register before the first day of class.

   c. Students don't have to register before the first day of class.

Some of these sentences have errors. Find the errors and correct them.

1. We have leave tonight.
   to

2. They must wear uniforms to school.

3. I should take chemistry next year.

4. U.S. voters should be at least 18 years old.

5. You must to finish before 6:00.

6. Does she has to leave immediately?

7. You should not studying every night.

8. Didn't you see the sign? You don't have to smoke here.

 # Beyond the Classroom

Searching for Authentic Examples

Look in an English-language newspaper or on the Internet for advice about health and fitness. Find three examples of sentences that use modals of advice, necessity, or prohibition. Write them in your notebook and share them with your class.

Writing

Follow the steps below to write a paragraph about the laws in your country.

1. Use these questions to make notes.
   - Do people have to carry an ID with them?
   - Do drivers need to keep their driver's license in their car?
   - Do drivers have to have car insurance?
   - Do young men and women have to join the army?
   - Do adults have to vote in elections?

2. Write a first draft. Use *must, must not,* and *don't have to.*

3. Read your work carefully and circle grammar, spelling, and punctuation errors. Work with a partner to decide how to fix the errors and improve the content.

4. Rewrite your paragraph.

   All men and women over the age of 18 must carry an ID with them at all times. People must also have their driver's license with them when they drive. . . .

Objects, Infinitives, and Gerunds

Object Pronouns; Direct and Indirect Objects

A Holidays Around the World

A1 Before You Read

Discuss these questions.

What is your favorite holiday? How do you celebrate this holiday?

A2 Read

Read this book excerpt. How many holidays did you read about? Did you know about these holidays before you read the excerpt?

HOLIDAYS AROUND THE WORLD

All countries have special holidays. Some holidays are religious or cultural. Other holidays are political. Holidays around the world have many characteristics in common. On many holidays, people make special food for their friends and family. Often, they also give gifts to each other. For some holidays, people send cards to friends and relatives, or sing special
5 songs. Holidays are important because they teach children the traditions of their culture. Read below to learn what holidays some people around the world celebrate.

Day of the Dead (Mexico)

The Day of the Dead is not a sad holiday. On this day (November 1), Mexicans remember their
10 ancestors and tell their children stories about them. Everyone eats cookies and candy in the shape of skeletons, and decorates their houses with skeletons. Many Mexican families go to the cemetery on this day, too. Often they have a picnic
15 at the cemetery, and they offer food and drink to their ancestors. Families also clean the gravestones and plant flowers.

Shichi-Go-San (Japan)

Shichi-Go-San means "seven, five, three" in Japanese. This is a special celebration for
20 children who are seven, five, and three years old. Families go to a temple and pray for good health for their children. At the temple, a priest gives the children *omiki*, a kind of rice wine. After that, the parents buy the children candy.

Boxing Day (Britain and Canada)

Boxing Day began hundreds of years ago in England. At that time, rich people gave boxes of
25 gifts to their servants on December 26, the day after Christmas. Today, people in Britain and
Canada spend the day with family and friends. They eat a special meal of ham or roast lamb.

Loy Krathong (Thailand)

On Loy Krathong, Thais pray to the goddess of
water. They make small boats from banana leaves.
30 The boats usually contain a candle, flowers, incense,
and coins. In the evening, people carry their boats
to the water. They light the candles and the incense.
Then they make a wish and put their boats in the
water. Thais believe that the boats will bring them
35 good luck.

ancestors: relatives from a long time ago
cemetery: the place where people bury dead bodies
gravestones: stone markers on graves with the
person's name, and dates of birth and death

incense: a substance that releases a pleasant smell when it
burns
skeleton: the structure formed from all the bones of the
body

A3 After You Read

Match the words and phrases to the correct holiday. Check (✓) the correct column.

		DAY OF THE DEAD	SHICHI-GO-SAN	BOXING DAY	LOY KRATHONG
1.	Mexico	✓			
2.	a holiday for children				
3.	remember ancestors				
4.	Thailand				
5.	Great Britain				
6.	the day after Christmas				
7.	make boats				
8.	Japan				

B Object Pronouns

Examining Form

Read the sentences and complete the tasks below. Then discuss your answers and read the Form chart to check them.

1a. Call Mrs. Allen.   **2a.** I spoke to the manager.
1b. Call her.   **2b.** I spoke to him.

1. An object follows a verb or a preposition. Underline the objects in the sentences.

2. Which objects are nouns? Which are pronouns?

	Object Pronouns	
SUBJECT PRONOUN	**OBJECT PRONOUN**	**EXAMPLES**
I	**me**	I helped my sister. She thanked **me**.
you	**you**	You will be late. I will drive **you**.
he	**him**	He needed some money. I helped **him**.
she	**her**	She is a ballerina. I admire **her**.
it	**it**	It is under the table. I can't find **it**.
we	**us**	We play soccer every day. Tom often joins **us**.
you	**you**	You need to work harder. I will help **you**.
they	**them**	They are outside. I'll get **them**.

- An object pronoun replaces a noun in the object position (after a verb in a sentence).
- When talking about a pair or group that includes you, mention yourself last.
  Betty talked to **him and me**.
⚠ Use *me* as the object of a verb or a preposition, not *I*.
  My friend invited John and **me**.
  *My friend invited John and I. (INCORRECT)

B1) Listening for Form

🎧 Listen to the sentences. Check (✓) the object pronouns you hear.

	ME	HIM	HER	IT	US	THEM
1.						✓
2.						
3.						
4.						
5.						
6.						

B2) Working with Object Pronouns

Complete each sentence. Use the correct object pronoun related to the underlined noun.

1. <u>Diego</u> is worried. Please speak to ____*him*____.

2. There are <u>two new students</u> in class. We are waiting for _____.

3. *Star Wars* is a good <u>movie</u>. I watched _____ last night.

4. <u>I</u> don't have a watch. Please tell _____ the time.

5. <u>Jack and I</u> are at home. Please call _____.

6. <u>Elena</u> was sick yesterday. We visited _____.

B3) Using Subject and Object Pronouns

Complete the paragraph. Use the correct subject pronouns and object pronouns.

In the United States, ____*we*____ celebrate Halloween on October 31. On this day,
     1
people wear creative costumes. People wear _____ to parties. Children go trick-
                                               2
or-treating with their parents. _____ knock on neighbors' doors and ask for
                                     3
candy. When _____ was young, my mother always made beautiful costumes for
                4
my brothers and me. Then on Halloween night, my brothers and _____ went
                                                                    5
trick-or-treating. _____ always had a great time.
                        6

C Direct Objects and Indirect Objects

Examining Form

Read the sentences and complete the tasks below. Then discuss your answers and read the Form charts to check them.

> **a.** We sang a folk song.
> **b.** We sang it.
> **c.** We sang a folk song to the children.

1. Direct objects usually follow verbs. Underline the verb in each sentence. Circle the direct object.

2. An indirect object often occurs after the prepositions *to* or *for*. Draw two lines under the indirect object.

VERBS WITH DIRECT OBJECTS

Direct Objects		
SUBJECT	**VERB**	**DIRECT OBJECT**
People	make	**special food.**
Some people	send	**cards and gifts.**

VERBS WITH DIRECT AND INDIRECT OBJECTS

Direct Object + *To/For* + Indirect Object				
SUBJECT	**VERB**	**DIRECT OBJECT**	*TO/FOR*	**INDIRECT OBJECT**
People	send	**cards and gifts**	to	**them.**
	make	**special food**	for	**their friends.**

Indirect Object + Direct Object			
SUBJECT	VERB	INDIRECT OBJECT	DIRECT OBJECT
People	make	their friends	special food.
	send	them	cards and gifts.

Verbs with Direct Objects

- Some verbs have a direct object.
- A direct object is a person or a thing that receives the action of a verb. A direct object can be a noun or an object pronoun.
- A direct object follows a verb.

    Many people send **cards**.   Some people make **them**.

Verbs with Direct Objects and Indirect Objects

- Some verbs have two objects: a direct object and an indirect object.
- An indirect object is a person who receives the direct object. An indirect object can be a noun or an object pronoun.

Direct Object + To/For + Indirect Object

- All verbs with both direct and indirect objects can follow this pattern: direct object + *to/for* + indirect object. In this pattern, the indirect object comes after the direct object. It follows *to* or *for*.

    I gave a book **to Irina**.   I cooked a meal **for Lee**.

- We can use this pattern with the verbs below.

TO + INDIRECT OBJECT			*FOR* + INDIRECT OBJECT	
bring	offer	send	bake	fix
describe	owe	show	build	get
explain	repeat	teach	buy	leave
give	say	tell	cook	make
mail	sell	write	do	prepare

Indirect Object + Direct Object

- Some verbs with both direct and indirect objects can also follow this pattern: indirect object + direct object. In this pattern, the indirect object comes before the direct object, without the prepositions *to* or *for*.

    I cooked **Lee** a meal.   *I cooked for Lee a meal. (INCORRECT)

- We can use this pattern with the verbs below.

bake	give	save
bring	leave	sell
build	mail	send
buy	make	show
cook	offer	tell
do	owe	write
get	read	

A. 🎧 Listen to the sentences. Write the words or phrases you hear.

___DO___ 1. In the United States, many people celebrate _Christmas_____ .

_____ 2. They buy gifts for _____ .

_____ 3. A lot of people also cook _____ special foods.

_____ 4. Many children bake _____ .

_____ 5. A lot of families decorate _____ before the holidays.

_____ 6. Santa Claus brings children _____ .

B. Look at your answers in part A. Write *DO* if your answer is a direct object and *IO* if your answer is an indirect object.

Read each sentence. Circle the direct object. Put an ✗ after the sentence if there is no direct object.

1. Brad joined (the army) four months ago.

2. He is very lonely.

3. He misses his friends and family a lot.

4. Last week Brad sent Carol a letter.

5. He asked an important question.

6. Carol was surprised.

7. Brad wants a wife.

8. Carol wants a career.

9. She is giving him an answer.

10. She is writing him a letter right now.

C3 Identifying Direct Objects and Indirect Objects

Read the letter. Look at the underlined words in each sentence. Write *DO* above the direct objects and *IO* above the indirect objects.

Dear Laura,

Last night I went to the Loy Krathong festival here in Thailand. Let me describe
$$\underset{1}{\overset{DO}{\underline{it}}}\ \underset{2}{\overset{IO}{\underline{for\ you}}}.$$ A *krathong* is a small boat. People make $\underset{3}{\underline{them}}$ from banana leaves. They

put $\underset{4}{\underline{a\ candle,\ incense,\ flowers,\ and\ coins}}$ in the krathong. They offer $\underset{5}{\underline{the\ krathong}}$ to

$\underset{6}{\underline{the\ goddess\ of\ water}}$. Then they put $\underset{7}{\underline{the\ krathong}}$ into the river and make $\underset{8}{\underline{a\ wish}}$.

My friend Somchai made $\underset{9}{\underline{a\ krathong}}$ for $\underset{10}{\underline{me}}$. After we left the river, we went to a

party. Somchai taught $\underset{11}{\underline{me}}$ $\underset{12}{\underline{a\ special\ Loy\ Krathong\ song}}$.

Wish you were here,

Erica

C4 Forming Sentences with Direct and Indirect Objects

Form sentences with direct and indirect objects. Use the words and phrases.

1. Nancy/us/sent/a postcard/from Spain

Nancy sent us a postcard from Spain.

2. bought/I/him/a present/yesterday

3. gave/her/a birthday cake/we

4. got/for/a glass of water/Mrs. Johnson/him

5. she/an essay/for/the school newspaper/wrote

6. they/photos/us/are showing/their

Direct Objects and Indirect Objects

Examining Meaning and Use

Read the sentences and answer the questions below. Then discuss your answers and read the Meaning and Use Notes to check them.

a. Greg bought a book for his teacher.
b. My boss announced his retirement to everyone this afternoon.

1. Underline the direct objects and circle the indirect objects in the sentences.

2. Look at sentence a. What did Greg buy? Who received Greg's gift?

3. Look at sentence b. What did the boss announce? Who did he make the announcement to?

Meaning and Use Notes

Direct Objects

1A A direct object can be a person, place, or thing that a verb affects or changes in some way. It answers the questions *Who/Whom?* or *What?*

A: <u>Who/Whom</u> did he see?
B: He saw **his sister**.

A: <u>What</u> is she explaining?
B: She is explaining **her ideas**.

1B Some verbs always have a direct object. Without an object their meaning is not complete. Some common verbs that need direct objects are *bring, buy, get, have, like, make, need, say, take, turn on/off,* and *want*.

Lynn **needs a car**.
*Lynn needs. (INCORRECT)

Indirect Objects

2 An indirect object is a person or group. It is the person that receives the direct object. It answers the questions *To whom?* and *For whom?* An indirect object can be an institution such as a library or a bank.

A: <u>To whom</u> did he send the check?   A: <u>For whom</u> did you buy a book?

B: Corey sent the check **to the bank**.   B: I bought a book **for Marta**.

Direct Object + *To/For* + Indirect Object vs. Indirect Object + Direct Object

3A There is no difference in meaning between direct object + *to/for* + indirect object and indirect object + direct object.

He is writing **a letter to us**. = He is writing **us a letter**.

She bought **a dress for me**. = She bought **me a dress**.

3B Some verbs have similar meanings but follow different patterns. For example, the verbs *say* and *tell* have similar meanings, but only *tell* can have an indirect object before a direct object.

Direct Object + To/For *+ Indirect Object*	*Indirect Object + Direct Object*
He told **his name to the teacher**.	He told **the teacher his name**.
He said **his name to the teacher**.	*He said the teacher his name. (INCORRECT)

D1 ## Listening for Meaning and Use ▶ Notes 1A–3B

🎧 Listen to the story about Sally. Is the word in the chart the direct object or the indirect object of the sentence? Check (✓) the correct column.

		DIRECT OBJECT	INDIRECT OBJECT
1.	Sally	✓	
2.	her		
3.	her		
4.	her		
5.	Sally		
6.	her		
7.	Sally		
8.	her		

Complete the sentences. Use direct objects.

1. I need _a new car_ .

2. My town needs _____ .

3. I want _____ for my birthday.

4. Next year, I'm going to buy _____ .

5. My best friend has _____ .

6. I really like _____ .

Alex organized a party for his friend Amy's twenty-fifth birthday. Read his notes about things to do for the party. In your notebook, write full sentences to describe his preparations. Add an appropriate indirect object to each sentence.

1. Send an e-mail about the party

   Alex sent an e-mail about the party to Amy's brother.

2. Mail the invitations

3. Give directions

4. Bake a chocolate cake

5. Buy a birthday gift

6. Write a short speech

A. Answer the questions about a special holiday in your notebook. Use direct objects or indirect objects in your answers.

1. What special holiday do you celebrate every year?

   We celebrate Thanksgiving.

2. What foods do you cook?

3. What other things do you buy?

4. What other special things do you make?

5. What special clothes do you wear?

6. Who do you invite to celebrate with you?

B. Tell a partner about the holiday in part A. Use verbs such as *give, cook, bake,* and *make.* Use both sentence patterns for direct and indirect objects in your description.

   People cook special treats on this day.
   My aunt bakes pumpkin pie for the whole family.

E ## Combining Form, Meaning, and Use

Complete each conversation. Then discuss your answers in small groups.

1. **A:** Dan bought me a book for my birthday.

   B: _____

   a. Did you buy it for him?

   b. Was it good? *(circled)*

   c. Was it delicious?

2. **A:** They owe the bank a lot of money.

   B: _____

   a. They arrived yesterday.

   b. Did the bank pay them?

   c. That's terrible!

3. **A:** When did he speak to you about Mike's project?

   B: _____

   a. He talked to me last week.

   b. He worked on the project.

   c. He spoke to Mike.

4. **A:** She sent them money for Christmas.

   B: Really? _____

   a. They didn't get it.

   b. She didn't get it.

   c. They didn't get them.

5. **A:** Who taught you German?

   B: _____

   a. Ms. Werner taught me.

   b. I taught her.

   c. It did.

6. **A:** Paul invited Ana to dinner.

   B: _____

   a. Did he accept?

   b. Did she invite him?

   c. Did she accept?

Some of these sentences have errors. Find the errors and correct them.

1. They explained the situation ^to us.

2. I made for you a cake.

3. He sends to us a Christmas card every year.

4. Frank's mother gave him the house.

5. We bought a bicycle my daughter.

6. He is cooking a meal for us.

7. They said me good-bye.

8. Let me tell she the answer.

Beyond the Classroom

Searching for Authentic Examples

Look on the Internet or in the library for information about a holiday from another country. Find two examples of sentences with direct object + *to/for* + indirect object and two examples with indirect object + direct object. Write them in your notebook and share them with your class.

Writing

Follow the steps below to write a paragraph about a friend or classmate. Find out how your partner's family celebrates his or her birthday.

1. Use these questions to make notes.
   - Does your family celebrate birthdays?
   - Are any birthdays more significant than others? Why?
   - Do you sing any special songs? What are they?
   - What special activities are there for birthdays?
   - Do you buy presents?
   - Do you eat any special foods on birthdays? What are they?

2. Write a first draft. Use the verbs on page 351 with direct objects and indirect objects. Use both patterns.

3. Read your work carefully and circle grammar, spelling, and punctuation errors. Work with a partner to decide how to fix the errors and improve the content.

4. Rewrite your draft.

   Marta's family celebrates her birthday every year. They had a big party for her on her eighteenth birthday. . . .

Infinitives and
Gerunds After Verbs

Advice to Business Travelers

A1 Before You Read

Discuss these questions.

Is it important to be on time for work meetings? for parties?

A2 Read

🎧 Read the magazine article on the following page. What kinds of information should international business travelers find out about the country they will visit?

A3 After You Read

Linda Marsh went to Tokyo on business. Here are some of the things she did. According to the article, were they mistakes or not? Check (✓) the correct column.

		MISTAKE	NOT A MISTAKE
1.	She didn't read about Japanese culture.	✓	
2.	She learned greetings in Japanese before she went.		
3.	She arrived the day before a national holiday.		
4.	She spoke to a Japanese colleague about working hours in Japan.		
5.	She was on time for her meeting.		
6.	She is friendly, so she called everyone by their first name.		

Advice to Business Travelers

International business travelers <u>need to</u> <u>know</u> something about the customs of foreign countries. Otherwise, the business trip may not be successful. How do experienced
5 business travelers prepare for a trip to another country? Many people like to talk to someone from the country. Some people prefer to read about the country. Others even learn to say a few simple phrases in the native language of
10 the country. Business travel to a foreign country is always difficult at first. But, according to experienced business travelers, things begin to improve after a few trips.

Here are a few helpful hints for any
15 **business trip abroad:**

Find out about office hours.
When do your foreign colleagues start work each day? When do they like to eat lunch? When do they (finish working)? What days
20 do they work? You need to know these things so you can schedule appointments at the right time.

Find out about religious and national holidays.
25 For example, experienced business travelers don't expect to do much business during the week before and after Easter in countries like Italy and Spain. Employers and employees around the world enjoy celebrating holidays.

30 Do you need to travel to the Middle East or Hong Kong? You probably don't want to plan a business trip during Ramadan or the Chinese New Year. Check with someone from your host country before you make final arrangements.

35 ## Find out about business customs.
In countries like Japan, business people expect to start meetings on time. In other countries, people are more relaxed and they don't expect to start on time. In some cultures, business
40 people don't like discussing business at the start of a meeting. They prefer beginning a discussion with small talk about the weather, art, or sports. There are also different customs about names and titles, so avoid using first
45 names immediately.

---

arrangements: plans, preparations
avoid: stay away from

experience: having the knowledge required for something
small talk: polite conversation about topics that are not very serious

B Infinitives and Gerunds After Verbs

Examining Form

Look back at the article on page 361 and complete the tasks below. Then discuss your answers and read the Form charts to check them.

1. The underlined phrase is an example of a verb + infinitive. Find three more examples.

2. What two words form the infinitive?

3. The circled phrase is an example of a verb + gerund. Find three more examples.

4. How do we form the gerund?

Verb + Infinitive		
SUBJECT	VERB	INFINITIVE
I	need	
You	hope	
She	decided	**to work.**
They	wanted	

Verb + Gerund		
SUBJECT	VERB	GERUND
I	keep	
You	enjoy	
She	discussed	**working.**
They	finished	

Verb + Infinitive/Gerund		
SUBJECT	VERB	INFINITIVE/GERUND
I	like	
You	prefer	**to work.**
She	started	**working.**
They	began	

Verb + Infinitive

- To form the infinitive, add *to* to the base form of a verb.
- Infinitives can follow many verbs. For example:

decide	need
expect	plan
hope	want
learn	agree

Verb + Gerund

- To form the gerund, add *-ing* to the base form of a verb.
- Gerunds can follow many verbs. For example:

avoid	finish
discuss	keep
dislike	practice
enjoy	

Verb + Infinitive/Gerund

- We can use some verbs with either the gerund or the infinitive. For example:

begin	prefer
like	start
love	try
hate	

B1 **Listening for Form**

Listen to each sentence. Do you hear an infinitive or a gerund? Check (✓) the correct column.

	INFINITIVE	GERUND
1.	✓	
2.		
3.		
4.		
5.		
6.		
7.		
8.		

A temple in Thailand

B2) Identifying Infinitives and Gerunds

Read each sentence. If the sentence contains an infinitive, write *I*. If the sentence contains a gerund, write *G*. If it doesn't contain an infinitive or a gerund, write **X**.

_G_ 1. Paul and Lisa enjoy playing tennis.

_____ 2. Julia goes to class three days a week.

_____ 3. My parents plan to buy a new car.

_____ 4. She is learning to play the guitar.

_____ 5. Juan wants to buy a new car.

_____ 6. He really enjoys working with other people.

_____ 7. She is learning Polish.

_____ 8. Magda finished writing her dissertation last year.

B3) Building Sentences with Infinitives and Gerunds

A. Build two affirmative and two negative statements with a verb + infinitive. Use each word or phrase only once. Make any changes necessary to the verbs in the second and third columns. Punctuate your sentences correctly.

the students	want	pass this course
her boss	need	speak Chinese
our teacher	learn	sign the contract
his parents	plan	move to California

The students want to pass this course.

B. Build two affirmative and two negative statements with a verb + gerund. Use each word or phrase only once. Make any changes necessary to the verbs in the second and third columns. Punctuate your sentences correctly.

most of my friends	enjoy	take piano lessons last year
my cousin and I	keep	speak in front of a large audience
Philip	discuss	make mistakes
I	avoid	open a business together

Most of my friends enjoyed taking piano lessons last year.

B4) Forming Questions with Infinitives and Gerunds

A. Form questions with a verb + infinitive or a verb + gerund. Use the words and phrases. Punctuate your sentences correctly.

1. What/do/you/plan/do/this evening

   What do you plan to do this evening?

2. What/do/you/want/do/this summer

3. Where/do/your/friends/enjoy/go/on/weekends

4. What kinds of/films/do/you/avoid/watch

5. What/do/you/hope/do/in the future

6. Where/do/you/expect/live/in ten years

B. Work with a partner. Take turns asking and answering the questions in part A.

A: What do you plan to do this evening?
B: I plan to go to that new restaurant on Smith Street.

B5) Choosing the Infinitive or the Gerund

Choose the correct form. In some cases both answers are possible.

1. I like _____ cakes.
   - **(a.)** to bake
   - **(b.)** baking

2. Paul enjoys _____ to classical music.
   - **a.** to listen
   - **b.** listening

3. Pat is finally learning _____.
   - **a.** to drive
   - **b.** driving

4. Lee prefers _____ slowly.
   - **a.** to work
   - **b.** working

5. She needs _____ harder.
   - **a.** to work
   - **b.** working

6. Maria started _____ more carefully after the accident.
   - **a.** to drive
   - **b.** driving

7. At the meeting, we discussed

   _____ a new employee.
   - **a.** to hire
   - **b.** hiring

8. At the age of 60, she began

   _____ the piano.
   - **a.** to learn
   - **b.** learning

Infinitives and Gerunds

Examining Meaning and Use

Read the sentences and answer the questions below. Then discuss your answers and read the Meaning and Use Notes to check them.

    a. We like Mexican food.
    b. We like eating Mexican food.
    c. We like to eat Mexican food.

1. Which sentences talk about an activity? Which sentence does not?

2. Which two sentences have exactly the same meaning?

Meaning and Use Notes

Referring to Activities and States

1A   We use infinitives and gerunds to refer to activities or states. We can use them in the same position in the sentence as a direct object.

Activities	*States*
He <u>loves</u> **tennis**.	They <u>hate</u> **cold weather**.
He <u>loves</u> **to play** tennis.	They <u>hate</u> **to be** cold.
He <u>loves</u> **playing** tennis.	They <u>hate</u> **being** cold.

1B   After the verbs *like*, *hate*, *love*, *prefer*, *begin*, and *start*, we can use an infinitive or a gerund with little or no difference in meaning.

I <u>like</u> **to travel** alone. = I <u>like</u> **traveling** alone.   She <u>started</u> **to leave**. = She <u>started</u> **leaving**.
They <u>prefer</u> **to walk**. = They <u>prefer</u> **walking**.   It <u>began</u> **to rain**. = It <u>began</u> **raining**.

Expressing Likes and Dislikes

2   We often use verbs with infinitives and gerunds to discuss our like or dislike of an activity or state.

I <u>enjoy</u> **cooking**, but I <u>dislike</u> **cleaning**.   We <u>love</u> **to ski**.
Marta <u>loves</u> **being** healthy and <u>hates</u> **being** sick.   They <u>hate</u> **to be** late.

🎧 Listen to the sentences. Choose the sentence that has the same meaning as the one you hear.

1. **a.** Susan hates her house.
   b. Susan hates cleaning her house. *(circled)*

2. **a.** Josh dislikes sleeping late.
   b. Josh likes sleeping late.

3. **a.** Holly didn't enjoy the party.
   b. Holly doesn't like to go to parties.

4. **a.** Rob dislikes working on Saturdays.
   b. Rob prefers to work on Sundays.

5. **a.** We decided to work late.
   b. We don't like to work late.

6. **a.** Derek dislikes taking tests.
   b. Derek prefers taking tests.

A. Complete each sentence with a gerund or infinitive. Use an appropriate form of one of the phrases below or use your own ideas.

be a vegetarian	clean my room	jog in the park	study for exams
borrow money	eat red meat	shop for clothes	take a vacation

1. I hate _cleaning my room_____.

2. I always avoid _____.

3. Next month I expect _____.

4. Last summer I enjoyed _____.

5. As a child, I avoided _____.

6. A few months ago I really needed _____.

7. I strongly dislike _____.

8. Last year I decided _____.

B. Work in small groups. Share your answers to part A. Discuss the structures you used.

1. In which sentences can you use only a gerund?

2. In which sentences can you use only an infinitive?

3. In which sentences can you use either a gerund or an infinitive?

A. Answer the questions with complete sentences in your notebook. Use gerunds or infinitives in your answers.

1. What two things do you enjoy doing on Sunday?

   On Sunday I enjoy riding my bicycle and playing tennis.

2. What holiday do you love to celebrate? What two things do you like to do on this day?

3. What three things do you enjoy doing after a stressful day?

4. What two household chores do you dislike doing?

5. What three things do you want to do in the near future?

6. What two things did you love to do as a child?

7. What two things did you hate doing as a child?

8. What three things do you want to do in the next year?

B. Work with a partner. Take turns asking and answering the questions in part A. Use the chart to take notes on your partner's answers.

1.	likes sleeping late, going for long walks, renting DVDs
2.	loves to celebrate Thanksgiving . . .
3.	
4.	
5.	
6.	
7.	
8.	

C. Exchange partners. Tell you new partner about your first partner's answers.

On Sunday Ana enjoys sleeping late, going for long walks, and renting DVDs.

D Combining Form, Meaning, and Use

D1 Thinking About Meaning and Use

Complete each conversation. Then discuss your answers in small groups.

1. **A:** Do you like making cookies?

   B: _____

      (**a.**) No, but I like to eat them.

      b. I like chocolate cookies.

      c. No, I don't like them.

2. **A:** Do you usually drive to New York?

   B: _____

      a. Actually, I prefer to fly.

      b. Yes, I decided to drive this time.

      c. No, I decided to fly.

3. **A:** Do you go to a gym?

   B: _____

      a. No, I like to exercise.

      b. No, I dislike exercising.

      c. No, the gym is new.

4. **A:** My brother likes to wake up early.

   B: _____

      a. I am too.

      b. Yes, I do.

      c. I don't. I prefer sleeping late.

5. **A:** He quit his job last week.

   B: _____

      a. Did he dislike working there?

      b. Does he like to leave?

      c. Does he enjoy working there?

6. **A:** Do you avoid taking the train?

   B: _____

      a. No, I don't like to take the train.

      b. Yes, I like to take the train.

      c. No, I like taking the train.

D2 Editing

Find the errors in this paragraph and correct them.

    Keisha plans ~~going~~ _to go_ to college next year, so she is starting apply to different schools. She wants to go to a school in Chicago because she wants live at home. In this way, she'll avoid to spending a lot of money on room and board. She enjoys to study biology and chemistry, and she likes help people. She wants to becoming a nurse. Her grades are good so she expects get into several schools in the area.

Beyond the Classroom

Searching for Authentic Examples

Look at advice columns in English-language newspapers and magazines, or on the Internet. Find at least two verb + infinitive and two verb + gerund combinations with the verbs in this chapter. Write them in your notebook and share them with your class.

Writing

Follow the steps below to write one or two paragraphs with advice for business travelers visiting your country for the first time. Use verbs with infinitives and gerunds.

1. Use these questions to make notes.
   - Do business people expect others to be on time?
   - Do they prefer to use first names or formal titles?
   - When do they avoid doing business?
   - What do people in your country expect visitors to do? For example, do they expect visitors to bring a gift?
   - Should visitors avoid doing certain things in a person's home?

2. Write a first draft.

3. Read your work carefully and circle grammar, spelling, and punctuation errors. Work with a partner to decide how to fix the errors and improve the content.

4. Rewrite your draft.

   Business customs in Japan are very formal. For example, business people bow to each other and they prefer calling their business associates by their last names. . . .

Comparatives and Superlatives

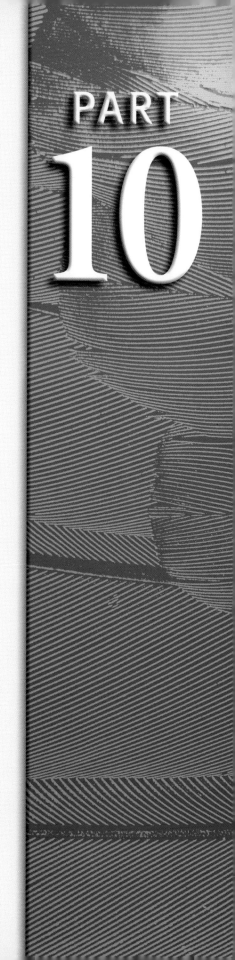

Comparatives

What's So Great About QWERTY?

A1 Before You Read

Discuss these questions.

Can you type? Do you type quickly or slowly? How many fingers do you use?

A2 Read

Read the article about keyboards on the following page. How many kinds of keyboards does the article discuss? What are the names of the keyboards?

A3 After You Read

Read the statements. Check (✓) the correct column.

		QWERTY KEYBOARD	DVORAK KEYBOARD
1.	This keyboard is more popular.	✓	
2.	Many people believe that this keyboard is better.		
3.	Typists work more efficiently with this keyboard.		
4.	The name comes from the first six letters of the keyboard.		
5.	This keyboard is more difficult to learn.		
6.	This keyboard is older.		

Typewriter keyboard

Computer keyboard

What's So Great About QWERTY?

Typewriters and computers are very different, but look closely at their keyboards. What do you notice about them? They are the same.

5 QWERTY is the name for the arrangement of the letters on an English keyboard. The name QWERTY comes from the first six keys in the second row of the keyboard. The letters were arranged in
10 this order on the first typewriters. The keys on old typewriters often got stuck together. The inventor of the QWERTY keyboard tried to prevent this. Even though most people no longer use typewriters, the
15 QWERTY keyboard is still <u>more popular</u> than any other English keyboard.

Although the QWERTY keyboard is still in use, many people think that it is not very efficient. Experts think another keyboard,
20 the Dvorak, is much better. The Dvorak keyboard is named for its inventor, August Dvorak. Dvorak studied films of typists. He noticed the keys people used a lot. He decided to make a <u>more efficient</u> keyboard.
25 Many people believe that he was successful.

Why is the Dvorak keyboard better than the QWERTY? First, it's easier to use because it uses the middle row of keys a lot. It is simpler to type on the middle row of keys
30 than on the other rows. A typist can type

The Dvorak Keyboard

thousands of words with only the middle row of a Dvorak keyboard. On the middle row of a QWERTY keyboard a typist can only type about a hundred English words.

35 Second, people type <u>more slowly</u> on a QWERTY keyboard than on a Dvorak keyboard. With a QWERTY keyboard, typists use both hands and move all around the keyboard so they work (harder). With the
40 Dvorak keyboard, the typist can type much (faster). Also, most people have (weaker) left hands than right hands. With a QWERTY keyboard, more than three thousand English words use the left hand alone.
45 Only about three hundred use the stronger right hand alone.

So why do people continue using the QWERTY? The Dvorak is faster, more accurate, and easier to learn than QWERTY.
50 The simple answer is that QWERTY is (older) and people don't usually like change.

---

accurate: without mistakes
arrangement: order

efficient: working well with little effort or energy
inventor: the first person to make something

B The Comparative with Adjectives and Adverbs

Examining Form

Look back at the article on page 375 and complete the tasks below. Then discuss your answers and read the Form charts to check them.

1. Look at the circled words. These are the comparative forms of the adjectives and adverbs below. Write the comparative form next to each adjective or adverb below. How do we form the comparatives of these words?

   Adjectives   *Adverbs*

   weak _____   fast _____

   old _____   hard _____

2. Look at the underlined phrases. These are the comparative forms of the adjectives and adverbs below. Write the comparative form next to each adjective or adverb below. How do we form the comparatives of these words?

   Adjectives   *Adverb*

   popular _____   slowly _____

   efficient _____

REGULAR COMPARATIVE FORMS

One-Syllable Adjectives

ADJECTIVE	COMPARATIVE
big	**bigger**
strong	**stronger**
young	**younger**

Two-Syllable Adjectives

ADJECTIVE	COMPARATIVE
simple	**simpler**
easy	**easier**
famous	**more famous**

Three-Syllable Adjectives

ADJECTIVE	COMPARATIVE
efficient	**more efficient**
popular	**more popular**

One-Syllable Adverbs

ADVERB	COMPARATIVE
fast	**faster**
hard	**harder**

Two- or Three-Syllable Adverbs

ADVERB	COMPARATIVE
slowly	**more slowly**
frequently	**more frequently**

Adjectives with One Syllable

- Add -*er* to form the comparative. If the adjective ends in -*e*, add -*r*.
- For adjectives that end with a single vowel and a consonant, double the final consonant and add -*er*.

Adjectives with Two Syllables

- Some two-syllable adjectives use -*er*. Other two-syllable adjectives use either -*er* or *more*. See Appendix 10 for adjectives that use both forms of the comparative.

  Jenny is **friendlier/more friendly** than her sister.

- If an adjective ends in a consonant + -*y*, change the *y* to *i* and add -*er*.

Adjectives with Three or More Syllables

- Use *more* with adjectives of three or more syllables.

Adverbs with One Syllable

- Add -*er* to form the comparative.

Adverbs with Two or More Syllables

- For adverbs of two or more syllables ending in -*ly*, use *more* instead of -*er*.

IRREGULAR COMPARATIVE FORMS

ADJECTIVE	ADVERB	COMPARATIVE
good	well	**better**
bad	badly	**worse**

THE COMPARATIVE IN SENTENCES

	COMPARATIVE	*THAN*	SUBJECT (+ VERB OR AUXILIARY)
A mile is	**longer**	**than**	a kilometer.
Vanilla ice cream is	**more popular**		chocolate ice cream is.
Chris drives	**faster**		Gloria drives.
My grandfather talks	**more slowly**		my father does.

- Use the comparative form of an adjective or adverb + *than*.
- Use *than* to connect the two parts of a comparative sentence.
- We sometimes use the main verb or an auxiliary verb *(be, do)* in the second part of a comparative sentence.

Listening for Form

🎧 Listen to each sentence. What comparative form do you hear? Check (✓) the correct column.

	REGULAR FORM WITH -*ER*	REGULAR FORM WITH *MORE*	IRREGULAR FORM
1.	✓		
2.			
3.			
4.			
5.			
6.			
7.			
8.			

B2 **Forming Comparatives**

A. Write the comparative form of the adjectives and adverbs.

Adjectives

1. thin   thinner

2. easy   _____

3. intelligent _____

4. expensive _____

Adverbs

5. fast   _____

6. happily   _____

7. quietly   _____

8. carefully   _____

B. Write the base form of the comparative adjectives and adverbs.

Adjectives

1. bigger   big

2. nicer   _____

3. taller   _____

4. prettier   _____

Adverbs

5. worse   _____

6. better   _____

7. more slowly   _____

8. more efficiently _____

B3) Making Comparative Statements

Complete the statements. Use the comparative form of the adjectives and adverbs in parentheses.

1. Color printers are _more expensive than_ (expensive) black-and-white printers.

2. Faxing a document is _____ (fast) mailing a document.

3. E-mail works _____ (quickly) regular mail.

4. Computers are _____ (good) typewriters, but typewriters are

   _____ (cheap) computers.

5. Cell phones are _____ (convenient) regular phones, but regular

   phones are _____ (reliable) cell phones.

6. Computers can solve some problems _____ (fast) and

   _____ (accurately) humans.

B4) Working on Comparative Adjectives and Adverbs

Complete the conversations. Use the comparative form of the adjectives and adverbs in parentheses.

Conversation 1

Hiro: Let's rent the movie *Blazing Saddles.*

Yuki: I want to see something _more serious_ (serious). How about *Gone with the Wind*?
   1

Hiro: It's too long! I'll fall asleep. What about *Blade Runner*? It's _____ (short).
   2

Yuki: But it's a lot _____ (violent).
   3

Hiro: I know. Let's rent both, and we'll see which one is _____ (enjoyable).
   4

Conversation 2

Elena: Lee should be the new manager. He works _____ (hard) than Rick.
   1

Andre: Well, Lee supervises _____ (effectively) than Rick does, but Rick is
   2

   _____ (friendly). Everyone likes him.
   3

Elena: I agree that Rick is _____ (popular), but can he do a _____
   4   5

   (good) job than Lee does?

C Making Comparisons

Examining Meaning and Use

Read the sentences and answer the questions below. Then discuss your answers and read the Meaning and Use Notes to check them.

> **a.** Ruth and Sara are sisters. Ruth is younger.
> **b.** George drives more slowly than Meg.
> **c.** My car is newer than Lee's car.

1. Which sentence compares people?

2. Which sentence compares things?

3. Which sentence compares actions?

Meaning and Use Notes

Comparing People, Things, or Actions

1A We use comparatives to talk about the differences between people, things, or actions. We often use comparatives to express opinions.

> Holly is **taller than** Carl.
> Buses are **slower than** trains.
>
> Paris is **more beautiful than** Rome.
> Joanna dances **more gracefully than** Laura.

1B *Less* is the opposite of *more*.

> Computers are **less expensive** than they were ten years ago. Computers are **more efficient** than they were ten years ago.

1C We do not always use a phrase or a clause with *than* to make a comparison in every sentence. Often, the second part of the sentence with *than* is not necessary in the context.

> Computers are **faster than** typewriters. They are much **more efficient**, too. They work **better**, and they're **easier** to use.

Listen to the information. Choose the correct answer for each question.

1. **a.** Yes. 3. **a.** Jack. 5. **a.** A sports car. 7. **a.** Mr. Ryan's.
   b. No.   **b.** Paul.   **b.** An SUV.   **b.** Mr. Larkin's.

2. **a.** Tyrone. 4. **a.** Brad. 6. **a.** Keiko. 8. **a.** A typewriter.
   b. Tamika.   **b.** Sasha.   **b.** Koji.   **b.** A computer.

C2 **Making Comparisons** ▶ Notes 1A–1C

Work with a partner. Compare the people or things in the pictures. Use the adjectives and adverbs below or others of your choice. Use *more* or *less*. Make as many sentences as you can.

dangerous	fast	loyal	slow	useful
exciting	high	safe	strong	well

1a. _A bicycle is safer than a motorcycle._ 2a. _____ 3a. _____

1b. _____ 2b. _____ 3b. _____

C3 Expressing Similarities and Differences

► Notes 1A–1C

A. Choose three of the categories below. Think of two things or people to compare in each category. Write at least three comparisons for each in your notebook. Use adjectives and adverbs. Try to alternate the subjects in your sentences.

airports	cities	kinds of food	styles of music
athletes	holidays	members of your family	TV shows

Classical music is calmer and more restful than rock music. Rock music is . . .

B. Work with a partner. Share your comparisons.

C4 Expressing Opinions

► Notes 1A–1C

A. Read the two paragraphs. What is Paragraph 1 about? What is Paragraph 2 about?

Paragraph 1

Modern technology is bringing people together. We now have cell phones, pagers, and, of course, the Internet. Calling people in other places is much less expensive than it was just a few years ago. And e-mail is faster than regular mail and cheaper than a telephone call. With these inventions it's easy to communicate frequently with our friends, our family, and the whole world.

Paragraph 2

People don't communicate in the world today. First, TV replaced family time. Instead of talking together, people started sitting quietly in front of the TV. Now, we have the Internet. People talk to strangers, but they don't talk to the people in their own homes! We need to communicate more effectively with our own families.

B. Work with a partner. Answer the questions. Use comparatives.

1. Which paragraph do you agree with? Why?

   I agree with paragraph 1. Technology is bringing people together because . . .

2. How is communication different today compared to the past?

3. Is life better today, or was it better before? Why?

D Combining Form, Meaning, and Use

D1 Thinking About Meaning and Use

Complete each conversation. Then discuss your answers in small groups.

1. **A:** He's taller than everyone in his class.

   B: _____

   a. Is he taller than his father too?
   b. Don't worry. He'll grow soon.
   c. Is he shorter than his friends?

2. **A:** That Volvo is more expensive than this Ford.

   B: _____

   a. Yes, Fords are very expensive.
   b. Yes, Volvos are very cheap.
   c. Yes, the Ford is cheaper.

3. **A:** You're smarter than Paul.

   B: _____

   a. Then why are my grades worse?
   b. You're always criticizing me.
   c. Yes, you are.

4. **A:** Soo-jin is much more responsible than she was before.

   B: _____

   a. Her boss is going to make her a manager.
   b. That's too bad.
   c. She never comes to work on time.

5. **A:** Paul was sick yesterday, and he's worse today.

   B: _____

   a. We should call the doctor.
   b. Then he can go to work.
   c. That's great!

6. **A:** Thank goodness it's cooler today.

   B: You're right. _____

   a. It is hotter today.
   b. It was really hot yesterday.
   c. Let's turn on the air conditioner!

Some of these sentences have errors. Find the errors and correct them.

1. Carl is a ~~good~~ *better* student than you are.

2. Davis High School is large than Union High School.

3. Who is more tall?

4. Ling sings beautifully than Sam.

5. My new teacher is nicer than my old teacher.

6. Erica is friendlier from Luiz.

7. My shoes are more newer than yours.

8. Is Mike more efficient than Anna?

▶ Beyond the Classroom

Searching for Authentic Examples

Look at articles in English-language newspapers and magazines, or on the Internet. Find three examples of comparative adjectives and adverbs. What things are they comparing? Write them in your notebook and share them with your class.

Writing

Think of two people you know. Follow the steps below to write a paragraph comparing the two people. Use comparative adjectives and adverbs.

1. Use these questions to make notes.
   - Describe the two people's appearances.
   - Do they have similar personalities? Compare them.
   - How do you feel about them?

2. Write a first draft.

3. Read your work carefully and circle grammar, spelling, and punctuation errors. Work with a partner to decide how to fix the errors and improve the content.

4. Rewrite your draft.

   I have two younger brothers, Stefan and Sasha. Stefan is younger than Sasha, but Stefan is taller. . . .

Superlatives

A And Europe's Worst Language Learners Are . . .

A1 Before You Read

Discuss these questions.

How many languages do you speak? Do many people you know speak more than one language? Do you think that it is important to speak a second language?

A2 Read

Read the newspaper article on the following page. Which Europeans are the best language learners?

A3 After You Read

Write the correct percentage next to each statement.

_66%_ **1.** monolingual people in Britain

_____ **2.** monolingual people in Denmark

_____ **3.** people in Denmark, Sweden, and the Netherlands who speak English well

_____ **4.** people in the European Union who are monolingual

_____ **5.** Europeans who think foreign language skills are useful

_____ **6.** Europeans who think everyone should speak English

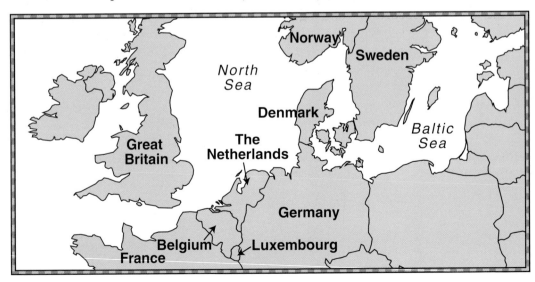

And Europe's Worst Language Learners Are . . .

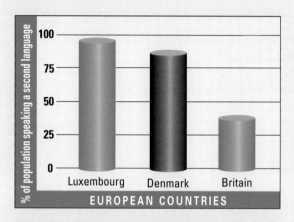

A recent survey on language learning in the European Union (EU) found that Britons are the worst language learners in Europe. According to a survey of 15
5 European nations, almost 66 percent of Britons do not speak a second language. However, British travelers to Europe do not need to worry. English is growing the fastest of all the European languages,
10 and it is now the most popular second language in the EU. So which European country has the best record on language learning?

According to the survey, the smallest
15 country in Europe earned that honor—the people of Luxembourg are the best language learners. Only 2.2 percent of Luxembourg's population does not speak a second language. Denmark also scored
20 well: only 12.3 percent of its population is monolingual.

It is not surprising that English is the most popular second language in the EU. Forty-one percent of EU citizens
25 speak English. In some countries, the percentage is much higher. The populations of Denmark, Sweden, and the Netherlands speak English the most fluently: at least 78 percent of the people
30 in those countries speak English well.

Although 47 percent of all EU citizens are monolingual, many of them believe that speaking a foreign language is a good thing. Seventy-two percent of Europeans
35 believe foreign language skills are useful. Seventy-one percent said everyone should know one foreign language, and sixty-nine percent said everyone should speak English. The survey also asked people
40 why they do not know a foreign language. The most common answer: it is expensive, and it takes a long time.

---

monolingual: speaking only one language
record: performance or rating

survey: a set of questions for a study

The Superlative with Adjectives and Adverbs

Examining Form

Look back at the article on page 387 and complete the tasks below. Then discuss your answers and read the Form charts to check them.

1. Look at the underlined phrases. These are superlative forms of the adjective and adverb below. Write the superlative form next to the adjective and adverb below. How do we form the superlative of these words?

   Adjective   *Adverb*

   small _____   fast _____

2. Look at the circled phrases. These are the superlative forms of the adjectives and adverb below. Write the superlative form next to the adjectives and adverb below. How do we form the superlative of these words?

   Adjectives   *Adverb*

   popular _____   fluently _____

   common _____

REGULAR SUPERLATIVE FORMS

One-Syllable Adjectives		
ADJECTIVE	COMPARATIVE	SUPERLATIVE
old	older	**the oldest**
weak	weaker	**the weakest**
big	bigger	**the biggest**

Two-Syllable Adjectives		
ADJECTIVE	COMPARATIVE	SUPERLATIVE
simple	simpler	**the simplest**
easy	easier	**the easiest**
famous	more famous	**the most famous**

Three-Syllable Adjectives		
ADJECTIVE	COMPARATIVE	SUPERLATIVE
efficient	more efficient	**the most efficient**
popular	more popular	**the most popular**

One-Syllable Adverbs		
ADVERB	COMPARATIVE	SUPERLATIVE
fast	faster	**the fastest**
hard	harder	**the hardest**

Two- or Three-Syllable Adverbs		
ADVERB	COMPARATIVE	SUPERLATIVE
slowly	more slowly	**the most slowly**
frequently	more frequently	**the most frequently**

Adjectives with One Syllable

- To form the superlative, use *the* + adjective + *-est*.
- For adjectives that end with a single vowel and a consonant, double the final consonant and add *-est*.

Adjectives with Two Syllables

- Some two-syllable adjectives add *-est*. Some two-syllable adjectives add *the most*. See Appendix 10 for adjectives that use both forms of the superlative.
    John is **the friendliest / the most friendly**.
- If an adjective ends in a consonant + *-y*, change the *y* to *i* and add *-est*.

Adjectives with Three or More Syllables

- Use *the most* with adjectives of three or more syllables.

Adverbs with One Syllable

- Add *-est* to form the superlative.

Adverbs with Two or More Syllables

- Use *the most* with adverbs of two or more syllables.

IRREGULAR SUPERLATIVE FORMS

ADJECTIVE	ADVERB	SUPERLATIVE
good	well	**the best**
bad	badly	**the worst**

THE SUPERLATIVE IN SENTENCES

	SUPERLATIVE	
Tom is	**the tallest**	student in the class.
Kim speaks	**the most fluently**	of all the students.

(Continued on page 390)

> ⚠ Do not use *than* after superlatives. Use prepositional phrases such as *in the . . .* and *. . . of all.*
>
> They are the greatest language learners **in the world.**
>
> They are the greatest language learners **of all.**
>
> *They are the greatest language learners than all. (INCORRECT)

B1) Listening for Form

🎧 Listen to each sentence. Do you hear a comparative or a superlative? Check (✓) the correct column.

	COMPARATIVE	SUPERLATIVE
1.		✓
2.		
3.		
4.		
5.		
6.		
7.		
8.		

B2) Forming Superlatives

A. Write the superlative form of the adjectives and adverbs.

Adjectives

1. tall ____the tallest____

2. easy _____

3. intelligent _____

4. new _____

Adverbs

5. happily _____

6. gracefully _____

7. fluently _____

8. carefully _____

B. Write the base form of the superlative adjectives and adverbs.

Adjectives

1. the biggest _big_____

2. the prettiest _____

3. the thinnest _____

4. the happiest _____

Adverbs

5. the fastest _____

6. the worst _____

7. the most quickly _____

8. the best _____

B3 Working with Superlative Adjectives and Adverbs

Complete the conversations. Use the superlative form of the adjectives and adverbs in parentheses.

Conversation 1

A: How's Dan doing in your Latin class? He says that he's _____the worst_____ (bad)
                                                                        1

in the class.

B: Nonsense! He should get the _____ (high) grade. He works
                                              2

_____ (hard).
        3

Conversation 2

A: I'm going to fire Linda. She is _____ (careless) of all my employees.
                                          1

B: Who are _____ (good) workers?
                    2

A: Derek and Ruth work _____ (efficiently).
                                    3

Conversation 3

A: Who is _____ (bad) driver in your family?
                  1

B: My older sister. She's terrible. My younger sister drives the _____
                                                                            2

(carefully).

Conversation 4

A: What is _____ (long) river in the world?
                  1

B: I think it's the Nile in Africa. But the Amazon in South America carries

_____ (large) volume of water.
        2

Superlatives

Examining Meaning and Use

Read the sentences and answer the questions below. Then discuss your answers and read the Meaning and Use Notes to check them.

a. Dan walks faster than Rick.
b. Dan is slower than Bob.
c. Bob walks the fastest of the three. Rick walks the slowest.

1. Which sentence compares two actions?

2. Which compares two people?

3. Which sentences show that something is first or last in a group of three or more?

Meaning and Use Notes

Comparing Three or More People, Things, or Actions

1A We use superlatives to compare people, things, or actions in a group of three or more. We often use superlatives to express opinions.

Hong Kong is **the most expensive** place to live.
Kyoto is **the most beautiful** city in Japan.

1B *Least* is the opposite of *most.*

Ferraris are **the most expensive** cars in the world. Fords are **the least expensive**.
My math class is **the least interesting** of all my classes this semester.

1C We do not always use an expression with *in* or *of* in sentences with superlatives. Often it is not necessary in the context.

Sam is **the tallest** in the family. John is **the shortest** and Ana is **the most intelligent**.

🎧 Listen to the conversation. Check (✓) the school that is the best in each category.

		LIGHTHOUSE UNIVERSITY	WESTBROOK COLLEGE	CRANBERRY UNIVERSITY
1.	reputation	✓		
2.	cheap			
3.	close to home			
4.	easy to get in			
5.	comfortable dorms			
6.	famous professors			
7.	friendly students			
8.	beautiful campus			

C2 **Expressing Opinions** ▶ Notes 1A–1C

A. There are many different ways to compare languages. Write sentences using the notes below. Use superlatives to describe which language is first or last in each category.

1. easy to learn   _Spanish is the easiest to learn._

2. hard to read   _____

3. useful for business   _____

4. easy spelling rules   _____

5. simple grammar   _____

6. difficult pronunciation   _____

B. Discuss your opinions in small groups. Do you agree?

A. Work with a partner. Make guesses about the animals below. Match each of the animals to one of the world records.

anaconda   blue whale   hummingbird   sea turtle
bar-headed goose   cheetah   peregrine falcon   sea wasp jellyfish

	ANIMALS	WORLD RECORDS
1.	hummingbird	Some of these birds are only 2 inches long.
2.		This bird can dive at speeds of 270 miles per hour.
3.		This snake can grow to a length of 30 feet.
4.		This animal can reach a speed of 70 miles per hour.
5.		This animal can weigh up to 30 tons.
6.		This sea animal is 30 times more deadly than a cobra.
7.		This sea animal can live to 200 years.
8.		This bird can fly above 29,000 feet.

B. Now see Appendix 12 to check your answers. How many right answers do you have?

C. Write a statement in your notebook about each animal using a superlative adjective or adverb.

The hummingbird is the smallest bird in the world.

Make one comparative and one superlative statement about each category below. Use the adjectives in parentheses. Use *the least* and *the most* in some of your statements. Discuss your answers with a partner.

1. **ice cream flavors (delicious):** chocolate   vanilla   strawberry

   Vanilla ice cream is more delicious than strawberry.
   Chocolate is the most delicious ice cream flavor of all.

2. **cities (expensive):** Beijing   Paris   New York

3. **languages (difficult):** Russian   Arabic   Chinese

4. **careers (dangerous):** race car driver   jet pilot   stuntman

D Combining Form, Meaning, and Use

D1 Thinking About Meaning and Use

Complete each conversation. Then discuss your answers in small groups.

1. A: Mr. Day's class is the most popular.

   B: I know. _____

     a. Nobody likes him.

     b. It's very boring.

     c. Everyone wants to take it.

2. A: My computer is faster than yours.

   B: _____

     a. But is it better?

     b. I know, but mine is the fastest.

     c. Is it slower than mine?

3. A: I need smaller gloves. These don't fit.

   B: _____

     a. Can you get some larger ones?

     b. Sorry, these are the smallest in the store.

     c. You can buy less expensive gloves.

4. A: She's the best dancer I know.

   B: _____

     a. I agree. A lot of people are better.

     b. You're right. She's the greatest!

     c. Yes, she should practice more.

5. A: How hard are diamonds?

   B: _____

     a. They're the hardest minerals on earth.

     b. They are the most difficult minerals on earth.

     c. They're harder.

6. A: Why should I take Latin?

   B: _____

     a. Because it's the least useful language offered.

     b. Because it's less interesting than Greek.

     c. Because the Latin teacher is the best in the school.

Some of these sentences have errors. Find the errors and correct them.

1. Rio is the ~~more~~ *most* exciting city in the world.

2. I'm the worst driver in my family.

3. He's an oldest person in the class.

4. July 28 was the hottest day of the year.

5. This restaurant is not the cheaper one in the city.

6. This is the most slowest bus in this town.

7. She is the smartest than all.

8. They're the carefullest students.

Beyond the Classroom

Searching for Authentic Examples

Look in an English-language reference book or on the Internet for superlatives describing people, places, and things. For example, look in *Guinness World Records*™ or in an almanac. Find three superlatives, such as the longest river or the oldest person. Write them in your notebook and share them with your class. Who found the most interesting or unusual information?

Speaking

Follow the steps below to make comparisons about your classmates.

1. Interview three classmates. Ask questions about each category below. Write their answers in your notebook.
   - Height
   - Size of family
   - House or apartment
   - Ability at sports
   - Ability at cooking

   Paul is six feet four inches. Alex is five feet four inches.

2. Make comparisons about your classmates. Use comparative and superlative adjectives and adverbs in your statements.

   Alex is shorter than Paul.

3. Share your comparisons with the class.

   Paul is the tallest in the group. Alex is the shortest.

Appendices

1 Spelling of Regular and Irregular Plural Nouns

Regular Plural Nouns

1. For most plural nouns, add *-s* to the base form.

   apple — apples   lake — lakes
   flower — flowers   river — rivers

2. If the base form ends with the letter *s, z, sh, ch,* or *x*, add *-es*.

   box — boxes   fax — faxes
   bush — bushes   gas — gases

3. If the base form ends with a consonant + *y*, change *y* to *i* and add *-es*.
   (Compare vowel + *y*: boy — boys; toy — toys.)

   baby — babies
   balcony — balconies
   dictionary — dictionaries

4. If the base form ends with a consonant + *o*, add *-s* or *-es*. Some words take *-s*,
   some words take *-es*, some take both *-s* and *-es*. (Compare vowel + *o*: radio —
   radios; zoo — zoos.)

-s	*-es*	**Both *-s* and *-es***
auto — autos	potato — potatoes	tornado — tornados/tornadoes
photo — photos	tomato — tomatoes	volcano — volcanos/volcanoes
piano — pianos		zero — zeros/zeroes
radio — radios		

5. If the base form of certain nouns ends with a single *f* or in *fe*, change the *f* or *fe* to
   v and add *-es*.

   calf — calves
   shelf — shelves
   knife — knives

   Exceptions

   belief — beliefs
   chief — chiefs
   roof — roofs
   scarf — scarfs/scarves

   Irregular Plural Nouns

   Singular – Plural

child – children	goose – geese	person – people
fish – fish	man – men	tooth – teeth
foot – feet	mouse – mice	woman – women

2 Common Noncount Nouns

Solids

bread
butter
chalk
cheese
chocolate
fish
meat
pasta
rope
soap

Gases

air
carbon dioxide
oxygen
smoke
steam

Materials

cotton
glass
gold
iron
metal
plastic
silver
steel
wood
wool

Liquids

coffee
cream
gasoline
juice
milk
oil
rain
shampoo
soda
soup
tea
toothpaste
water

Grains and Powders

cereal
detergent
dust
flour
pepper
rice
salt
sand
sugar
wheat

Feelings and Ideas

fear
freedom
happiness
independence
information
knowledge
love
sadness
time
work

School Subjects

biology
economics
English
history
mathematics
physical education
physics
science

Activities

baseball
basketball
chess
football
hiking
reading
soccer
swimming
tennis

General Categories

candy
clothing
education
equipment
food
fruit
furniture
jewelry
luggage
money
weather
work

3 Spelling of Verbs Ending in *-ing*

1. For most verbs, add *-ing* to the base form of the verb.

   sleep — sleeping   talk — talking

2. If the base form ends in a single *e*, drop the *e* and add *-ing* (exception: be – being).

   live — living   write — writing

3. If the base form ends in *ie*, change *ie* to *y* and add *-ing*.

   die — dying   lie — lying

4. If the base form of a one-syllable verb ends with a single vowel + consonant, double the final consonant and add *-ing*. (Compare two vowels + consonant: eat — eating.)

   hit — hitting   stop — stopping

5. If the base form of a verb with two or more syllables ends in a single vowel + consonant, double the final consonant only if the stress is on the final syllable. Do not double the final consonant if the stress is not on the final syllable.

   admit — admitting   begin — beginning   develop — developing   listen — listening

6. Do not double the final consonants *x*, *w*, and *y*.

   fix — fixing   grow — growing   obey — obeying

4 Spelling of Verbs Ending in *–s* and *–es*

1. For most third-person singular verbs, add *–s* to the base form.

   live – lives
   swim – swims

2. If the base form ends with the letter *s*, *z*, *sh*, *ch*, or *x*, add *–es*.

   miss – misses
   teach—teaches

3. If the base form ends with a consonant + *y*, change *y* to *i* and add *–es*.

   study – studies
   try – tries

4. If the base form ends with a consonant + *o*, *–es*.

   do – does
   go – goes

5 Pronunciation of Verbs and Nouns Ending in *-s* and *-es*

1. If the base form of the verb or noun ends with the sound /s/, /z/, /ʃ/, /ʒ/, /tʃ/, /dʒ/, or /ks/, then pronounce *-es* as an extra syllable /ɪz/.

Verbs		**Nouns**	
slice — slices	watch — watches	price — prices	inch — inches
lose — loses	judge — judges	size — sizes	language — languages
wash — washes	relax — relaxes	dish — dishes	tax — taxes

2. If the base form ends with the voiceless sound /p/, /t/, /k/, /f/, or /θ/, then pronounce *-s* and *-es* as /s/.

Verbs		**Nouns**	
sleep — sleeps	work — works	grape — grapes	book — books
hit — hits	laugh — laughs	cat — cats	cuff — cuffs

3. If the base form ends with any other consonant or with a vowel sound, then pronounce *-s* and *-es* as /z/.

Verbs	**Nouns**
learn — learns	name — names
go — goes	boy — boys

6 Spelling of Verbs Ending in *-ed*

1. To form the simple past of most regular verbs, add *-ed* to the base form.

   brush — brushed   play — played

2. If the base form ends with *e,* just add *-d.*

   close — closed   live — lived

3. If the base form ends with a consonant + *y,* change the *y* to *i* and add *-ed.* (Compare vowel +*y*: play — played; enjoy — enjoyed.)

   study — studied   dry — dried

4. If the base form of a one-syllable verb ends with a single vowel + consonant, double the final consonant and add *-ed.*

   plan — planned   shop — shopped

5. If the base form of a verb with two or more syllables ends with a single vowel + consonant, double the final consonant and add *-ed* only when the stress is on the final syllable. Do not double the final consonant if the stress is not on the final syllable.

   prefer — preferred   enter — entered

6. Do not double the final consonants *x, w,* and *y.*

   fix — fixed   snow — snowed   stay — stayed

7 Pronunciation of Verbs Ending in *-ed*

1. If the base form of the verb ends with the sounds /t/ or /d/, then pronounce *-ed* as an extra syllable /ɪd/.

/t/	/d/
start — started	need — needed
wait — waited	decide — decided

2. If the base form ends with the voiceless sounds /p/, /k/, /f/, /s/, /ʃ/, /tʃ/, or /ks/, then pronounce *-ed* as /t/.

jump — jumped	laugh — laughed	wish — wished	fax — faxed
look — looked	slice — sliced	watch — watched	

3. If the base form ends with the voiced sounds /b/, /g/, /dʒ/, /m/, /n/, /ŋ/, /l/, /r/, /ð/, /v/, /z/, or with a vowel, then pronounce *-ed* as /d/.

rob — robbed	hum — hummed	call — called	wave — waved
brag — bragged	rain — rained	order — ordered	close — closed
judge — judged	bang — banged	bathe — bathed	play — played

8 Irregular Verbs

Base Form	Simple Past	Base Form	Simple Past	Base Form	Simple Past
be	was/were	dive	dove (OR dived)	go	went
become	became	do	did	grow	grew
begin	began	draw	drew	hang	hung
bend	bent	drink	drank	have	had
bite	bit	drive	drove	hear	heard
blow	blew	eat	ate	hide	hid
break	broke	fall	fell	hit	hit
bring	brought	feed	fed	hold	held
build	built	feel	felt	hurt	hurt
buy	bought	fight	fought	keep	kept
catch	caught	find	found	know	knew
choose	chose	fly	flew	lay (= put)	laid
come	came	forget	forgot	lead	led
cost	cost	freeze	froze	leave	left
cut	cut	get	got	lend	lent
dig	dug	give	gave	let	let

Base Form	Simple Past	Base Form	Simple Past	Base Form	Simple Past
lose	lost	sell	sold	take	took
make	made	send	sent	teach	taught
meet	met	shoot	shot	tear	tore
pay	paid	show	showed	tell	told
put	put	shut	shut	think	thought
quit	quit	sing	sang	throw	threw
read	read	sit	sat	understand	understood
ride	rode	sleep	slept	wake	woke
ring	rang	speak	spoke	wear	wore
run	ran	spend	spent	win	won
say	said	steal	stole	write	wrote
see	saw	swim	swam		

9 Common Adjectives

Quality/Opinion	Size	Color	Age	Origin	Shape
athletic	big	black	ancient	African	oval
awful	huge	blue	antique	American	rectangular
bright	large	brown	modern	Asian	round
brilliant	little	green	new	Australian	square
cheap	long	grey	old	Brazilian	triangular
cloudy	narrow	orange	old-fashioned	Canadian	
delicious	small	pink	young	Chinese	
expensive	short	purple		European	
famous	tall	red		French	
fantastic	thick	white		German	
handsome	thin	yellow		Indian	
intelligent	tiny			Italian	
interesting	wide			Japanese	
noisy				Korean	
rainy				Latin American	
serious				Middle Eastern	
strong				South American	
terrible				Spanish	
unusual					
useless					
valuable					
wonderful					

🔟 Adjectives with Two Comparative and Superlative Forms

Adjective	Comparative	Superlative
friendly	friendlier more friendly	the friendliest the most friendly
handsome	handsomer more handsome	the handsomest the most handsome
happy	happier more happy	the happiest the most happy
polite	politer more polite	the politest the most polite
quiet	quieter more quiet	the quietest the most quiet

🔟🔟 Contractions with Verb and Modal Forms

Contractions with *Be*

I am	=	I'm
you are	=	you're
he is	=	he's
she is	=	she's
it is	=	it's
we are	=	we're
you are	=	you're
they are	=	they're

I am not	=	I'm not
you are not	=	you're not / you aren't
he is not	=	he's not / he isn't
she is not	=	she's not / she isn't
it is not	=	it's not / it isn't
we are not	=	we're not / we aren't
you are not	=	you're not / you aren't
they are not	=	they're not / they aren't

Contractions with *Will*

I will	=	I'll
you will	=	you'll
he will	=	he'll
she will	=	she'll
it will	=	it'll
we will	=	we'll
you will	=	you'll
they will	=	they'll

will not	=	won't

Contractions with *Was* and *Were*

was not	=	wasn't
were not	=	weren't

Contractions with *Be Going To*

I am going to	= I'm going to
you are going to	= you're going to
he is going to	= he's going to
she is going to	= she's going to
it is going to	= it's going to
we are going to	= we're going to
you are going to	= you're going to
they are going to	= they're going to
you are not going to	= you're not going to / you aren't going to

Contractions with *Do* and *Did*

do not	= don't
does not	= doesn't
did not	= didn't

Contractions with *Can, Could* and *Should*

cannot	= can't
could not	= couldn't
should not	= shouldn't

12 Answers to Exercises

C3: page 179

		PLACE OF BIRTH	YEAR OF BIRTH
2.	Columbus	Italy	1451 A.D.
3.	Confucius	China	about 551 B.C.
4.	Marie Curie	Poland	1867 A.D.
5.	Einstein	Germany	1879 A.D.
6.	Picasso	Spain	1881 A.D.
7.	Rembrandt	the Netherlands	1606 A.D.
8.	Shakespeare	England	1564 A.D.

C3: page 394

	ANIMALS	WORLD RECORDS
2.	peregrine falcon	This bird can dive at speeds of 270 miles per hour.
3.	anaconda	This snake can grow to a length of 30 feet.
4.	cheetah	This animal can reach a speed of 70 miles per hour.
5.	blue whale	This animal can weigh up to 30 tons.
6.	sea-wasp jellyfish	This sea animal is 30 times more deadly than a cobra.
7.	sea turtle	This sea animal can live up to 200 years.
8.	bar-headed goose	This bird can fly above 29,000 feet.

⑬ Phonetic Symbols

Vowels

i	**see** /si/	u	**too** /tu/	oʊ	**go** /goʊ/
ɪ	**sit** /sɪt/	ʌ	**cup** /kʌp/	ər	**bird** /bərd/
ɛ	**ten** /tɛn/	ə	**about** /ə'baʊt/	ɪr	**near** /nɪr/
æ	**cat** /kæt/	eɪ	**say** /seɪ/	ɛr	**hair** /hɛr/
ɑ	**hot** /hɑt/	aɪ	**five** /faɪv/	ɑr	**car** /kɑr/
ɔ	**saw** /sɔ/	ɔɪ	**boy** /bɔɪ/	ɔr	**north** /nɔrθ/
ʊ	**put** /pʊt/	aʊ	**now** /naʊ/	ʊr	**tour** /tʊr/

Consonants

p	**pen** /pɛn/	f	**fall** /fɔl/	m	**man** /mæn/
b	**bad** /bæd/	v	**voice** /vɔɪs/	n	**no** /noʊ/
t	**tea** /ti/	θ	**thin** /θɪn/	ŋ	**sing** /sɪŋ/
t̬	**butter** /'bʌt̬ər/	ð	**then** /ðɛn/	l	**leg** /lɛg/
d	**did** /dɪd/	s	**so** /soʊ/	r	**red** /rɛd/
k	**cat** /kæt/	z	**zoo** /zu/	y	**yes** /yɛs/
g	**got** /gɑt/	ʃ	**she** /ʃi/	w	**wet** /wɛt/
tʃ	**chin** /tʃɪn/	ʒ	**vision** /'vɪʒn/	x	**Chanukah** /'xɑnəkə/
dʒ	**June** /dʒun/	h	**how** /haʊ/

Glossary of Grammar Terms

ability modal *See* **modal of ability**.

action Something that you do, usually involving movement, such as *open a door, drink some water, wash your face.*

action verb A verb that describes a thing that someone or something does. An action verb does not describe a state or condition.

　　Sam **rang** the bell.

　　I **eat** soup for lunch.

　　It **rains** a lot here.

activity A lot of action or movement over a period of time, such as *running, dancing, eating, swimming.*

adjective A word that describes or modifies the meaning of a noun.

　　the **orange** car

　　a **strange** noise

adverb A word that describes or modifies the meaning of a verb, another adverb, an adjective, or a sentence. Many adverbs answer such questions as *How? When? Where?* or *How often?* They often end in **-ly**.

　　She ran **quickly**.　　She ran **very** quickly.

　　a **really** hot day　　**Maybe** she'll leave.

adverb of degree An adverb that makes adjectives or other adverbs stronger or weaker.

　　She is **extremely** busy this week.

　　He performed **very** well during the exam.

　　He was **somewhat** surprised by her response.

adverb of frequency An adverb that tells how often a situation occurs. Adverbs of frequency range in meaning from *all of the time* to *none of the time.*

　　She **always** eats breakfast.

　　He **never** eats meat.

adverb of manner An adverb that answers the question *How?* and describes the way someone does something or the way something happens. Adverbs of manner usually end in **-ly**.

　　He walked **slowly**.

　　It rained **heavily** all night.

adverb of opinion An adverb that expresses an opinion about an entire sentence or idea.

　　Luckily, we missed the traffic.

　　We couldn't find a seat on the train, **unfortunately**.

adverb of time An adverb that answers the question *When?* and refers to either a specific time or a more indefinite time.

　　Let's leave **tonight** instead of **tomorrow**.

　　They **recently** opened a new store.

adverbial phrase A phrase that functions as an adverb.

　　Amy spoke **very softly**.

affirmative statement A sentence that does not have a negative verb.

　　Linda went to the movies.

agree To have a grammatical relationship with. In English subjects and verbs agree in person and number, for example, *I am . . . , You are . . . , He is . . .*

agreement The subject and verb of a clause must agree in number. If the subject is singular, the verb form is also singular. If the subject is plural, the verb form is also plural.

　　He comes home early.　　**They come** home early.

article The words **a, an,** and **the** in English. Articles are used to introduce and identify nouns.

　　a potato　　**an** onion　　**the** supermarket

auxiliary verb A verb that is used before main verbs (or other auxiliary verbs) in a sentence. Auxiliary verbs are usually used in questions and negative sentences. **Do, have,** and **be** can act as auxiliary verbs. Modals (**may, can, will,** and so on) are also auxiliary verbs.

Do you have the time?

I **have** never been to Italy.

The car **was** speeding.

I **may** be late.

base form The form of a verb without any verb endings; the infinitive form without *to*. Also called *simple form*.

sleep   be   stop

clause A group of words that has a subject and a verb. *See also* **dependent clause** and **main clause**.

If I leave, . . .

The rain stopped.

. . . when he speaks.

. . . that I saw.

common noun A noun that refers to any of a class of people, animals, places, things, or ideas. Common nouns are not capitalized.

man   cat   city   pencil   grammar

comparative A form of an adjective, adverb, or noun that is used to express differences between two items or situations.

This book is **heavier than** that one.

He runs **more quickly than** his brother.

A CD costs **more money than** a cassette.

consonant A speech sound that is made by partly or completely stopping the air as it comes out of the mouth. For example, with the sounds /p/, /d/, and /g/, the air is completely stopped. With the sounds /s/, /f/, and /l/, the air is partly stopped.

contraction The combination of two words into one by omitting certain letters and replacing them with an apostrophe.

I will = **I'll**   we are = **we're**   are not = **aren't**

count noun A common noun that you can count as an individual thing. It usually has both a singular and a plural form.

orange — oranges   woman — women

definite article The word **the** in English. It is used to identify nouns based on information the speaker and listener share about the noun. The definite article is also used for making general statements about a whole class or group of nouns.

Please give me **the** key.

The scorpion is dangerous.

demonstrative adjective This, that, these, and those are demonstrative adjectives when they occur before nouns. They tell whether the noun is near or far from the speaker.

This house is nice. **That** house isn't.

These books are due at the library. **Those** books aren't.

demonstrative pronoun This, that, these, and those are demonstrative pronouns when they take the place of a demonstrative adjective + noun.

This is new. (This book is new.)

That is old. (That book is old.)

These are ready. (These cookies are ready.)

Those aren't ready. (Those cookies aren't ready.)

dependent clause A clause that cannot stand alone as a sentence because it depends on the main clause to complete the meaning of the sentence. Also called *subordinate clause*.

I'm going home **after he calls**.

determiner A word such as **a, an, the, this, that, these, those, my, some, a few,** and **three** that is used before a noun to limit its meaning in some way.

those videos

direct object A noun or pronoun that refers to a person or thing that is directly affected by the action of a verb.

John wrote **a letter**.

Please buy **some milk**.

first person One of the three classes of personal pronouns. First person refers to the person (*I*) or people (*we*) who are actually speaking or writing.

formal A style of speech or writing where the speaker or writer is very careful about pronunciation, choice of words, and sentence structure. Formal language is used at official functions, ceremonies, speeches, in the law and in other types of serious writing.

> "Ladies and Gentlemen, allow me to introduce a man **to whom** I owe a great deal of gratitude . . . "

future A time that is to come. The future is expressed in English with **will, be going to,** the simple present, or the present continuous. These different forms of the future often have different meanings and uses.

> I **will** help you later.
> David **is going to** call later.
> The train **leaves** at 6:05 this evening.
> **I'm driving** to Toronto tomorrow.

general quantity expression A quantity expression that indicates whether a quantity or an amount is large or small. It does not give an exact amount.

> **a lot of** cookies   **a little** flour
> **a few** people   **some** milk

general statement A generalization about a whole class or group of nouns.

> Whales are mammals.
> A daffodil is a flower that grows from a bulb.

gerund An **-ing** form of a verb that is used in place of a noun or pronoun to name an activity or a state.

> **Skiing** is fun.   He doesn't like **being sick**.

imperative A type of sentence, usually without a subject, that tells someone to do something. The verb is in the base form.

> **Open** your books to page 36.
> **Be** ready at eight.

impersonal *you* The use of the pronoun **you** to refer to people in general rather than a particular person or group of people.

> Nowadays **you** can buy anything on the Internet.

indefinite article The words **a** and **an** in English. Indefinite articles introduce a noun as a member of a class of nouns or make generalizations about a whole class or group of nouns.

> Please hand me **a** pencil.
> **An** ocean is **a** large body of water.

independent clause *See* **main clause.**

indirect object A noun or pronoun used after some verbs that refers to the person who receives the direct object of a sentence.

> John wrote a letter **to Mary**.
> Please buy some milk **for us**.

infinitive A verb form that includes **to** + the base form of a verb. An infinitive is used in place of a noun or pronoun to name an activity or state expressed by a verb.

> Do you like **to swim**?

informal A style of speech, and sometimes writing, used in everyday conversations between friends, co-workers, and family members. In informal speech, the speaker is casual about pronunciation, choice of words, and sentence structure. Informal speech is often fast speech with a lot of reduced and contracted forms. Short notes, e-mail messages, and written dialogues are often informal.

information question A question that begins with a **wh-** word.

> Where does she live?
> Who lives here?

intonation The change in pitch, loudness, syllable length, and rhythm in spoken language.

intransitive verb A verb that cannot be followed by an object.

> We finally **arrived**.

irregular verb A verb that does not form the simple past by adding *-d* or *-ed* endings.

> put — put
> buy — bought

main clause A clause that can be used by itself as a sentence. Also called *independent clause*.

> I'm going home.

main verb A verb that can be used alone in a sentence. A main verb can also occur with an auxiliary verb.

> I **ate** lunch at 11:30.
> Kate can't **eat** lunch today.

modal The auxiliary verbs **can, could, may, might, must, should, will,** and **would.** They modify the meaning of a main verb by expressing ability, authority, formality, politeness, or various degrees of certainty. Also called *modal auxiliary.*

You **should** take something for your headache.
Applicants **must** have a high school diploma.

modal of ability **Can** and **could** are called modals of ability when they express the ability to do something.

He **can** speak Arabic and English.
Can you play the piano?
Yesterday we **couldn't** leave during the storm.
Seat belts **can** save lives.

modal of permission **May, could,** and **can** are called modals of permission when they are used to ask for, give, or refuse permission to do something.

A: **May** I leave early?
B: Yes, you **can.**
A: Mom, **could** I stay up late tonight?
B: No, you **may not.** You have school tomorrow.

modal auxiliary See **modal.**

modify To add to or change the meaning of a word.

Adjectives modify nouns (**expensive** cars).
Adverbs modify verbs (**very** fast).

negative statement A sentence with a negative verb.

I **didn't see** that movie.
He **isn't** happy.

non-action verb See **stative verb**

noncount noun A common noun that cannot be counted. A noncount noun has no plural form and cannot occur with **a, an,** or a number.

information   mathematics   weather

noun A word that typically refers to a person, animal, place, thing, or idea.

Tom   rabbit   store   computer   mathematics

noun phrase A phrase formed by a noun and its modifiers. A noun phrase can substitute for a noun in a sentence.

She drank **milk.**
She drank **chocolate milk.**
She drank **the milk.**

object A noun, pronoun, or noun phrase that follows a transitive verb or a preposition.

He likes **pizza.**
She likes **him.**
Go with **her.**
Steve threw **the ball.**

object pronoun The pronouns **me, you** (sg., pl.), **him, her, it, us,** and **them** are object pronouns when they act as the object of a verb or preposition.

past continuous A verb form that expresses an activity in progress at a specific time in the past. The past continuous is formed with **was** or **were** + verb + **-ing.** Also called *past progressive.*

A: What **were** you **doing** last night
   at eight o'clock?
B: I **was studying.**

past progressive See **past continuous.**

phrasal modal A verb that is not a true modal, but has the same meaning as a modal verb. Examples of phrasal modals are **ought to, have to,** and **have got to.**

phrase A group of words that can form a grammatical unit. A phrase can take the form of a noun phrase, verb phrase, adjective phrase, adverbial phrase, or prepositional phrase. This means it can act as a noun, verb, adjective, adverb, or preposition.

The **tall man** left.
Lee **hit the ball.**
The child was **very quiet.**
She spoke **too fast.**
They ran **down the stairs.**

plural The form of a word that refers to more than one person or thing. For example, **cats** and **children** are the plural forms of **cat** and **child.**

preposition A word such as **at, in, on,** or **to,** that links nouns, pronouns, and gerunds to other words.

prepositional phrase A phrase that consists of a preposition followed by a noun or noun phrase.

on Sunday
under the table

present continuous A verb form that indicates that an activity is in progress, temporary, or changing. It is formed with **be** + verb + **-ing**. Also called *present progressive*.

> **I'm watering** the garden.
> Ruth **is working** for her uncle.
> He**'s getting** better.

present progressive *See* **present continuous**.

pronoun A word that can replace a noun or noun phrase. **I, you, he, she, it, mine,** and **yours** are some examples of pronouns.

proper noun A noun that is the name of a particular person, animal, place, thing, or idea. Proper nouns begin with capital letters and are usually not preceded by **the**.

> Peter   Rover   India   Apollo 13   Buddhism

quantity expression A word or words that occur before a noun to express a quantity or amount of that noun.

> **a lot of** rain
> **few** books
> **four** trucks

reduced form A shortened form of a word or phrase that is common in fast, informal speech.

> "Need any help?" (Do you need any help?)
> "I'm gonna call you." (I'm going to call you.)

regular verb A verb that forms the simple past by adding **-ed, -d,** or changing **y** to **i** and then adding **-ed** to the simple form.

> hunt — hunted
> love — loved
> cry — cried

response An answer to a question, or a reply to other types of spoken or written language.

> A: Are you hungry?
> B: **Yes, in fact I am. Let's eat.**

second person One of the three classes of personal pronouns. Second person refers to the person (**you,** singular) or people (**you,** plural) who are the listeners or readers.

short answer An answer to a *Yes/No* question that has *yes* or *no* plus the subject and an auxiliary verb.

> A: Do you speak Chinese?
> B: **Yes, I do. / No, I don't.**

simple form *See* **base form**.

simple past A verb tense that expresses actions and situations that were completed at a definite time in the past.

> Carol **ate** lunch.
> She **was** hungry.

simple present A verb tense that expresses general statements, especially about habitual or repeated activities and permanent situations.

> Every morning I **catch** the 8:00 bus.
> The earth **is** round.

singular The form of a word that refers to only one person or thing. For example, **cat** and **child** are the singular forms of **cats** and **children**.

standard form A form of language that is based on the speech and writing of educated native speakers of a language. Standard language is used in the news media and other public speech, in literature, in textbooks, and other academic materials. It is described in dictionaries and grammar books.

state Physical conditions, senses, possession, knowledge, feelings, and measurements are states that are expressed with *be* and other non-action (stative) verbs.

> She **is tall**.
> The flower **smells good**.
> He **owns a house**.

stative verb A type of verb that is not usually used in the continuous form because it expresses a condition or state that is not changing. **Know, love, resemble, see,** and **smell** are some examples. Also called *non-action verb*.

stress The pronunciation of a syllable or word with more force than the pronunciation of surrounding syllables or words. Stressed syllables or words often sound louder and longer than surrounding syllables or words.

> I didn't see **Sara**, I saw **John**.

subject A noun, pronoun, or noun phrase that precedes the verb phrase in a sentence. The subject of a sentence with *be* tells who or what the sentence is about. The subject of a sentence with an action verb tells who did or caused the action.

> **The park** is huge.
> **Erica** kicked the ball.

subject pronoun The pronouns **I, you** (sg., pl.), **he, she, it, we**, and **they** are subject pronouns when they act as the subject of a clause.

subordinate clause *See* **dependent clause.**

superlative A form of an adjective, adverb, or noun used to compare a group of three or more people, things, or actions. The superlative shows that one member of the group has more (or less) than all of the others.

> This perfume has **the strongest** scent.
> He speaks **the fastest** of all.
> That machine makes **the most noise** of the three.

syllable A word or part of a word that contains one vowel sound.

> **Happy** has two syllables: **hap-py**
> **Dictionary** has four syllables: **dic-tion-ar-y**

tense The form of a verb that shows past, present, and future time.

> He **lives** in New York now.
> He **lived** in Washington two years ago.
> He**'ll live** in Toronto next year.

third person One of the three classes of personal pronouns. Third person refers to some person (**he, she**), people (**they**), or thing (**it**) other than the speaker/writer or listener/reader.

time expression A phrase that functions as an adverb of time.

> She graduated **three years ago**.
> I'll see them **the day after tomorrow**.

transitive verb A verb that is followed by an object.

> I **read** the book.

verb A word that refers to an action or a state.

> Gina **closed** the window.
> Tim **loves** classical music.

verb phrase A phrase that has a main verb and any objects, adverbs, or dependent clauses that complete the meaning of the verb in the sentence.

> She **is talking**.
> Who **called you**?
> He **walked slowly**.

voiced Refers to speech sounds that are made by vibrating the vocal cords. Examples of voiced sounds are /b/, /d/, and /g/.

> **b**at   **d**ot   **g**et

voiceless Refers to speech sounds that are made without vibrating the vocal cords. Examples of voiceless sounds are /p/, /t/, and /f/.

> u**p**   i**t**   i**f**

vowel A speech sound that is made with the lips and teeth open. The air from the lungs is not blocked at all. For example, the sounds /a/, /o/, and /i/ are vowels.

***wh*- word** Who, whom, what, where, when, why, how, and which are **wh**- words. They are used to ask questions and to connect clauses.

***Yes/No* question** A question that can be answered with the words **yes** or **no**.

> Can you drive a car?
> Does he live here?

Index